Energy, Cities and Sustainability

According to some estimates, humanity has now passed the point at which city dwellers outnumber country dwellers. This simple fact encapsulates a multitude of historical trends and contentions; not the least being "is this sustainable"?

Energy, Cities and Sustainability aims to illuminate this question by tracing the evolution of the modern city, the energy sources that power it and the motivations behind increasing urbanisation. The book examines changing energy use across history, analysing the origins and significance of the Industrial Revolution to reveal how the modern city came into being. Transport, population size, housing, electricity use and growing consumption are each discussed, showing how the cultural aspects of energy use have influenced urban form in the developed world and developing countries. Finally, in contemplating the future, it is considered whether this model of modern urban life is sustainable.

This book is a valuable resource for researchers, academics and policy-makers in the areas of planning, energy policy and environment and sustainability.

Harry Margalit is an Associate Professor in Architecture at the University of New South Wales, Australia.

Routledge Studies in Energy Policy

For further details please visit the series page on the Routledge website:
http://www.routledge.com/books/series/RSIEP/

Energy, Cities and Sustainability

An historical approach

Harry Margalit

Routledge
Taylor & Francis Group

LONDON AND NEW YORK

from Routledge

First published 2016
by Routledge

2 Park Square, Milton Park, Abingdon, Oxfordshire OX14 4RN
711 Third Avenue, New York, NY 10017

Routledge is an imprint of the Taylor & Francis Group, an informa business

First issud in paperback 2017

British Library Cataloguing in Publication Data
A catalogue record for this book is available from the British Library

Library of Congress Cataloging in Publication Data
Names: Margalit, Harry, author.
Title: Energy, cities and sustainability : an historical approach /
Harry Margalit.
Description: Abingdon, Oxon ; New York, NY : Routledge, 2016. | Series:
Routledge studies in energy policy
Identifiers: LCCN 2015035522| ISBN 9781138852396 (hb) |
ISBN 9781315723501 (ebook)
Subjects: LCSH: Cities and towns--Energy consumption. |
Urbanization--Environmental aspects. | Energy development. | Sustainable
urban development. | Urban policy--Environmental aspects.
Classification: LCC HT361 .M387 2016 | DDC 307.76--dc23
LC record available at http://lccn.loc.gov/2015035522

ISBN: 978-1-138-85239-6 (hbk)
ISBN: 978-0-8153-5906-7 (pbk)

Typeset in Goudy
by Taylor & Francis Books

Contents

Illustrations

Figures

Tables

Units and measurements

This book is not intended for readers with advanced technical expertise. Due to the nature of its material, though, some use of technical units has been necessary to make comparisons, and to give an idea about the relative size of things such as power and energy. For non-technical readers the following points may help to avoid confusion.

Energy

Energy is the capacity to do work – to move things about, to heat objects or materials, or to emit light, for example. The amount of energy in a particular fuel can be estimated, and fuels that contain a lot of energy are considered "energy dense". Gasoline (petrol) has an energy density of 32.5 megajoules per litre (MJ/l). This means that each litre in a tank can provide 32.5 million joules of energy when put to work. However, when this fuel is put to work in the average car, all this energy is not translated directly into the car moving forward. The internal combustion engine that powers the car is not particularly efficient, and in the process of burning the gasoline through a sequence of controlled explosions within the car's cylinders, only about 25% of the available energy in fuel is actually converted into motive power. So even if we say that our 10 litre gasoline tank contains 325 million joules of energy, in the end only a quarter of that will appear as work done to move the car. This is important in energy accounting, where the amount of energy used by the final consumer may be considerably less than that fed into the system as primary energy.

In the metric system energy is expressed in joules, and I have used this unit wherever possible. In some cases other units are used for comparison. Two of these are British Thermal Units (Btu) and tonne of oil equivalent (toe). The first is a unit of heat, and is a good expression of how much heat a quantity of fuel can produce. Since a joule can also be a measure of heat, Btu's and joules can be converted to each other, with one Btu equal to about 1,055 joules. Tonne of oil equivalent measures energy as the amount released when a tonne of oil is fully burned. Although different oils produce differing amounts, by convention one toe is about 42 billion joules

(42 gigajoules, abbreviated as GJ). It is generally used as a way of visualising large amounts of energy.

Power

Power is a measure of how quickly work can be done, or the rate of energy conversion. We may know that the energy in our gasoline tank can move our car 100 kilometres, but this could take minutes, hours or days depending on the kind of engine we have. Thus power introduces time into the equation, and its unit of the watt is equal to one joule expended over one second. A 100 kilowatt engine (100 kW) produces 100,000 joules of motive power per second, and would probably shift our car the 100 km in an hour. Watts can also express electrical power, and are often multiplied by how long that power is produced or consumed. If a household appliance uses 1 kW continuously, over a full day it will use 24 kilowatt hours (kWh). The same applies to a source of power. If a wind turbine produces 2 million watts, or 2 MW (megawatts), continuously for 5 hours, then it has generated 10 megawatt hours, abbreviated as 10 MWh. Typically, a wind turbine will only produce its maximum power for a fraction of the year. A turbine rated as capable of producing 2 MW may only do so for 8 hours a day. It will therefore have generated 16 MWh for that day, or a third of its theoretical maximum of 48 MWh for 24 hours. The ratio between the amount it can produce in theory, and its actual production, is termed its capacity factor. In this case the capacity factor is a third, or 33.3%. Taking the capacity factor into account is critical when comparing different electricity generating options.

Introduction

There are many books that deal with energy and urban form in a prescriptive way. This is not one of them. I am an architect by training, as well as an architectural historian. My interest in cities is as historical artefacts, since they are the most complex creations of humanity. They are the locus of modernity, the places where the full array of human possibilities plays out. In our time they exert an irresistible pull, and we are witnessing an urbanisation of populations that is historically unique.

My immediate concern was to understand these movements as history, but viewed through the lens of energy systems. By energy I mean the physical means by which cities and the civilisations they foster are powered and sustained. The interaction of energy sources and urban forms seems to me to be a fundamental relationship where energy is used by the city to power daily life, but the specific ways that energy is put to work in turn shapes the forms and limits of urban life. The issue of limits is the key one here. Pre-industrial cities were markedly different to industrial cities in both scale and functioning. Nonetheless they contained the precursors for modern urban life, and in one view we can see the modern city as the elaboration of pre-existing aspects of city life through the application of unprecedented amounts of energy.

Both cities and energy have been extensively studied, and references to their respective histories appear throughout the text. What seemed to be missing was an historical examination of their interaction. There have been a number of contemporary accounts of urban energy systems such as Austin Troy's *The Very Hungry City* which show the many hidden applications of energy in running modern cities, but my intention was to see if there were broader lessons that could be drawn from looking at cities and energy over time. The challenge here was in the integration of different kinds of history. Most of the raw material of this book is gleaned from conventional sources. The degree of integration I sought was the motivating project of the book.

Weaving together different kinds of history is never a neutral exercise. It entails, invariably, some larger notions about the mechanisms of history itself. I have not attempted to impose a specific schema over the project, but invariably biases emerge as a consequence of historical writing. What I was conscious of was the inevitability of any study in energy being used to inform current objectives in energy policy and urban planning. I am not sure if this book will be useful to others in that respect, but writing it has clarified certain relationships in my thinking.

It is easier to explain these in relation to current books on the topic. Most books in the area are prescriptive, that is they propose solutions to energy dilemmas in the form of planning suggestions or principles. However, these strike me as generally ahistorical, in that they seldom take into account the historical forces that created the dilemmas. Many exist in the form of an orthodoxy that favours making cities denser and reducing car use, two suggestions that appear attractive in current advanced economies.

However, on careful examination these policy trends have unintended consequences. These will be looked at more closely in later chapters, but the complexity of the city makes its aspects interdependent. At heart the question is: if one aspect is altered in pursuit of a specific goal, what else will change? The answer, for me, involves teasing out whatever mechanisms of urban interdependence we can, using history as the means to understand how they were constituted.

This is not always easy. The tendencies within the pre-industrial city manifested in the later industrial city, but the advent of planning and sophisticated urban governance in the late 19th and early 20th centuries created an avenue for the injection of ideological aims into shaping the city. Thus the early, almost organic, creation of the 19th century city gave way to a process of development that involved critique of the existing city, and attempted rectification of its deficiencies. Needless to say the law of unintended consequences became widely evident in the results. Much of my career in writing the architectural history of the 20th century has been around this topic.

This accounts for the structure of the book. It is roughly chronological in structure, and the first chapter sketches out the relationship between energy and cities in pre-industrial societies. Political entities play a large part in this story, as all these societies were essentially solar in their powering. The second chapter looks at the breaking of the nexus between conversions of solar energy, and city form and size, as fossil fuels were adopted. This enabled the development of the modern city, and most of the book concerns its growth and evolution. One of the aims of the book is to maintain a degree of complexity in dealing with technology. A history that charts the rise of inventions and their subsequent adoption would be both dull and inaccurate. Technical advances act upon existing institutions, and in many cases transform them comprehensively. How this happens is a story of institutions, beliefs and group interests as much as one of innovation. Capturing this has proved a challenge.

Thus chapter 5 is concerned with critiques of the modern city in which energy is bound up, but not necessarily dominant. I felt this was important in understanding the ideological underpinnings of contemporary ideas about how to fix cities, and in particular how to reduce their energy use.

The ideological mechanism I am interested in is not so much what is the proposed solution, but rather what was the perceived problem? In many cases this is constituted partly as a technical issue and partly as a matter of group perception. Distinguishing between the two is not always easy.

It is for this reason that the idea of sustainability may not always appear in these pages in familiar guise. In my view societies or regimes are as likely to fail through a loss of confidence as they are for lack of markets, or raw materials or any objective material reason. Having witnessed the swift dismantling of the Iron Curtain and the Apartheid regime, I remain of the view that it was not economics alone that made this happen. The commonplace definition of sustainability as having social, ecological and economic dimensions turns out to be useful even in complex systems, where each of these can be seen as playing an equal role.

I take social sustainability very seriously. It is easy to regard the passing of Stalinism or Apartheid as evidence that history can be innately just, but that would be a mistake in my opinion. Progress is a contingent thing, dependent on many factors. One thread that I have attempted to weave through the book is that of demographics, which provides indicators of social sustainability. The demographics of the modern world are telling, and in many cases not what one would expect. The statistics and projections of the United Nations Population Division present a paradigm shift that will play out in ways that are hard to visualise. This too is part of the story of what abundant energy has brought about.

Above all I hope that the book makes the point that energy must be respected. Many people have become wedded to opinions on the matter, but there seems to be a disturbing deficiency in understanding how engineering works. I am not an engineer, but the key concepts of how energy is distilled, distributed and generated can be understood with basic mathematics. Too many claims are taken at face value, when it is a simple matter to check them on a notepad using a calculator. The amount of energy in a litre of fuel, how much energy a solar panel generates on average – these can be ascertained with some accuracy, even allowing for improvements in technology. If not absolute figures, they at least give some sense of the magnitude of things which is critical in energy policy.

It is a puzzle to me why engineers have not played a bigger role in public debate. They are, after all, central to any aspect of implementation. When engineers do develop a sense of history, it can be revelatory. There are many references to Vaclav Smil in this book, a testimony to the pre-eminent rank he holds in the field of energy history. In Australia Pat Troy has for years used engineering to inform planning and a view of social justice, to convincing effect.

There are other key texts that have helped shape the book. Foremost among these is Chandler and Fox's *3000 Years of Urban Growth*, which remains a critical source for the raw figures that tell the story. Also essential was Massimo Livi-Bacci's *A Concise History of World Population*. Read in conjunction with Smil's *Energy in World History*, these three works inform the basic thesis of the book. Of course there is more, and Kenneth Jackson's *Crabgrass Frontier* was a very useful account of the history of suburbia. In general I have tried to use mainstream sources for data in the last chapters. There are an enormous number of websites these days with reasonably credible national and regional data around energy, cities and populations. The challenge is to create a unified picture from these sources.

I am aware that the argument of this book is not mainstream in planning or architectural circles. I have not gone out of my way to make it so. It is simply the story that seems to me to fit the data, and history, that is widely available. Along the way I have had colleagues who have disagreed with me, but have seen nothing personal in it, and I respect then immensely for that. Others have assisted me through extended discussion, or generous editing. My colleague Alan Peters was a patient sounding board, and Maryam Gusheh has been a great friend and critic. Many thanks to Cath Lassen, who told me to just get on with the book at the start. Needless to say they don't necessarily agree with my views or interpretation. The Built Environment faculty at the University of New South Wales kindly assisted with production costs. I also owe my gratitude to Khanam Virjee, Margaret Farrelly, Alanna Donaldson and the production team at Routledge for their invariably good-natured professionalism. I would thank my wife Anne for her endless patience, but I suspect she finds me easier when I'm writing, so it applies less to this than to almost everything else.

1 Energy and urban formation in the pre-modern city

The form of urban structures, or cities, is studied in a number of ways. Depending on the home discipline of the scholar, the techniques and emphasis can vary enormously. For the field of urban morphology, the prevailing discipline is geography, and the published studies often, but not exclusively, take an historical slant. This view is inclusive, and seeks the explanation of urban form in historical, economic and cultural factors that act on urban growth over extended periods. The field owes much to the work of M.R.G. Conzen, whose seminal influence in Britain is acknowledged in publications such as *The Built Form of Western Cities*, a *festschrift* devoted to Conzen on his eightieth birthday. The list of contributors, drawn almost exclusively from geography, underlines how geographers have dominated the study of the form of Western cities within the field (Slater 1990).

However, this is not the complete picture. As Ivor Samuels points out, urban morphology has in recent decades attempted to reconcile with other schools of thought that have an interest in urban form and structure. If urban morphology has been linked to explanations of how cities have come to look and function as they are, other disciplines have had an interest in the field as a way of informing the design of buildings, precincts and cities. Thus the intention is to use an understanding of existing urban form to make good decisions about how projects and buildings not yet built will sit in their urban context (Samuels 1990).

This intention has been manifest in a range of attitudes to the city. When it first emerged, in the 1950s in Italy under Saverio Muratori, the emphasis was on discovering persistent types of buildings and urban structures that characterise cities and that recur over time (Muratori & Cataldi 1984). The manifestation of these, in the work of architects such as Aldo Rossi, was to create buildings which were similar to the persistent types in appearance and organisation, but which had a contemporary expression. Thus Rossi's work created a resonance with historical form, but also had a strong sense of being of its time, and critical of prevailing modes of development (Rossi & Moschini 1979).

Other architects also took up the study of pre-modern city form to inform their own work, as post-war developments in Western countries replaced

19th century, and earlier, buildings with modern, rationalist, types. In part this was the result of a changed building industry, where the craft necessary to produce traditional buildings was either absent or simply too expensive. In part, too, it was the result of the desire for new spaces that were precise in their intention, and not subject to the vagaries of historical influence and the cycles of decay and maintenance. As the prospect of the loss of whole historic town cores to development loomed, the value of these cores became evident to planners and architects. They were held up against new development as examples of charm, whimsy and texture which gave scale and comfort to users and those passing through.

The rediscovery of the historic town has what might be called a class aspect. In many cities the historic centres were largely abandoned by those who could afford to move to the suburbs. The degradation of historic housing stock meant that the poor were left in the cores, and the prevalence of middle-class values drove families to homogenous suburbs precisely because they presented a predictable and safe living environment. Whatever charm the streets of the historic core may have had was often counteracted by the poor internal amenity of its houses and flats. The sheer space of the suburbs alleviated this.

Thus the picturesque aspects of old towns and cities retained their value as exemplary spaces between buildings, but the spaces within were often unsuitable for the expectations of modern life. The effort of renovating old houses was generally uneconomic, at least until the age of gentrification when the huge amount of labour required was undertaken by the owner, who then reaped a profit through the collective revitalisation of old neighbourhoods by similar owners.

The motive for studying urban form can therefore oscillate between nostalgia for the human-scale street-and-square networks of the pre-industrial town or city, with the dense human interaction they appeared to encourage, and the desire to understand the city in an abstract way to inform new development and building. This latter intent, with more than a dash of the former, is behind the revival of interest in the city that suffused architecture in the 1950s and 60s. In recent years it has appeared as part of an ongoing debate on sustainability, since urban form clearly has an influence on how people go about their lives, and how much energy they use in the process. This principle has grown stronger in recent years, to the point where it could be described as the dominant paradigm for the planning and development of contemporary Western cities.

Although this is widely evident and understood, the imperatives of sustainable urban development have driven a singular understanding of the effect of urban form on energy use. The sheer complexity of the urban system is often poorly represented, and the suburban/urban split of contemporary cities is oversimplified to encourage the revitalisation of the latter and the demise of the former. This is not always helpful, as the tendency towards efficiency has been at work within all types of urban development. The rising cost of petrol may skew the equation, but it doesn't efface those things that suburbia does, or did, well.

To view the question of urban development as suburban or urban also denies the many historic phases of development away from the centre, producing suburbs or demi-suburbs of great variety in form and density. Many of these are now characterised as inner-city, despite their early history as places to escape the poor conditions that prevailed in the urban core when they were first developed.

The drivers of urban morphology vary from city to city, depending on age, periods of rapid growth and geographical factors. The surprisingly high density of Los Angeles, by American standards, may be the consequence of its constrained water supply which encouraged city-wide compact development (Kahrl 1982). London has its ancient city with its Medieval layout, its subsequent economic power and its post-war green belt. Sydney has a vast harbour dividing north from south whose bridging in 1932 gave the north shore its distinctive suburban texture. The newness of Vancouver has meant that almost all the forms of 19th century urban development are absent, and suburb abruptly meets city. In addition patterns of subdivision, forms of land title and cultural preferences have made their mark.

The influence of energy consumption and availability might have assumed a significant role in how the contemporary city would develop, but it has been surprisingly poorly understood in historical context. This appears to be a function of the ideological role this factor has assumed – in order to support specific ideas as to how cities should develop, those parts that represent an opposing vision have been painted in a poor light. A developed and historically aware account of urban development which emphasises energy use has yet to be written – that is one which simply attempts to understand the innate logic prevailing at the time when specific forms of development made sense. We might criticise the suburb as car-dependent and hence energy intensive, but its development as an alternative to the evils of the Victorian city was undertaken as a matter of social imperative for the expanding middle classes. In modern times urban development has too often been reactive, where the driving vision is to correct the perceived inadequacies of the status quo.

The move from country to city that characterises our time has also changed perceptions of the social function of the city. With this shift the city becomes the locus of modern life. All its aspects are accommodated in the modern metropolis, from work to leisure, from consumption to production. The US passed from a rural to an urban majority around 1920, but many Southern states retained significant rural majorities into the latter part of the 20th century. A map of current urbanisation rates shows large urban majorities in Europe, North America and Australia, as well as much of South America. India and South Asia are distinctly rural, despite having very large cities. Africa, with significant exceptions, is also predominantly rural (United Nations Population Division n.d.).

Given the prevalence of cities, and their undoubted role as attracters of all strata of society, it seems perhaps unusual that advocates of urbanity were moved to defend the city and its social role in the 20th century. Yet urbanisation had a poor press for much of the modern era, with its dynamic overriding attempts to plan in an orderly fashion for urban growth. The dilemma for developing economies was that investment in manufacturing required concentrations of labour, such as occur in cities. Drawing workers from the countryside with the prospect of employment also meant a swelling urban population, which could shift the balance of demography and power over a generation.

China currently is grappling with this shift, and the control on population movement is enforced through the *hukou* household registration document. Access to social services is determined by legal residency, and attaining a *hukou* for major cities like Beijing, Guangzhou and Shanghai remains difficult for poor rural dwellers. Recent reforms have made residency in smaller cities easier, but the system remains as a determinant of where rural migrants can settle, and which cities are encouraged to grow.

Perhaps the most infamous system of this type was Apartheid, the system of race-based movement control implemented by the National Party government of South Africa in the 1950s and 60s. The intention of the system was to bring rural labour to the industrial and mining centres of the Witwatersrand but without granting rights of residency. Rural workers would return to their villages of birth for annual holidays, but were deemed to be continuing residents of these villages. A man might work for 30 years in Johannesburg but have a wife and children in a rural location, and see them rarely. Needless to say many led double lives, and the social dislocation engendered has continued after the passing of Apartheid.

The effect of this migration, where uncontrolled, has been massive informal or unplanned settlements around established cities. The favelas of Brazil are among the best known, but the Iranian Revolution of 1979 owed much of its driving discontent to the rural poor who had migrated to a small number of large cities, particularly Tehran. Iran became predominantly urban in the early 1980s (Kazemipour & Mirzaie 2005).

In the US, the abolition of slavery established the free movement of labour as a right nationwide. This is a fundamental tenet of an efficient capitalist economy – that capital and labour move freely to exploit differences in opportunity and cost. Many Southern black families took advantage of this right and settled in the expanding manufacturing centres of Chicago and Detroit in the early 20th century. America continues to be a highly mobile society, where moving cities to pursue job opportunities is a commonplace occurrence supported by traditions such as attending college in a distant city or town.

The free movement of populations in search of economic opportunity shaped many advanced economies, and their cities, through the 20th century. Large conurbations, such as Buenos Aires or Tokyo–Yokohama or

Los Angeles, have all served as major attractors of internal and international migrants. Many of these cities have seen their manufacturing base shrink, and are faced with reinventing themselves as cities, moving from making to consuming in economies that are becoming increasingly characterised by growth in service jobs.

Thus the determinants of urban form may vary from the incremental, as in ownership patterns and subdivisions dating from pre-industrial times, to the driving compulsion to absorb millions of migrants seeking work in manufacturing centres where they can sell their labour and diligence. In addition, the period in which these movements take place, and the political conditions under which they happen, all add to the distinctive urban form that emerges.

The 21st century manifestations of urban growth may seem to reflect a compelling urgency, with the city representing the promise of contemporary life as well as offering access to the most up to date services and opportunities. But this is only a modern view, and rests on that unsettling aspect of modern life that arises from the enormous changes that seem to characterise the modern era. For much of history cities held only a small proportion of the population, and this proportion was as likely to decline as to grow. Often the city played a role in history greater than its size might suggest, and empires are identified by their capitals more than by the masses who sustained their rulers and bureaucracies.

Thus Rome is synonymous with its early Empire, and London with a later one. Florence looms large in the story of Renaissance Italy, and the story of St Petersburg encapsulates the rise of Russia. The city is a cultural entity as well as an economic one, and the kind of lives lived in cities over time have fascinated historians of architecture and of urbanity for millennia. In the English-speaking world few figures have shaped the historical view of cities as comprehensively as Lewis Mumford.

Born in Flushing, New York, in 1895, Mumford's interests and writings ranged across literary criticism, philosophy, history, technology and architecture. His best known work is an integrated historical volume titled *The City in History: Its origins, its transformations and its prospects* (Mumford 1961). The book presents a view of the city influenced by both American naturalism, where the city and country exist as a duality, and a Freud-inspired schema of the city as embodying a social psychology from the outset. This latter idea has Mumford introducing psychological terms to describe the social effect, and the underlying, continuing tensions of the city as a social organism. He writes of the "paranoid claims and delusions" of kingship, the "normalized schizophrenia" engendered by the coercion between social classes, and neurosis resulting from "repetitious labor" (Mumford 1961, p.46).

The idea of societies being marked by collective psychological states or maladies has its roots in the social philosophers who fled Germany in the 1930s and settled in America, where they combined Freudian notions of psychological imbalances with sociological concepts such as class, and the tensions it produced. A key figure in this was Theodor Adorno, who led a group of American academics in the production of a volume titled *The Authoritarian Personality*, an attempt to explain the rise of fascism as a collective phenomenon in the years preceding the Second World War (Adorno 1950). Thus the idea that specific social phenomena can be expressed as collective psychology, with one or more traits predominating, found its way into Mumford's work.

While the groups in ancient cities may have exhibited their collective neuroses or psychoses, the cities themselves fulfilled a powerful and seductive symbolic role. For Mumford the king was the catalyst and creator of the ancient city, but the city itself had both "a despotic and divine aspect". This latter symbolic dimension is, for Mumford, the compelling power of the ancient city, which comes to be not only a collective creation, but also a place that physically embodied a cosmology, or all-encompassing belief system. As the place of residence of the king and the priesthood, it was also the site of the most fulfilled life available (Mumford 1961, p.49).

It is impossible to verify this dual idea of the significance of early cities. Whereas we might with confidence say that cities generally rely on agriculture, or at a minimum herding of cattle as in the large 19th century Zulu proto-cities of Southern Africa, the idea that the king, as the embodiment of a centralised and hierarchical social structure, is necessary to hold the endeavour together and to connect to gods has overtones of Freud's *primal father* who monopolises power and pleasure in the primal horde (Marcuse 1987, p.15).

For Mumford this characterisation of the early city contains within it his ambivalence towards modern life. For the city is not only a commercial agglomeration, or a symbolic entity: it is the seat of a civilisation, which contains both codified and streamlined laws, and the capacity to wreak destruction through its very organisation. Mumford proposes that as the city achieves greater consistency and peace within, it assumes greater menace towards those outside its confines (Mumford 1961, p.51). This same idea is reflected in the first of a series of six documentaries Mumford created for the Canadian Film Board in 1963, which he titled *The City – Heaven and Hell* (Mumford 1963).

For someone of Mumford's learning, the modern city he was confronted by in the early 1960s undermined the social cohesion he saw as part of the traditional function of cities. For him the industrial city – the "paleotechnic paradise", as he called it with some irony – was an abrogation of the promise of the city, and his contempt was visceral. He considers that the industrial city is unique in history not for its misery or squalor, which existed in previous periods, but in its normalisation and acceptance of ugliness and poor civic life (Mumford 1961, p.474).

The industrial city, as we shall see, was not only unusually grim, it was also unusually large historically. With growth came a need to divide the city into discrete units, the better for social function and identity. Venice is held up by Mumford as the paradigm of this, and he proposes its neighbourhoods and precincts as exemplars whose "recovery today, as an essential cellular unit of planning, is one of the fundamental steps towards re-establishing a new urban life" (Mumford 1961, p.321).

Thus we can see that any attempt to understand the city historically – and there have been myriad – is bound up in the concerns and ideologies prevailing at the time of writing. This may be a truism in the practice of history, but it does explain why the view of the city as an historical phenomenon is constantly shifting. A counter view to that of Mumford has been put forward by Leonardo Benevolo, author of the graphically lush *The History of the City*, first published in Italian in 1975 and in English five years later (Benevolo 1980).

Benevolo's book is influenced by his training as an architect, as evident in the copious use of photographs and drawings, and by his mid 20th century education in Rome. The organisational schema, or organising intellectual framework, is a modified version of Marx's view of history. This view influenced all the social sciences with its reductive, yet compelling premise that expressed in one simple sentence one great organising principle: "The history of all hitherto existing society is the history of class struggles". Out of this arose the whole gamut of Marxist and neo-Marxist histories, including urban histories. The beauty of this idea is that societies – and cities represented complex societies in themselves, even when part of a greater empire – could be analysed with reference to a simple duality, the ruling and the ruled (Marx & Engels 1977).

Marx and Engels saw things in more complex detail, for they write that "In the earlier epochs of history, we find almost everywhere a complicated arrangement of society into various orders, a manifold gradation of social rank" (Marx & Engels 1977, p.222). However, the simplicity of the basic proclamation fostered analyses that looked at the role of each class and order within the prevailing power structure. Whereas Mumford maintains the power of physical archetypes such as the citadel to give shape to the city in a symbolic hierarchy, Benevolo (1980) asserts certain Marxist notions in his view of the origin of cities.

Foremost amongst these is the idea of surplus. The major transition necessary for the earliest cities to arise was the conversion in ways of living from the Palaeolithic to the Neolithic, or from hunter–gatherer to farmer. Although the shift appears gradual, it had profound effects on social organisation and created the necessary conditions for permanent settlements, and ultimately cities. While hunter–gatherer groups may have enjoyed good food sources under optimal conditions, they were essentially mobile, and they exploited wild food sources where they found them. The domestication of animals and plants for settled farming not only gave humans some control over the location of food, it also influenced its relative abundance. Harvested crops can be stored, and animals bred through husbandry. If farmers produce more than they consume, a surplus is created, and this arrangement allows the freeing of some people from the work of food production. They may form an administrative or spiritual elite, but it is the continued existence of a food surplus that makes viable the existence of all those not directly farming or hunting.

The notion of surplus became widespread through its role in Marx's analysis of capitalism (Marx 1969). Surplus represented the value contributed by the worker over and above their wage or recompense, and as such it is the increment of value they have created that is appropriated by the capitalist. In capitalism it has a monetary value: if the concept is applied to pre-capitalist societies, it may be in the form of food or work that is given over to sustaining groups such as priests, courtiers or soldiers. However, the creation of a surplus may be a necessary condition for urban life, but it is hardly sufficient to create the great diversity of cities and urban structures through history.

While surplus in pre-capitalist societies has traditionally referred to food, it can be broken down even further. We may think of food as necessary for life, and in modern society we understand the energy content of different foods varies greatly, but we use this understanding to avoid those foods that contain excess energy and are thus stored as fat. However, the varying energy content of different foods had a more profound importance in ancient times, and energy contained in food surpluses played a large role in the development of particular societies.

In simple terms, in a foraging or hunting society, the greater the energy content of the food being gathered or hunted, the less was needed. Conversely if the time and effort required for two foods was equal, then the one providing more energy would be favoured. Gathering roots appears to provide the best energy returns for foragers, with up to 40 times as much energy gleaned compared to that expended in digging and collecting. In contrast, the effort to hunt small tropical animals can take as much energy as the animals yield as food, a poor prospect in energy returns (Smil 1994, p.21). Large fatty animals also provide a far better energy return for the effort expended than small lean ones, so group hunts of mammoths or bison become attractive feeding strategies. Some areas are particularly well endowed. The Pacific Northwest had an annual cycle of berry gathering, mountain goat hunting and a great abundance of salmon that could be caught. This was supplemented by seasonal catching of eulachon, a small fish so rich in fat that it was sometimes known as "candlefish" as it could be burned as a candle when dried. These food sources were reliable enough, and dense enough, to sustain large permanent communities (Czapp 2009).

As with any species, the population densities of foragers depended on the amount of energy that could be harvested over a given range. Generally the yield was low, with correspondingly low numbers of people. In these sparse and isolated bands, the balance of life was precarious and no complex social organisation could emerge. Where food was more abundant, greater numbers of people could live in close proximity. Storage of food allowed greater population densities to exist, with the greater opportunities that this supported. As Smil asserts, once the benefits and specialisation provided by greater densities became established, humanity was committed to more complex societies and their attendant need to harness greater energy flows (Smil 1994, p.22).

The foods chosen for cultivation and domestication thus needed to be, from the outset, energy rewarding, given the intensive effort required for primitive agriculture compared to foraging. However, the reliability of the resulting food supply, and the greater overall energy yield and hence population densities, secured its dominance over foraging and hunting. Yet early agriculture suffered from the limitations of humans as a species. Our ability to sweat profusely gives us the capacity to exert ourselves over long periods, a useful attribute for hunting and running down prey. But we are poor machines, with little power. We are relatively ineffectual at heavy work – digging, slashing or pulling ploughs. The effort required in early agriculture consisted not only of fieldwork, in which fields were cleared and ploughed, seeds sown and the resulting crops harvested: the crops also needed to be processed, with the grain separated from its inedible casing for storage and eating.

The domestication of wild grasses to yield cereals is a fascinating story, popularised by Jared Diamond. Cereals have innate advantages over other seed forms, in that they provide substantial energy as carbohydrate, contain typically around 15% protein, and are dense and dry, which suits storage (Smil 1994, p.36). When combined with pulses, or derivatives of the pea family, a broad spectrum of dietary requirements is met. Diamond describes a biological "package" that emerged in the Fertile Crescent of the Middle East, which consisted of cereals, pulses, domesticated animals and flax for fibre and oil (Diamond 1998, p.142). The particular package varied across Eurasia, with rice and soybeans playing a larger role in China, and lentils and chick-peas more common in India. In pre-Columbian America maize and beans formed the staples, but at higher elevations grains such as quinoa were derived from broad leaved plants and were not strictly cereals.

Thus, through trial, error and observation, traditional agriculture took the limited number of grains suitable for domestication and moulded them to its purpose. This involved selective breeding of the attributes useful to people, such as high energy yields and convenient processing. The package as a whole may have varied, but the essential principles remained constant, shaped locally by opportunity and preference. When we consider how these forms of agriculture supported specific instances of social organisation, we can speak of differing energy economies. Smil provides estimates of the kind of effort required for various tasks in traditional farming, and they underline the labour-intensive nature of this form of subsistence. Without the aid of animals, hoeing can consume up to 180 hours per hectare for a single crop, weeding up to 300, harvesting 30–55 hours and flailing to separate the wheat from the chaff can take up to 100 hours. Even this represents an incomplete picture, with many additional tasks required to bring the grain to table (Smil 1994, p.85).

The shift to traditional farming naturally led to a search for greater efficiencies. Crop rotation was needed to prevent a single crop denuding the soil of nutrients, and fluctuations in rainfall across seasons and cycles produced variable yields, with famine when rains failed. The first could partly be overcome with fertiliser derived from human and animal waste, the second with irrigation. In terms of energy and effort, the greatest advance was the employment of animals for the tasks that needed greater power, such as ploughing, transport and threshing. Domestic animals can digest grain by-products such as chaff (straw), so there is an immediate gain in their employment despite the food's low nutritional content. In an energy economy, the grazing required to maintain work animals must be subtracted from the overall gain in energy yield they produce. Nonetheless draught animals were a major factor in the increase in energy yields needed for the establishment of early cities and empires.

The superiority of farming allowed population densities up to ten times greater than those supported by shifting cultivation. However, this left little margin for natural variability, and famines could be devastating. With advanced techniques an upper limit of 12–15 people per hectare of cultivated land could be supported by traditional farming. By the time of the late Roman Empire, the energy budget for a wheat harvest, using oxen to aid the heavy tasks such as ploughing, hauling and treading to break up the grain stalks, consumed about 177 hours of human effort and 180 of animal power per hectare. This produced about 400 kg of wheat, containing some 23 times as much energy as that expended in its production (Smil 1994, pp.80–89).

Thus we can see how a surplus of energy arises in developed ancient agriculture using animals, fertiliser and irrigation. These sorts of yields, together with trade and a range of exotic foods, formed the nutritional backbone of the late Roman Empire. But this is only part of the energy story, albeit a crucial one. The Roman Empire extended across a wide geographic range, and holding together a political entity of such size took additional amounts of energy for transport. Despite their reputation for excellent road building – and the Roman network was extensive – the primary means of bulk transportation was by ship. The use of the network of some 80,000 km of paved roads was still hampered by the physics of carts drawn by oxen, which have a limited load capacity and are subject to friction only partly overcome by ancient lubricants and axle bearings. Loads were restricted under the Theodosian Code to 1000 Roman pounds (327 kilograms) for the *rhœda*, and 1500 pounds (491 kg) for the heavier *angeria* (Usher 1954, p.155). The hard surface of the Roman road made for considerably more efficient travel than a rutted track, with less energy required to keep a wagon moving, but compared to sea transport it remained highly uneconomic over long distances.

However, it is easy to see that as a civilisation, the energy benefit over centuries of constructing paved roads compared to tracks would be substantial even for foot traffic. Thus for Rome the high degree of social organisation achieved enabled large public works to be undertaken, with a corresponding efficiency gain that could be reaped over long periods of time. The Roman legion marching to Gaul would gain speed from the even surface, expend less energy due to the gentle gradient of the road, and subsist on a complex and vast distributed food supply. The existence of a surplus food supply looms large in any consideration of the Roman military expansion. For the two centuries preceding the birth of Christ, Rome maintained vast armies with soldiers numbering in the hundreds of thousands (Roth 1999, p.224).

The means by which these armies were supplied were a reflection of the imperial structure itself. Taxation on Roman citizens provided funds in the initial period, and Roman allies sent gifts of grain supplies to cement alliances and show good faith. However, by 200 BC the grain production of both Rome and its allies was insufficient to sustain the imperial armies. Grain was bought from Egypt in market transactions, but the acquired territories were also coerced into giving over agricultural produce to the Roman legions. In Sicily, for example, the first Roman governor conducted an island-wide survey of farmland, and quickly gleaned a significant surplus which was sent both to field armies and to Rome. Spain, too, was required to pay tribute to the armies in the form of clothing and grain.

The burden on colonies continued to grow to the extent that in 170 BC Carthage, for example, contributed over 6,700 tonnes of wheat for military supplies, and half as much barley. In Imperial Rome direct taxation of farm produce was instituted, and could amount to 10% of total production. The logistical sophistication of Rome became part of its tactics, as it maintained a continual supply of men and food for its field armies, and could thus outlast its foes. The shipping routes used were extensive and ambitious: for the campaign against the Seleucid Antiochus III, grain was shipped from Sicily, Sardinia, Carthage (Tunis) and Numidia (North Africa west of Carthage).

The sophistication of these logistics shows how, ultimately, the Roman conquest was fuelled by transporting grain, and hence energy, across vast distances to changing locations. The collection of food as a form of taxation yielded a centralised grain surplus that sustained continual expansion and colonisation. A typical Roman soldier needed about 12,500 kJ per day to stay effective. The capacity of Rome and its vicinity to supply these needs, and its own citizenry, was quickly exhausted. At its peak the city, and its armies, were importing over 400,000 tonnes of grain from Roman provinces. The situation was exacerbated by the numerous estates surrounding Rome given over to the leisure and hobbies of the upper classes, where only fruit and vegetables might be grown.

The extensive trading networks of ancient Rome meant a large variety of foods such as nuts, spices and preserves were imported from as far as India. These supplemented the Roman diet, in particular of the upper classes, but hardly provided the basic energy requirements of the population. Given the preponderance of imported grain in the later Republic and in Imperial Rome, the importance of Ostia as Rome's major port cannot be underestimated. The Forum may have been the most important cultural space in Rome, but the stretch of the Tiber traversed by barges which bore imports from the Harbour of Trajan west of Ostia to the landing docks at the Emporium may well have been its most important artery.

Given the extensive trade conducted by the Roman merchant navy, the actual size of Rome remains surprising. Population estimates at 100 AD put the number at perhaps 650,000, a provincial city in modern terms (Chandler & Fox 1974, p.368). The road network was clogged with traffic, and the limitations of ox-wagons meant that its links with the surrounding countryside diminished rapidly with distance. This had two consequences for the city, both elucidated in graphic terms by Mumford.

The first was the effective decentralisation of the Empire, and the establishment of regional cities that mirrored Rome, and served as its symbolic proxies. Since the technological limits precluded the physical centralisation of the Empire, it dispersed its form in a manner which created an imagined unity. In Mumford's words, the Roman Empire was "a vast city-building enterprise: it left the imprint of Rome on every part of Europe, Northern Africa and Asia Minor" (Mumford 1961, p.205). This cultural transformation, this export of Roman forms and order, served to strengthen Rome as an ideal as much as a city. Alexandria in 100 AD housed 400,000 people, and Seleucia (on the Tigris, in present day Iraq) held 600,000 inhabitants. Rome was not uniquely populous within its known world, but it was uniquely potent (Chandler & Fox 1974, p.81).

The second consequence was that the shipping network that sustained Roman conquests also fed the city as it outgrew its regional food supply. Rather than absorbing a larger population, a difficult task with the internal transport system overwhelmed and the water supply and sewage system limited, this surplus created a skewed social structure and a city where leisure assumed unprecedented forms. Whereas the noble families, perhaps 1800 of them, had spacious urban compounds or at least a large *domus* or urban house, functionaries and merchants made do in closer quarters, and the bulk of the population lived in crude tenements (*insulae*). Yet the extremes of class which underlay this physical separation still supported the privileged position of the city as a whole, through the increasing part that leisure and spectacle played in the daily life of Imperial Rome.

Mumford subjects this to a scathing diagnosis, pointing to the emergence of a parasitic social structure which produced a crippling sense of dependence, and a consequent self-hatred. It is this dynamic, in his view, that led to the murderous spectacles that grew more common, allowing the populace to project their self-hatred onto helpless victims. This process, however, could not have arisen without the imports of grain produced elsewhere. Vast handouts of bread from public stores, unearned and taken for granted, appeased the population and bought a measure of social cohesion. It also led to increasing expectations. By the 4th century AD the Roman calendar had 200 public holidays, a situation unimaginable without a massive transfer of food and agricultural effort within the Empire even when the proportion of slaves (about 35%) is taken into account.

The indolence and the collective brutality that, for Mumford, marked the latter days of Rome were thus enabled by the ceaseless traffic of grain, as well as slaves and exotic foods and animals, from the provinces to Rome. The mere existence provided by a basic food surplus to support a hierarchy of priests and rulers was superseded comprehensively for centuries, and the public works of the city such as the Colosseum, the baths or the racecourse catered for the mass scale of leisure and pleasure cultivated in the city. The image of its decadence remains a potent one, and can be found in many explanations for its decline.

The failure of Rome to cultivate a civic mission that would allow its colonial citizens to match the standing of its Italian citizens, particularly in developing a civic and political life that would be decentralised but equal to the centre, was no doubt one explanation. But supply to the city of essentials fell away as the organising entity withered: as Mumford observed, when the supply of water to the baths of Caracalla ceased in 537, it simply followed the cessation of wood supply for heating many years earlier (Mumford 1961, p.234).

With the collapse of the Roman Empire comes the passing of the most sophisticated energy economy of ancient times. Crucial to this was the harnessing of horses and particularly oxen for haulage and agriculture. But the key transport for large quantities was of course the ship, wind and oar driven but subject to enormous efficiencies of size and friction. The enclosure of the Mediterranean aided this, with its slight tides and limited swells.

Lower population densities than in modern times also explain the predominance of shipping. Despite the reach of Rome at its height, all territories apparently under its control were not uniformly so. Even within Italy bandits presented a constant threat to travellers (Grunewald & Drinkwater 2004, p.18). At sea piracy remained a threat, and sail-driven supply ships were escorted by faster galleys for defence. Even crucial towns were at risk, for in 68 BC Ostia was sacked and held for the better part of a year. With the collapse of Rome and the rise of Constantinople as its eastern successor, the Mediterranean trade routes diminished into local trading opportunities. The centralised surplus that sustained Rome withered away, and the edifice of its legal system that sustained trade through sophisticated notions of contract and laws of evidence passed into obscurity for half a millennium.

The decline of Rome reduced the volume of trade that took place within the Mediterranean that fed and supplied the city itself. While the productivity of European farming is not reflected in the growth of cities in the rest of Europe in the first millennium, the harnessing of horses with the shoulder collar allowed these animals to replace oxen as draught animals (Smil 1994, p.66). Outside of Europe cities grew on the basis of unifying political forces and agricultural advances, such as the corn-based economies of Mesoamerica, in particular the Aztec civilisation and its capital at

Tenochtitlan. A distinct innovation was the construction of raised fields within the lake system surrounding the city, known as *chinampa*, which proved significantly more productive than farming cleared terrain. Transport from outlying areas was restricted to pack animals, but the location of the city made water-borne transport viable for everyday tasks using the lake itself and a grid of canals within the city. When discovered by Spanish conquistadores in 1519, it was barely two centuries old but contained perhaps 200,000 inhabitants, although some estimates put the figure at only 80,000. Its energy economy was sufficient to provide food and labour to build significant public monuments and allow extensive masonry construction. The thriving city shows that lack of animal-drawn transport is no impediment to the growth of pre-industrial cities, if the location can sustain intensive agricultural practices.

The relative advantages of water-borne transport, in energy terms, remained a factor even as local influences vied for control of trading zones and resources. The list of largest cities in 900 AD, according to Chandler and Fox (1974), is instructive: Baghdad, Chang'an (Xi'an), Constantinople (Istanbul), Kyoto, Hangzhou, Alexandria, Cordoba. The first is a creation of the rise of Islam, the last two are beneficiaries of Islamic conquest. Constantinople remained the foremost city of Christianity, heir to Rome and dominant in its westward influence. Baghdad sits astride the Tigris, Cordoba is on the Guadalquivir River and Constantinople commands a key maritime position on the Bosphorus.

Xi'an and Hangzhou represent Chinese centralised government at the close of the Tang dynasty, and its advanced agriculture and transportation. Hangzhou also has the distinction of being at the southern end of the Beijing–Hangzhou Grand Canal, a vital constructed waterway which reached completion around 600 AD. The tonnage of trade accommodated along its 1776 km was impressive, matching Roman proportions: some 150,000 tonnes annually traversed its route by 735 AD. Although the canal was not connected to Xi'an, the city of Luoyang bordered the canal and served as the outlet for Xi'an.

The Grand Canal became part of a more complex set of waterways over time, and its completion in the Sui dynasty involved ambitiously connecting a pre-existing set of disparate canals. Luoyang was at the apex, as roughly the midpoint between Beijing and Hangzhou, and westward enough to facilitate transport to Xi'an. For some commentators the Canal was a pre-requisite for the expansionary events under the Tang dynasty. Initially connecting the Wei and Yellow River basins to Hangzhou, by 608 AD the system extended north to Beijing. Its importance in the distribution of grain was underlined by the construction of enormous granaries between Luoyang and Xi'an, with the largest holding over 900,000 tonnes (Gernet 1982, p.240). However, the choice of Xi'an as a capital proved limiting in the long run. As the city grew it exhausted the agricultural capacity of its surrounds, and it became reliant on the Canal to supplement its food supply (Cotterell & Morgan, 1975). The section of the Yellow River connecting the city with Luoyang was not easily navigable due to currents, and grain transfer to Xi'an was restricted in volume. This constraint made the capital vulnerable not only to military isolation but also to recurrent famine, when the organs of government were forced to relocate to Luoyang to be closer to the trunk route of the Canal.

The extraction of a grain surplus to support the court and government was not without its social consequences. The rebellion of An Lu-Shan (755–766 AD) marked the beginning of the decline of the Tang dynasty. The rebel commander's personal ambition, by some accounts, meshed with the grievances of peasant farmers who bore the burden of the immense transfer of grain required to support the centralised administration and its retinue. This was not the only burden the system imposed. Its construction a century and half earlier had required immense quantities of labour. Using a corvée labour system where peasants were obliged to give a certain period per year, perhaps 20 days, to state service, the emperor Yang-ti demanded over a million such obligations for the northern section of the Canal in 605 AD (Wright 1978, p.135). Taken together, the immensity of labour and food extraction under the Tang dynasty is indicative not only of its social power, but also of the capacity, indeed the necessity, under its rule of transferring food energy, in the form of grain, in massive quantities to enable the existence of an imperial capital like Xi'an. Estimates for its population at its height in the 8th century range from 750,000 to 2,000,000, when its surrounding towns are included. The annual importation of 160,000 tonnes of grain was thus crucial to its survival.

The importance of the Grand Canal, and its subsequently expanded network, for political cohesion in China illustrates the reliance large cities had historically on regional transportation. Until the advent of rail, this was primarily by water. The energy budget of pre-industrial cities nonetheless precluded cities growing to over a million inhabitants. Indeed the situation at 900 AD was unusual in there being two cities, Baghdad and Xi'an, with over 750,000. This was not to be repeated until 1800, when London had swelled to 861,000 and Beijing had continued its rise to just exceed one million (Chandler & Fox 1974).

Size alone was not the only determinant of power or influence. The Italian cities of the Renaissance have left an indelible mark on Western culture, but none approached in population the largest cities of their time. They remain among the most extensively studied cities, and records reveal a complex relationship between city and country as a city's ascent to prominence transformed local economies. At 1500 Florence's population, for example, numbered perhaps 70,000 at a time when its cultural and economic powers were greatest in relative terms. As it grew in power its command of the surrounding countryside increased proportionately. Italy had always retained traces of urban settlements established under Rome, and by 1300 exhibited a highly urbanised character with as many as 20% of people living in cities. This was unusually high for Europe, and in Florence this created an increasing demand for food that could not be met locally. Some 35 tonnes of grain were required by the city daily, a demand that could only be met by imports from southern Italy. Annually the city also consumed 30,000 pigs and twice that number of sheep (Curtis 2012). These volumes too exceeded local production.

The reliance on imports made the city vulnerable both to price variations and poor harvests. To secure a local supply of food, the city drew its surrounds more tightly into its control in order to extract such surplus as it might. The existence of a surplus of produce and grain was not always assured in Medieval times. The Belgian cities of Bruges and Ghent, for example, drew supplies from northern France, as their local farmers worked within a system of land subdivision and farming practices that produced little more than subsistence yields. Florence, in attempting to bind its countryside to the city for food supply, produced widely differing results in its surrounds. For the area immediately encircling the city, the results were dire, with a reduction in population of some two-thirds by 1427. The process gained momentum as the harsh demands of the city increased the burden on those remaining, and a series of natural calamities hardly helped matters. However, in the further-flung districts, the looser bonds and strong local economies ensured not only survival but prosperity (Curtis 2012).

The general principle of expanding pre-industrial cities, with their agriculturally unproductive populations exploiting an increasingly larger agricultural base, thus manifests in a range of ways but with the same result – the collecting of a surplus either through coercion or markets. The 13,000 tonnes of grain required annually by Florence is an order of magnitude less than the appetite of Imperial Rome or Tang Xi'an, but it nonetheless demanded a level of coercion at local level that strained city–country relations. In many other respects, the city developed on the basis of far-flung trade in goods such as cloth. Its location on a navigable portion of the Arno River upstream from the port of Pisa allowed Florence access to the well-developed trade links forged by Italian traders and merchants across Europe and the Middle East. These facilitated the flow of many types of goods of high value but small bulk, such as cloth, spices and pottery. These may represent compressed value, but they are not part of the food supply needed to feed an urban population. Despite its economic success, the city could not sustain population growth, and an apogee of perhaps 100,000 inhabitants in 1300 slowly declined in number to under 40,000 in 1441. Plagues played a part in this, but for the survivors the economic prospects were reasonably bright as reduced population led to higher per capita wealth, as well as labour and skill shortages (Goldthwaite 1980, p.33). Another consequence was the low rents prevailing in Florence after the Black Death, due to the excess of dwellings.

The buildings of Renaissance Florence are testimony to the significant wealth flowing to the city in the 15th century, through clothmaking, trade and banking. Few cities displayed as much enthusiasm for spending on buildings both public and private. Naturally, at its core this required a skilled population of artisans and a secure supply of food and materials. As the quality of workmanship rose, the time taken to construct buildings also grew. For everyday construction the labour cost varied between 25 and 40% of total building costs, but for the elaborate *palazzi* of the nobility, with their hand-worked stone facings, this could rise to 50%. Modern architect-designed houses have similar ratios. The effort expended in labour, too, seems almost modern. Although the work week consisted of six days, workers also enjoyed some 50 religious holidays in addition to Sundays. The length of the workday itself is a matter of some debate, but in construction may have been eight or nine hours long (Goldthwaite 1980, pp.288–291).

The case of Florence raises a number of interesting points. First, many of the great buildings of the city, including the dome over the cathedral of Santa Maria el Fiore (completed in 1436) and the Palazzo Pitti (begun in 1458), were constructed in a period of declining population. They were the consequence of growing wealth rather than of a growing population. This is a phenomenon which bears some consideration, given population projections for modern societies the world over. Second, its relationship to its surrounding farmlands indicates that the extraction of an agricultural surplus to support urban life could be a fractious undertaking if productivity was low, and imports became crucial even for populations under 100,000. Third, the city seems to have found a natural upper size of about this figure despite international trading links and good water-borne transport, which underlines the difficulties for a city state in procuring sufficient surplus in comparison to a large empire whose coercion extended over hundreds or thousands of kilometres.

If Florence illustrates the power of finance in establishing influence, over and above physical population size, the story of Venice is even more remarkable. While the origins of the city as a defensible settlement on a series of islands sheltered from the Adriatic, but protected by shallow waters from mainland incursions, appear inventive if timid, the locality itself fostered a culture shaped by the very physical attributes of the city form. Forced from early on to forge a trading relationship with the neighbouring mainland, the Venetians developed both maritime skills and a boldness in pursuing opportunities by sea. Trading salt and fish, they slowly secured their city against the tides with oak piles driven into the mud, as well as the incremental construction of canals and their lining quay walls, which created the city itself. Dredged mud and fill were laid within the walls, and over time these were solidified into the series of islands that make up the city as it appears today (Ferraro 2012, p.5).

Thus Venice invested unusual energy in these two aspects: reclamation of land from the lagoon, and ambitious shipbuilding. By 1200 the power of this city of perhaps 70,000 inhabitants was established, but the events of the next four years would cement its prestige and secure its wealth. The story of the period is well recounted by Crowley (2011), and deserves some retelling. Always cognisant of its position linking Europe to the cultures and opportunities of the Middle East and Constantinople, the Venetians were the natural channel for Crusader ambitions in the Levant. The scale of the Fourth Crusade, in conception at least, was breathtaking. When the six knights representing France and the Low Countries arrived in Venice in 1201 to negotiate transport for the venture, they were confronted by the ambition of the doge Enrico Dandolo, already over 90 and sightless. The deal Dandolo drove was immense, on the back of the Crusading zeal. Venice undertook to convey 4,500 horses, 9,000 squires, 4,500 knights and 20,000 foot soldiers across the Mediterranean. Fifty armed galleys, to pursue Venetian interests in the wake of the Crusade, were thrown in free of charge. The proposed cost was 94,000 marks, equal to all French revenues for a year (Crowley 2011, p.25).

The ensuing debacle had a series of momentous but unintended consequences for Venice's great rival Constantinople, a city many times larger than Venice itself. Heir to Rome, the inhabitants of the Eastern capital held the Venetians in contempt for their obsession with trade and lack of idealism, but the city was nonetheless home to 10,000 Venetian merchants. Things first went awry when only a fraction of the anticipated Crusaders arrived – some 12,000 in total. For over a year the entire Venetian economy had been devoted to shipbuilding and provisioning, all effectively on credit. The debt remained despite the low numbers arriving, but in waiting the optimum sailing time had passed. Nonetheless Dandolo determined to make use of the opportunity provided to subdue the towns of the Dalmatian coast that had harassed Venetian ships as they made their way down the Adriatic. The largest of these, Zara, was attacked and sacked, despite papal dictates not to attack Christian cities. Further intrigues followed and the lasting consequence was the taking of Constantinople by the Venetian and Crusader fleet and army, a goal totally absent at the initial stages of planning and negotiation.

The looting of Constantinople transferred enormous wealth to Venice, but more importantly it cemented Venetian influence over key trade routes to the East. The influence of the city was secured, as was its economic base as a trading power. Significantly, all this was achieved without an agrarian base. In simple energy terms Venice needed to expand its network or die, since it commanded no natural agricultural lands. As its power grew it did indeed dominate the Veneto region, using the navigable sections of the Brenta, Po and Adige rivers for transportation and export. But its ambitions were wider, and a century and half after Constantinople was taken large volumes were traded with Beirut and Alexandria, and opportunities sought as far afield as India and China (Crowley 2011, p.xxvi).

Nonetheless the issue of food supply continued to trouble Venetian administrations. Maize was introduced in the wider Veneto region in the 16th century to supplement the cheaper cereals – sorghum, rye and oats – on which the poor of Venice traditionally fed. Venetians also invested heavily in the mainland. Marshes were reclaimed for agriculture, and fields were bought up at an increasing rate from the 13th century. By 1636 nearly 40% of the land in the mainland province surrounding Padova was owned by Venetians. The produce of these farms was also subject to legal restrictions, whereby crops were required to be brought to the city. Trading ships of the Republic were also encouraged to transport grain home through additional payments (Woolf 1968).

The Venetian expansion was achieved essentially through trade, land acquisition and military excursions rather than through an imperial project to subjugate large areas and establish military control. As such its food supply was obtained on the market, and the difference between a powerful but mercantile economy as opposed to a far-flung imperial one can be read in the city size. For all its pomp Venice, like Florence, never features high on the list of most populous cities. The contiguous conquests of Islam in North Africa and Spain were better suited to fostering large cities, as was the imperial bureaucracy of China.

By the time Venice reached its zenith and became synonymous with a complex urban canal network, the canal system in China had been sub-stantially enlarged and some sections doubled. Locks made the raising of barges and the retention of water at different levels within a canal system feasible, and the enormous mechanical advantage of animal-drawn barges where a single horse could move over 30 tonnes led to the adoption of canal building elsewhere in Europe (Smil 1994, p.136). The Naviglio Grande was commenced in 1177 as a trunk of the Ticino River, and by 1258 it reached into Milan. The Naviglio di Martesana, built between 1457 and 1465, further increased Milan's sphere of economic activity. Originally conceived as an irrigation canal, it was constructed to be navigable and give Milan access to the Adda River. Thus these two canals connected the city to rivers east and west, and the Milanese system was expanded to five *navigli* canals over ensuing centuries. Venice, too, expanded its river-based wider network through construction of 600 km of canals known collectively as the Litoranea Veneto.

Construction of canals in Europe illustrates again the dominance of water transport for any significant movement of goods. Northern Germany boasted the Stecknitz Canal by 1400, its 94 km length taking two weeks to traverse. The depth was a frugal 85 cm, so the draught of vessels it carried, and hence their load, would have been limited. The Loire and Seine valleys in France were connected in 1642 by the Briare Canal. Like the more famous Canal du Midi in southern France, the bulk transport of grain was a major reason for its construction. These waterways allowed grain from inland regions such as Languedoc to be exported, and in general allowed these regions to trade a range of produce.

The bucolic images of European canals today as leisure byways belie their importance in their heyday. As building projects they were challenging, and absorbed enormous resources, testament to their perceived payback. Some 12,000 workers, male and female, laboured on the Canal du Midi for 15 years with hand tools. The perfection of the pound lock was critical to the development of canal systems, as it allowed boats to be raised or lowered to sections of the canal without depleting the water level for the upper portions. The canals brought the mechanical benefits of river and sea transportation to the interior of landmasses themselves. Their benefits not only preceded the industrial age but were critical to the early functioning of manufacturing. The English network commenced relatively late with the Bridgewater Canal in 1761, but it heralded the start of the most complete system of the Industrial era.

Despite these developments, the overall urban population of Europe in towns with more than 5000 dwellers remained proportionately small, and only exceeded 11% in the mid 18th century (Hohenberg & Lees 1985, p.84). Thus urban life constituted a fraction of the total population, who remained overwhelmingly rural. Nonetheless our small survey of significant pre-industrial cities allows some general observations regarding energy and urban form. The primary energy requirement for the population is food, which must be available on a regular basis. No city can sustain shortfalls in supply, since the city contains limited opportunities for food production, in particular grain staples. The problem for larger cities is the relatively low surplus yield of traditional agriculture – perhaps 10% in Roman times, and rising only slowly in subsequent centuries. Smil estimates wheat yields, in energy terms, in Medieval England to be about 70% higher than in Roman Italy: significantly more, but still insufficient to alter settlement patterns at a large scale (Smil 1994, p.89). This is borne out by later Danish figures, which suggest a doubling in agricultural productivity between 1500 and 1800, with no increase in urbanisation (Pomeranz 2000, p.240).

With the limited surplus available, a very large city of half a million inhabitants needed to cast widely for its supply, often obtained with some coercion if the areas of supply were militarily or politically dominated. For cities under 100,000 the problems were less acute, and food supply could be met through trade and purchases, although this number still represented a large pre-industrial city.

And what of the specific forms that these cities took? When we consider the distribution of key resources such as food and water, this alone would encourage a compact form to lessen supply lengths. The Romans constructed an impressive aqueduct system to supply the city with gravity-fed water drawn from distant lakes and springs. Once in the city, the fountains and sluices ran constantly and helped flush sewage and waste into the Tiber. This was one of Rome's luxuries, but it made living at ground level more luxurious than in the upper storeys of the *insulae*. Internal distribution of goods in Rome was hampered by the network of narrow roads, which was in use day and night. The volume of grain imports would have presented the observer with a scene of oxen continuously plodding the towpath from Ostia, hauling the grain barges to feed a largely indolent population. In all the city suffered from its incremental growth, and the symbolic burden of its many temples and public places made it compelling but expensive to live in Rome.

If, as Mumford states, the city is indeed a version of heaven on earth, then its cosmology varies according to its culture. Seventh century Chang'an reflected a singular vision, and boasted an orderliness that eluded ancient Rome when the former was rebuilt around 600 AD. Defined by enclosing walls, the city occupied an area of 9.7 by 8.2 km, or 7954 hectares (Gernet 1982, p.241). If we accept an estimate of 800,000 inhabitants at its height, then this translates to an overall population density of 100 people per hectare, which is low to average by historical standards. The Aurelian Walls of Rome enclosed an area of 1305 hectares by the year 280 AD, and Chandler proposes a density of 500 people per hectare to reach his estimate of 650,000 inhabitants. These are gross figures: when roads and public spaces are subtracted, the actual living density may be much higher. Chang'an benefitted from a planned network of avenues which ran north–south and east–west. Varying in width from 25 to 150 metres for the major ceremonial axis of the Imperial Way, the broader avenues served to define the gridded quarters of the city, as well as acting as fire breaks.

To the north an Imperial compound sat adjoining the administrative precinct. Various gardens around the city provided contemplative relief or private settings for the Imperial family. Fruit trees were planted along the major avenues, increasing the penetration of nature into the city itself. A network of canals supplied water to gardens, as well as transporting household fuel.

The confluence of comprehensive planning, the symbolic arrangement of spaces linking divinity, the Imperial compound and the city administration, and the broad road network and enclosed gardens produced an orderliness that would also have diffused the urban experience, with its low population density. By contrast the qualitative aspects of Roman life, its restive masses and volatility, seem in some way connected to its opportunistic growth, rather than a planned development. The same seems true of Constantinople, where its polyglot community and urban slums made its defence against the Venetian and Crusader assault in 1204 incoherent and ultimately unsuccessful.

The walls surrounding Florence were enlarged to enclose 680 hectares by 1333. With a population estimated at between 60,000 and 94,000, this upper figure nonetheless translated to a gross population density of 138 people per hectare. The lower figure yields a density of 88, which is low historically. At their completion the walls were regarded as ambitious, indeed excessive, and the area contained could be given over in part to gardens and fields. The Black Death decimated the population in 1348, and the city struggled to regain its pre-plague numbers. Thus the city was not only characterised in its heyday by the generous proportions of its city walls, but rents remained cheap as a surplus of housing remained for its subsequent inhabitants. The population density of Renaissance Venice was determined not by its enclosing walls, but the extent of reclaimed and stabilised land. The six *sestieri* or districts cover a total of 725 hectares, a little larger than 14th century Florence, and hence with a population density varying from 151 people per hectare in 1347, to a peak of 251 in 1563 when the population reached 182,000. These figures relate to the modern extent of Venice, and would have been higher when the city was smaller, but the contemporary form of the city seems to have been established by 1300.

The pre-industrial city was not only reliant on an agricultural hinterland for food, but also for fuel. Power for many tasks could be supplied by waterwheels, which proliferated across northern Italy, but the basic heating and cooking requirements of households were met with wood and charcoal. These were drawn from surrounding woodland, and where demand exceeded the capacity of woodland to regenerate the results could be devastating. Where copper smelting took place the deforestation to fuel smelting operations could be extensive and lasting. For domestic energy uses, crop residues or the inedible portions of the harvest could be burned as fuel. These would need to be supplemented by wood harvested from woodland or forest. In France, for example, the ample wood supply that existed in 1550 had all but disappeared on the eve of the French Revolution. China also experienced local depletion of forests. By 1700 the northern provinces of Shandong and Henan were largely deforested, with less than 7% forest cover. Other northern provinces were reduced to less than 25% cover (Pomeranz 2000, p.234). Deforestation would have been exacerbated in periods of intensive timber construction or shipbuilding, as in Venice when preparations for the Fourth Crusade were underway.

Thus the limits of the pre-industrial city would have been set not only by problems of food supply, or the extraction and importation of a food surplus sufficient to feed the urban population. Fuel in the form of wood or charcoal would have presented its own problems. Forests regenerate at a fixed rate, converting sunlight into stored energy through photosynthesis. When the rate of harvesting of wood exceeds the rate of replenishment, deforestation occurs. Assuming a city is at the centre of this process, and it exhausts the woodland that immediately surrounds it, then the inhabitants are forced to look further afield for supply. With poor roads and basic wagons, the quantity of energy expended to bring the wood to the city becomes ever greater, and the energy return on effort expended increasingly smaller.

Great quantities of timber were indeed transported throughout the pre-industrial world by cart or wagon. For the short distances of local life this sufficed, and with small settlements this economy could be sustained, supplemented by high value and small volume goods such as cloth, salt, spices or pottery. But the growth and sustenance of larger cities was historically unusual for the population as a whole, and their continued existence precarious. The impulse for city construction, characterised by Mumford as the desire to create a vision of heaven on earth, where the cosmic order of gods, kings, priests and populace could be made physically manifest and represent the most fulfilled life being lived – this impulse required a confluence of resources, physical power, and political organisation. The exploitation of wind and sea for transport was always risky, with natural hazards supplemented by piracy and envy.

Despite these cyclical limitations, incremental advances were made in productivity and distribution over the course of decades and centuries.

While none were decisive, Chinese advances in irrigation and fertilisation sustained relatively high population densities. In broad terms the population of Asia doubled between 1500 and 1750 (to 500 million), and that of Europe increased by 66% to 111 million (Livi-Bacci 2001, p.27). The urban proportion still represented a small fraction, but increases in agricultural productivity sustained the higher overall densities and raised the prospect of surpluses sufficient to sustain cities as large as had been seen historically. Europe and China seemed, in many respects, to be equally well placed in 1750 to make some sort of leap into a new configuration of food supply, political coherence and urban development. The specifics of this convergence remain the topic of numerous studies, and the debate is as alive today as ever. Pomeranz's (2000) *The Great Divergence* proposes an account of why Europe and China parted ways developmentally, and the subject has been broached in numerous other publications. In some respects 1750 is already part of the story of the modern world, but how was this manifest in the seven largest cities of the time?

The list has changed between 900 and 1750, but not as dramatically as may appear if we look at it regionally. Beijing is first, with 900,000 people. Then come London, Constantinople, Paris, Edo (Tokyo), Canton (Guangzhou) and Osaka. The growth of the two European capitals follows population increases in both countries on the back of improved agricultural production and sophisticated state apparatuses. China retains its high population densities and centralising tendencies, Constantinople is prominent as the centre of the Ottoman Empire and Edo and Osaka testify to both intensive food production and a high degree of urbanisation in Japan, perhaps 22% or double that of Western Europe (Pomeranz 2000, p.35). The growth of Japanese cities followed the singular political order imposed on the country following the establishment of the Tokugawa shogunate, or regency, which ruled in the emperor's name from 1603 to 1868. The basic unit of rule was the domain of the *daimyo*, who numbered some 260 and were regarded as essentially equal, although in practice an hereditary and historical ranking system applied. Control over food production was severe and restrictive, and eventually perhaps 60% of rice production was taken in tax and obligations. Half of this went to the local daimyo who sold much of it at market in Osaka, and half went to the central Tokugawa family, followers and military corps.

Under the Tokugawa regime Edo, Kyoto and Osaka grew in size and status, but the largest, Edo, took in a large proportion of its population (60%) from its function as a large hostage compound. Each daimyo was required to lodge a large part of his court and followers in alternate years in the capital (*sankin-kotai*), a practice both costly and requiring large burdens of rice taxation that fell on the peasant farmers within each domain. The hostage retinue was not particularly hard worked, with one account having soldiers and functionaries working about ten days per month. The numbers also fluctuated depending on whether it was a residency year or not. The retinue of a mid-sized domain, Okayama, had 1394 members living long-term in Edo, which swelled to 3022 in a *sankin* year (Vaporis 2008, p.174).

Thus the picture of major cities at 1750 shows a geographic dispersal and a pattern of increased population growth in a number of localities around the world. As Pomeranz notes, there seems no evident reason for Western Europe to rise to global prominence from the base of 1750. But the constraints of the traditional city, already challenged by this date, were about to be comprehensively shattered.

Bibliography

Adorno, T. (1950). *The authoritarian personality.* New York: Harper.

Benevolo, L. (1980). *The history of the city.* Cambridge, MA: MIT Press.

Chandler, T., & Fox, G. (1974). *3000 years of urban growth.* New York: Academic Press.

Cotterell, A., & Morgan, D. (1975). *China: An integrated study.* London: Harrap.

Crowley, R. (2011). *City of fortune: How Venice ruled the seas.* New York: Random House.

Curtis, D. (2012). Florence and its hinterlands in the late Middle Ages: Contrasting fortunes in the Tuscan countryside, 1300–1500. *Journal of Medieval History, 38*(4), 472–499. doi:10.1080/03044181.2012.719830

Czapp, K. (2009, March 13). *Native Americans of the Pacific Northwest.* Retrieved July 24, 2015, from www.westonaprice.org/health-topics/native-americans-of-the-pacific-northwest

Diamond, J. (1998). *Guns, germs, and steel: The fates of human societies.* New York: W.W. Norton.

Ferraro, J. (2012). *Venice: History of the floating city.* New York: Cambridge University Press.

Garreau, J. (1991). *Edge city: Life on the new frontier.* New York: Doubleday.

Gernet, J. (1982). *A history of Chinese civilization.* Cambridge, UK: Cambridge University Press.

Goldthwaite, R. (1980). *The building of Renaissance Florence: An economic and social history.* Baltimore: Johns Hopkins University Press.

Goldthwaite, R. (2009). *The economy of Renaissance Florence.* Baltimore: Johns Hopkins University Press.

Grunewald, T., & Drinkwater, J. (2004). *Bandits in the Roman Empire: Myth and reality.* London: Routledge.

Hall, P. (1988). *Cities of tomorrow: An intellectual history of urban planning and design in the twentieth century.* Oxford: Blackwell.

Hohenberg, P., & Lees, L. (1985). *The making of urban Europe, 1000–1950.* Cambridge, MA: Harvard University Press.

Kahrl, W. (1982). *Water and power: The conflict over Los Angeles' water supply in the Owens Valley.* Berkeley: University of California Press.

Kazemipour, S., & Mirzaie, M. (2005). *Uneven growth of urbanization in Iran PO5–73* (Poster). IUSSP XXV International Population Conference, Tours, France, July 18–23, 2005. Retrieved August 5, 2015, from http://iussp2005.princeton.edu/papers/51663

Livi-Bacci, M. (2001). *A concise history of world population* (3rd ed.). Cambridge, MA: Blackwell.

Marcuse, H. (1987). *Eros and civilization: A philosophical inquiry into Freud.* London: Ark.

Marx, K. (1969). *Theories of surplus value.* London: Lawrence & Wishart.

Marx, K., & Engels, F. (1977). The Communist Manifesto. In D. McLellan (Ed.), *Karl Marx: Selected writings*. Oxford: Oxford University Press.

Mumford, L. (1961). *The city in history: Its origins, its transformations, and its prospects*. London: Secker and Warburg.

Mumford, L. (1963). *The city: Heaven and hell* [Motion picture]. National Film Board of Canada.

Muratori, S., & Cataldi, G. (1984). *Saverio Muratori, architetto (1910–1973): Il pensiero e l'opera* [*The thought and the work*]. Firenze: Alinea.

Pomeranz, K. (2000). *The great divergence: China, Europe, and the making of the modern world economy*. Princeton, NJ: Princeton University Press.

Rossi, A., & Moschini, F. (1979). *Aldo Rossi, progetti e disegni, 1962–1979* [*Aldo Rossi, projects and drawings, 1962–1979*]. New York: Rizzoli.

Roth, J. (1999). *The logistics of the Roman army at war (264 B.C.–A.D. 235)*. Leiden: Brill.

Samuels, I. (1990). Architectural practice and urban morphology. In T. Slater (Ed.), *The built form of Western cities: Essays for M.R.G. Conzen on the occasion of his 80th birthday*. Leicester: Leicester University Press.

Slater, T. (Ed.) (1990). *The built form of Western cities: Essays for M.R.G. Conzen on the occasion of his 80th birthday*. Leicester: Leicester University Press.

Smil, V. (1994). *Energy in world history*. Boulder, CO: Westview Press.

United Nations Population Division (n.d.). *Percentage urban and urban agglomerations by size class*. Retrieved October 19, 2015, from http://esa.un.org/unpd/wup/Maps/CityDistribution/CityPopulation/CityPop.aspx

Usher, A. (1954). *A history of mechanical inventions* (rev. ed.). Cambridge, MA: Harvard University Press.

Vaporis, C. (2008). *Tour of duty: Samurai, military service in Edo, and the culture of early modern Japan*. Honolulu: University of Hawai'i Press.

Woolf, S. (1968). Venice and the Terraferma: Problems of the change from commercial to landed activities. In B. Pullan (Ed.), *Crisis and change in the Venetian economy in the sixteenth and seventeenth centuries*. London: Methuen.

Wright, A. (1978). The Sui dynasty. In D. Twitchett (Ed.), *The Cambridge history of China* (Vol. 3, pp. 49–149). Cambridge, UK: Cambridge University Press.

2 The great transition

From solar sources to fossil fuels

The transition from the pre-industrial era to the industrial, or the related question of when modernity as a recognisable armature for everyday life emerged, are key concepts in understanding the shift in urban size and complexity that began about 300 years ago. Historians continue to think about, and debate, the remarkable transformation that certain countries underwent, and which has subsequently slowly spread across the globe. Indeed, the question as to why cities that had traditionally been limited to about one million inhabitants for millennia could suddenly transcend this figure was a motivating one for this study. Along with the whole spectacle of modern life, the contemporary city is a key creation of modernity. Yet even at the start of the modern era it was home to a small minority, despite exerting an influence beyond its numbers. This chapter deals in broad terms with the transformation that is loosely termed the Industrial Revolution, but on closer examination this term is misleading because the forces of social transformation were so much broader. In energy terms, those societies that have a low demand for energy may well have their needs met, and their stability assured, by simple solar-derived energy sources like wood or waterwheels. Those with greater energy needs may grow in power demand and complexity to the point where they outstrip the capacity of recurrent sources that are driven by the sun, such as wind, or evaporation for water power, or trees for biomass and crops for feed. This traditionally has meant decline and fall, but in the case of England from 1650 onwards it produced social dynamism and extraordinary invention, alongside social upheaval and unprecedented urban experiences.

The shift from recurrent and immediate solar-driven energy sources to ones that rely on the compaction, over geological time, of energy in the form of fossil fuels has been termed "the great transition" (Smil 1994, p.158). The principle is simple, but the consequences profound. Solar societies have their energy needs met through the incoming quantum of everyday solar irradiation. Plants grow, food is cultivated, the winds shift in response to solar-driven heating and cooling. Water evaporates and condenses, the potential energy of the clouds is converted into the force of rivers dropping to the sea. These processes are powerful but slow, and their harnessing for productive purposes determines a society's energy base and pace of life.

The transition to fossil fuels distorts this balance of incoming energy and its conversion to productive uses. Fossil fuels are, in effect, the compaction of millennia of incoming solar radiation – stored initially through photosynthesis in organic matter – by the combined effect of geological forces and very long timescales. This compaction produces material of great energy density, measured as the amount of usable energy capable of being released through combustion. A typical softwood such as pine releases about 16 MJ per kilogram of weight when burned efficiently. For coal the figure rises to about 24 MJ in each kilogram, and for petrol it almost doubles to 46 MJ. But the real difference is in the rate of replenishment. Trees grow slowly, but fossil fuels require geological time, ranging from "at least a few thousand years for young peat to hundreds of millions of years for hard coals" (Smil 1994, p.157).

A solar society may also outgrow its energy sources, leading to mass deforestation and decline. But fossil fuels occur in enormous deposits in many locations, an inter-millennial gift of energy abundance that remained untapped and unexploited until mid-way through the last millennium. The transition from antiquity to modernity had many facets, but as an objective measure the increasing use of fossil fuels is particularly telling. In England a shortage of local wood for burning around 1500 encouraged the extraction of local coal, which leapt from about 2.2 million tonnes mined annually in 1700 to more than 10 million tonnes by 1800 (Wrigley 2010, pp.37–39).

This rising rate of coal usage tells the story of the transition from solar to fossil-fuel societies, and it is reproduced in many accounts. Initially used for heating, the amount of coal mined was limited by the ancient sources of energy used in mining it – human and animal muscles. Indeed it was the use of early steam engines to pump water out of mineshafts that led to rapid advances in steam technology, a story graphically told in William Rosen's (2010) *The Most Powerful Idea in the World*. The significance of this event, or series of events, is given due attention in Rosen's account, but equally interesting is his speculation that the harnessing of steam power owed as much to the legal protection of patents in 18th century England as it did to a climate of innovation. In his account, culture, as much as necessity, makes progress possible (Rosen 2010).

The key story of this transition is not simply the burning of coal as a more abundant and efficient fuel than wood, but the development of machines that could convert these attributes of coal into motive power to drive a revolution in available energy. Using coal in abundance meant English manufacturing and transport could transcend the limits of replenishment imposed by a system reliant on solar energy. The energy budget that dictated a society could use no more energy than that provided by cropland, wood, wind and water was superseded, and the energy stored over millennia in coal could be added to the store of available energy sources.

What this allowed, in human terms, was an increase in the amount of energy available per capita in English society. Rosen puts this in context when he states that

> A skilled labourer – a weaver perhaps, or a blacksmith – in seventeenth-century England, France or China, spent roughly the same number of hours a week at his trade, producing about the same number of bolts of cloth, or nails, as his ten-times great-grandfather did during the time of Augustus. (Rosen 2010, p.xvii)

The transition to fossil fuels altered this – slowly in its initial stages, and then with increasing rapidity. This is reflected not only in increased productivity per person, although this is a significant marker, but in the transformation of everyday experience itself. A solar or somatic society, to use John McNeill's terms, relies on walking and labouring, supplemented by draught animals and horses to travel and transport goods (McNeill 2000). This limits the radius of experience in a particular generation, although large migrations might still occur in dire times. Sail opened up the possibility of travelling great distances, and encountering exotic experiences, but for the most part at the dawning of the fossil-fuel age lives were lived parochially, close to where one was born. Perhaps the most significant effect of the energy transition was the breaking of the traditional energy equation of the city or town, which allowed these crucibles of modernity to grow and flourish, and to provide unprecedented dynamism.

The energy equation here refers to the sources traditional cities relied on to meet their energy needs, and the relative contribution and efficiency of those sources. According to Vaclav Smil

> Traditional (solar) societies could support only a small number of large cities because the relatively high power densities of urban food and fuel consumption had to be supplied by harvesting biomass energy from large surrounding areas ... at least 40 times, and commonly about 100 times, larger than the settlement itself. (Smil 1994, p.208)

In other words the very low replenishment rate of trees cut down for fuel, as well as the low agricultural yields for traditional farming methods, dictated that what we might call the energy or food footprint of a traditional city quickly becomes many times the area of the city itself. This provides a natural limit to the radius of cultivated or harvested land surrounding these cities, as the means of transport for supplying the city will eventually fail if the loads or distances become too great. These factors define the limits of early urban sustainability.

For a typical pre-industrial city, then, the sheer effort of bringing food and fuel into the city from the surrounding countryside eventually reached the limits of both the countryside and the transportation methods employed. In addition, the surplus produced by agricultural production – the difference between what farmers produced in total, and what they consumed for their own sustenance – was relatively small. The city existed on this modest excess, its value underwritten by the efforts of a vast majority of the rural population, more than 80%, working the land.

Social organisation, too, reflected this energy balance. The feudal system represented a pyramid of energy flows, with a large labouring base contributing a portion of their produce to the nobility and their retinue. The power base of European feudalism lay in the country, a natural consequence of the land as source and converter of solar energy. As fossil fuels became available, they undermined this energy structure. The mine supplemented the field as an energy source, and the compact nature of coal compared to wood, together with the key role it played in the development of machines, provided a parallel energy budget to that of agrarian feudalism.

The growth of London is one significant example. In 1700 its population just exceeded half a million, equivalent to a large provincial town in current terms. A century later it had yet to top one million, but by 1901 it was over six and a half million. There are, of course, many reasons for this growth, but a necessary precondition was the breaking of the shackles of an urban energy budget which had precluded the growth of cities beyond about one million inhabitants, with most considerably smaller.

Wrigley provides a stark illustration of this phenomenon. He notes that "in 1700, when the English coal output is estimated at about 2.2 million tons, to have provided the same heat energy from wood on a sustained-yield basis would have required devoting 2 or 3 million acres to woodland" (Wrigley 2010, p.39). Had coal not emerged as a source of energy, he estimates London in 1800 would have drawn in about two million cartloads of firewood per year, requiring some 865,000 woodland acres without counting the land needed to feed the haulage animals. The use of coal thus enabled these acres to remain agriculturally productive, or forested, while the area taken by coal mines to make this energy available was a small fraction of the woodland acres.

We will revisit this concept a number of times, as it is central to any form of energy budgeting. It gives rise to the simple yet fundamental question: how much area is required to produce a given amount of energy? In the case cited above it is easy to see that coal, through its concentrated occurrence, produced an enormous amount of available energy when compared to the solar supply held in wood. In drawing on this inter-millennial energy subsidy, it allowed London to exceed the bounds of woodland energy supply and its corresponding displacement of agriculture and forest.

The exploitation of coal also allowed England to escape the confines of its poor road system. The advent of steam engines is one of the best-known indicators of the energy transition, with Richard Trevithick's clumsy but seminal 1804 locomotive running on rails heralding a phenomenon that went public when George Stephenson's *Rocket* powered trains between Liverpool and Manchester from 1830. The *Rocket* produced about 15 kW of power, about the same as a Model T Ford and less than the smallest petrol motor car engines manufactured today. Nonetheless it started a cycle of dramatic improvements in the size and efficiency of steam engines, which became the characteristic modern mode of land transport in the

19th century. The steamship, too, followed a similar trajectory, with the small paddle steamers of the early 1800s evolving into 200 metre behemoths half a century later.

As steam trains began to connect major cities, they engendered a host of secondary transport networks. Ironically the mass movement of goods by rail fostered a veritable explosion in the number of horses employed within cities. Harnessed to a variety of vehicles, working horses peaked in number just before the advent of the motor car at the beginning of the 20th century. In late Victorian London, or Paris of the Belle Époque, horses dominated street life. Many were used for private transport, another marker of rising affluence and energy abundance. The confines of a sustainable city, as understood in a solar economy, were well and truly burst by this time.

Although not specifically drawing on coal for motive power, the growth in English towns and cities between 1600 and 1800 was accompanied by a corresponding increase in agricultural output. The reasons for this are varied, but one cited factor is the heavy use in England of powerful horses, as opposed to oxen in continental Europe. Wrigley estimates an increase in agricultural output of at least threefold in the 17th and 18th centuries, with a proportion of the output going to feed the huge number of draught horses that played so key a role within industrialising England. Thus although agriculture *per se* had not mechanised, the substitution of coal for wood as a fuel meant less demand on wooded areas and cropland for biofuels such as wood and chaff. Consolidation of farms and the enclosure of common land, which caused widespread social upheaval, nonetheless allowed larger and more efficient farms to emerge, which aided productivity. Slowly, hand-in-hand, urbanisation and agricultural efficiency grew through these two key centuries, with coal adding incrementally but crucially to the available energy budget (Wrigley 2010, p.88).

The analogy could be of a train moving at a constant speed under solar power. When coal power is added, incrementally at first, the train accelerates slowly. Over time the acceleration increases, such that it attains an enormous momentum and coal becomes the prime energy source. The initial transformation in England was most evident in London, where urban growth had fostered qualitatively different experiences. These were often exhilarating, inspiring contemporary accounts such as that of Charles Lamb:

> London itself a pantomime and masquerade, all these things work themselves into my mind and feed me without a power of satiating me. The wonder of these sights impells me into night walks about the crowded streets, and I often shed tears in the motley Strand from fullness of joy at so much *Life*. (Jennings 1985, p.111)

The story of England is arguably the central one in understanding the mechanisms of nascent, and then triumphant, modernity. The exploitation of coal took place earlier in England than elsewhere. Urban growth was most pronounced there, and the increase in population until 1850 more profound, with a corresponding increase in agricultural production. The factors in favour of this transition in England have given rise to a massive literature, but the end result was a society which in 1850 was consuming a volume of coal that would have required an area of woodland greater than its entire land surface to produce the same amount of energy through burning wood. At this point the limits of the sun to replenish the energy consumed annually through photosynthesis, for both fuel and food, had been comprehensively exceeded.

Only the Netherlands in the 1600s, fuelled by peat, could match England's early energy abundance. However, through the 19th century most of northern Europe experienced a transition similar to England's. The colonial experience exported this transition, as well as creating a transport network that drew to Europe the results of exotic labour and resource extraction to add to the quantum of energy, represented in both raw materials and steam power, that transformed products like cotton in the factories and mills of European countries.

The essential part of this first transition ends around 1900. It is the period of growth in manufacturing and transport through the harnessing of the first of the significant fossil fuels, coal. The burning of coal may have had a profound influence on every aspect of life in England, France, the US or Australia, but the changes wrought would be still further extended and exacerbated when the internal combustion engine emerged as a mass technology. However, it is instructive to take stock of developments prior to cars and trucks, as it was coal that fostered the initial development and laid down the preconditions for the lived reality of modernity.

The term modernity in its current usage has been ascribed to Baudelaire, chronicler and poet of an emergent sense of newness, pace and dislocation. Marshall Berman described it thus in the 1980s:

> There is a mode of vital experience – experience of space and time, of the self and others, of life's possibilities and perils – that is shared by men and women all over the world today. I will call this body of experience "modernity". (Berman 1982, p.15)

Berman's 1982 book *All That Is Solid Melts into Air* draws its title from one of the most perspicacious of modernity's observers (if not prognosticators), Karl Marx. Despite being irrevocably associated with communism, the bulk of Marx's work was concerned with analysing and understanding modern capitalism. Marx's critique is particularly apt in a history of sustainability because he argued that capitalism was constrained by its social characteristics, while acknowledging its productive and transformative capacities. Indeed it was its very transformative powers that he credited with bringing into being the conditions for capitalism's supersession through the creation of a unique social class in history, the urban proletariat.

Marx's observations span a crucial period in England's industrial and social history. Although coal production had been rising since the 1600s, the early part of the 19th century showed the promise of the industrial age, without witnessing its full, accelerated, development. Hobsbawm comments that

> What strikes us retrospectively about the first half of the nineteenth century is the contrast between the enormous and rapidly growing productive potential of capitalist industrialisation and its inability, as it were, to broaden its base, to break the shackles which fettered it. (Hobsbawm 1977, p.47)

For Hobsbawm the great period of European expansion occurred between 1848 and 1875, its start marked by a series of revolutions and social movements growing out of an increasing, and increasingly urbanised, population, and the inability of the industrial establishment to meet their basic needs and aspirations. By 1875 the situation had altered markedly, and countries like Germany, which had seemed inured to rapid industrial progress, had fully entered the modern technological era.

Key amongst Marx's writings is, of course, the *Communist Manifesto*, authored with Frederick Engels in 1848. Its impressions bear out this sense of transformation, yet with an underlying limitation. Marx is breathless in his description of the effects of the bourgeoisie, the capitalist class, on all aspects of contemporary life as he saw it:

> Conservation of the old modes of production in unaltered form, was, on the contrary, the first condition of existence for all earlier industrial classes. Constant revolutionizing of production, uninterrupted disturbance of all social conditions, everlasting uncertainty and agitation distinguish the bourgeois epoch from all earlier ones. (Marx & Engels 1977, p.224)

Although he seems to imply increased energy use in his historic schema, it is nonetheless interesting to read Marx against an interpretation of history predicated both on energy use and sustainability. His statement that "The history of all hitherto existing society is the history of class struggles" seems to point to the importance of human effort as a source of energy until the widespread adoption of fossil fuels (Marx & Engels 1977, p.222). Indeed it can be read as a struggle over energy itself, where one class exploits the muscle power of another for its own gain and comfort. Yet the sense of the 19th century transcending the bounds of previous epochs is a constant in Marx, with his florid descriptions of vast productivity and social change: "a society that has conjured up such gigantic means of production and exchange, is like the sorcerer, who is no longer able to control the powers of the nether world which he has called up by his spells" (Marx & Engels 1977, p.226).

For Marx and Engels, though, the railway and the machine were of secondary interest to the social relations they brought into being. The ascent of science and its products, for them, simply laid bare exploitation that had been obscured for many years. They felt no nostalgia for much of what had been physically altered, crediting the bourgeoisie with increasing the urban population in proportion to the rural, and rescuing "a considerable part of the population from the idiocy of rural life" (Marx & Engels 1977, p.225). Yet what was obscured from Marx in 1848, or at least not fully appreciated, was the full potential held by modern capitalism acting in concert with coal as an energy source.

For Marx the unsustainable aspect of capitalism, when viewed at the middle of the 19th century, was not the pace of economic growth, nor its apparent wrecking of traditional society, but its apparent impoverishment of the worker in absolute terms. The *Communist Manifesto* is explicit on this point. Noting that in previous societies the oppressed were at least guaranteed some status that allowed them a living within the confines of class exploitation, the authors state that for capitalism

> The modern labourer, on the contrary, instead of rising with the progress of industry, sinks deeper and deeper below the conditions of his own class ... The bourgeoisie ... is unfit to rule because it is incompetent to assure an existence to its slave within his slavery, because it cannot help letting him sink into such a state, that it has to feed him, instead of being fed by him. (Marx & Engels 1977, p.226)

Thus we see that for Marx and Engels the limitation on the sustainability of capitalism, with all its attendant technological marvels, lay in the legal and social relationship it fostered between bourgeois and workers, where the latter suffered irreversible declines to their living standards, to the point where they could not survive.

We shall return to this argument in future chapters, partly because it is central to characterisations of capitalism, and partly because one of the reasons it has not come true is because of the vastly expanded quantum of energy available to anyone, even workers, in modern advanced societies. However, for now it serves to illustrate the threats perceived to the survival or sustainability of industrial England around 1850. These were even greater for other European countries. Observers in Germany of the same period despaired of the ability of their economy to provide employment for a rapidly growing and politically restive population (Hobsbawm 1977, p.48).

The rise in population had been mused over earlier in the century, and had encouraged speculation as to how unfettered growth might ultimately end, or at least play out. If Marx brought a relational mindset to the phenomenon of industrial capitalism, others in an earlier age were of a more empirical frame of mind. The classical economists, notably Smith and Ricardo, had wrestled with the contours and emergent tendencies of capitalism as it assumed distinct form, in sharp relief from an earlier mercantilism or trading economy. Of similar persuasion, but darker disposition, was a country clergyman of considerable learning named Thomas Robert Malthus. He is best remembered today for the adjective Malthusian, a reference to the school of thought he engendered through consideration of the dynamic, as he saw it, of population growth.

Malthus' ideas were first expounded in 1798 when he published *An Essay on the Principle of Population*. The work was subject to a number of revisions through his lifetime, as he sought to incorporate additional supporting material for his argument, and to address his critics. The impetus for his *Essay* was the idealism of earlier philosophers, particularly William Godwin and the Marquis de Condorcet. The context was the prospect, much discussed, of the idealistic ascent of humankind if the dead hands of nobility, religion and crude privilege were tossed aside through revolution. Both Condorcet and Godwin had written works expounding the perfectibility of society if certain conditions were met. Their contributions to political thinking mirrored an old division of belief that ran through social thinking in the 17th and 18th centuries – what was the natural repose of mankind? The colonial conquests of European powers had uncovered societies in the Americas, Africa and Asia that were at various stages of technological and social advancement. The nomadic tribes and hunter–gatherer societies observed by explorers evoked a certain envy for the apparent contentment that their simple lives bore. James Cook observed of the aboriginal tribes he encountered when circumnavigating Australia in 1770:

> From what I have said of the Natives of New-Holland they may appear to some to be the most wretched people upon Earth, but in reality they are far more happier than we Europeans; being wholly unacquainted not only with the superfluous but the necessary Conveniences so much sought after in Europe, they are happy in not knowing the use of them. (Cook 1971, entry for August 23, 1770)

The idea took root in English writings well before Cook, and the image of a pre-agricultural society of simplicity and equality remained powerful in the popular and literary imagination. Neither Godwin nor Condorcet advocated a return to this Eden, but they both imagined an evolution of social organisation towards a civilised but unfettered state of repose. This temper of extreme optimism, with its view of humanity as capable of transcending restraining social institutions, was at odds with Malthus' view of a cold and unrelenting struggle between procreation and sustenance, or population and food sources.

In this Malthus was the predecessor of Darwin, who also considered the problem, but at longer timescales. But Malthus was essentially contemplating the cycle of events that must follow even from a state of Eden-like abundance. For Malthus this situation would not produce static balance, and hence the preservation of abundance. On the contrary it would lead to a rapid increase in population, which would overturn the very conditions that enabled it to grow, creating a state of want and misery which would, in turn, limit or reverse population growth (Malthus 1973).

The distinction between these two contending ideas of the primitive state – one that it is happy despite its crudeness, the second that it is beset by the struggle against natural limits – has been termed "soft" and "hard" primitivism (Panofsky 1955). Malthus' attack on Godwin's idealism is an assertion of his "hard" stance. It originates not in response to the latter's belief in a primitive ideal, but rather from the question as to what type and degree of social coercion or structure is needed to maintain abundance and civic advancement. In this Malthus sided with Adam Smith, believing that

> It is to the established administration of property, and to the apparently narrow principle of self-love, that we are indebted for all the noblest exertions of human genius, all the finer and more delicate emotions of the soul, for everything, indeed, that distinguishes the civilized, from the savage state. (Malthus 1959, p.100)

The two notions of primitivism which underpinned the speculations of the period represent a significant essentialism, or innate view of human nature. The subtlety of Malthus, and of classical economics in general, is the idea of the transformation of self-interest into the common interest through the natural tendencies of the market – the saving grace of a system not generally associated with idealism. These contending notions, and the revival of classical economics through Friedrich Hayek and Milton Friedman in the Regan era, gives the work of Malthus a particular relevance in understanding the modern idea of sustainability.

For Malthus the mechanism by which population is checked is an oscillation, a to-and-fro movement between plenitude, population growth and natural checks on population. In revising his ideas, Malthus proposed that human populations are subject to two kinds of limitations, preventive and positive. The latter affects all of nature, and its human extreme is famine and starvation. The former, though, is confined to mankind, and is the result of an understanding of the dire consequences and suffering that too many children bring: "The preventive check, as far as it is voluntary, is peculiar to man and arises from that distinctive superiority in his reasoning faculties which enables him to calculate distant consequences" (Malthus 1973, p.12).

In introducing the preventive check, Malthus brings a crucial element into the debate around population and resources – the operation of self-restraint as a mitigating factor in population growth. He concludes that all checks are "resolvable into moral restraint, vice and misery" (Malthus 1973, p.14). Yet he contends that in most of the world there is "a constant effort to increase beyond the means of subsistence" which "tends to subject the lower classes of society to distress, and to prevent any great permanent melioration of their condition" (Malthus 1973, p.15).

What contemporary concerns, particularly around food supply, might we recognise in Malthus? One enduring theme is the spectre of unchecked population increase, to the point where food supply is exhausted or insufficient. For Malthus the potential increase in agricultural production was arithmetical, that is simply additive rather than compounding. Thus it could increase, but not in the compounding or geometrical (exponential) manner of population increase. The colonial experience was critical in the formation of these ideas. Malthus uses the colonised states of North America to estimate the rate of population increase, since in these areas "the means of subsistence have been more ample, the manners of the people more pure, and the checks to early marriages fewer than in any of the modern states of Europe" (Malthus 1973, p.7). He concludes that this results in a doubling of the population every 25 years, but that in more remote areas this period can be as short as 15 years. This represents what might be called the reference fertility rate, the rate at which populations grow under ideal circumstances.

Malthus' references encompass the lessons of colonial expansion, the evident growth of the population of England, and improving agricultural productivity, as well as his personal experience through pastoral activity among the poor. Collectively these informed his speculations, which were compatible with a theology that Winch has characterised as utilitarian, but imbued with a "teleology of improvement that acts as the religious equivalent of the secular perfectibilism which his Essay sets out to undermine" (Winch 1987, p.35).

These ideas endured well into modernity. They prefigure influential later notions, such as Freud's contention that repression is the price paid for civilisation. The significant error in the popular usage of the term Malthusian is the idea that the author imagined that growing populations would lead to catastrophe. On the contrary – he recognised that this does not generally come to pass, and much of his work is devoted to why that is.

Marx may have mocked Malthus, but they drew similar conclusions. For both, the capitalism they witnessed was harshest on the poor. Malthus imagined restraint, late marriage and fewer children as factors that could improve their lot. Marx saw the plight of the poor as a systemic issue, capable of being solved only by a reconfiguring of society as a whole. These two philosophers, among many, traverse the early years of industrial capitalism in its most advanced setting, England. Shaped by the evident growth and urbanisation around them, they sought to project this dynamic into the future and to examine its probable limits and consequences, in other words its apparent sustainability. Malthus died in 1834, too soon to appreciate the enormous acceleration which took place in Europe and its colonial corona after 1850. Marx survived him by a generation, and with Engels observed the maturation of the European industrial and commercial city.

The significance of 1850 as a watershed year in European development is graphically illustrated by Hobsbawm:

Capitalism now had the entire world at its disposal, and the expansion of both international trade and international investment measures the zest with which it proceeded to capture it. The world's trade between 1800 and 1840 had not quite doubled. Between 1850 and 1870 it increased by 260 per cent. (Hobsbawm 1977, p.49)

However, in light of Malthus' concerns, it is also instructive to look at what was happening to populations in Europe when the transition to coal was underway, but the full potential of an industrial and world-connected economy was yet to be revealed. The first point, elucidated by Wrigley but distinctly Malthusian, is that in a solar economy productive capacity fluctuated but was very much a limiting factor in how successfully populations could grow. In general, before fossil fuels were widespread, if a population grew by more than 0.5% per year, real wages fell and misery ensued for many. From about 1650 onwards, this nexus was broken in England and populations grew while wages and living standards did not decline as they had previously. This small shift translated to significant population growth over the next century. Even with growth, though, the difficulties of establishing a family during this period is reflected in the somewhat surprising age of women at first marriage in England. Around 1720 this was 26 years, but a century later it had fallen to 23½ as a greater food supply made new family formation less risky. Other factors also contributed to population growth, including declining rates of stillborn children and more mothers and children surviving birth and an increase in children born outside of marriage (Wrigley 2010, pp.147–148).

Thus Malthus was indeed wrestling with the issue of population growth, but without a full appreciation of its extent in historical terms. Across Europe population grew at unprecedented rates from 1800 to 1850. In Germany it grew at over six times the rate of a century earlier, in France at two and a half, and in England at over five. These rates generally exceed population growth in these countries, expressed as an annual percentage, for all of the 20th century. Little wonder, then, that Hobsbawm characterised this period as the age of revolutions, when the established social order struggled to accommodate the aspirations of rising populations. All of this had altered radically by 1875. In Europe the number of children per woman borne over her lifetime (Total Fertility Rate) declined markedly between 1850 and 1875. Sweden dropped from 4.28 to 3.51, Germany from 5.17 to 3.98 and France from 3.27 to 2.6. The US, too, was in step with the trend, with a decline from 4.48 to 3.53 (Livi-Bacci 1992, p.106). However, a declining fertility rate does not mean a shrinking population. The high birth rates of the 1830s translated into the workers, the dandies and the opportunists of the 1860s.

Where did all these extra souls, growing to maturity, go? In England, rural areas showed far less population increase than the overall figures would suggest. People moved towards employment, and this meant villages with industry, mining areas and of course the expanding cities. This became true for much of Europe, initiating a shifting half-century of change and migration, not only to the cities and industrial towns but to colonial out-posts and gold rushes. The Great Exhibition of 1851 in London may be remembered for its dramatic Crystal Palace, designed by Joseph Paxton to exploit recently developed glass making technology, but the true wonder was the products of 14,000 exhibitors from around the world contained within the building. These were testimony to the growth of manufacturing and agriculture, driven by colonial expansion and energised, crucially, by coal.

Steamships had shown that the technology was capable of long-distance powered travel. In 1827 the *Curacao* made passage across the Atlantic from the Netherlands to Surinam substantially under steam. By the end of the century modern ships had welded in place the links between Europe and the colonised world, transferring people and goods in quantities unimagined 50 years earlier. By 1890 the experience of the metropolitan world was recognisably modern, and the basis for the coming century was set.

The transformation brought with it its own distinct anxieties and obser-vations. The shift from a solar society where perhaps three-quarters of the population were employed in agriculture, to one where this figure was below half and dropping, changed politics fundamentally. A rural-based aristocracy was challenged, where it existed, by urban interests – manufacturers, financiers and traders. The growing cohorts of urban workers emerged as Marx's fabled proletariat, moulded by modernity and marked to play a key historical role. Though they may not have undertaken this in the manner Marx envi-saged, the rise of political parties dedicated to the rights and conditions of workers shaped politics the world over for the bulk of the 20th century. All of these things had become evident by 1890, as had some of the tendencies of the new age.

The energetics of urbanity

Of all the products and consequences of the industrialising process, none exceed the city in complexity and significance. It is now a truism that more of humanity lives in cities than in the countryside, but this relies on develop-ments originally set in train by the use of coal and the resulting shift in political power, slowly but certainly, towards cities. We take this for granted today, because the energy system that makes this possible has become mature and widespread. Today a city of one million inhabitants is commonplace. In 1750 probably no city worldwide had reached this figure, although a number (notably Chang'an and Baghdad) had come close. Even Imperial Rome, in 100 AD, housed just 650,000 inhabitants. Sometime between 1750 and 1800 Beijing passed the million mark, followed by London in the early 1800s. Table 2.1 gives some sense of the significance of a changed energy regime for city size.

In a solar society one million inhabitants represents the largest city size historically evident, and then only under conditions of imperial expansion and high levels of social organisation. London at 1800 may not have been

Table 2.1 Largest cities in the world, 100 AD to 1900

Date	Cities and population
100 AD	Rome 650,000
622	Constantinople 500,000
900	Baghdad 900,000 Chang'an 750,000
1200	Hangzhou 255,000 Fez 250,000 Cairo 200,000
1400	Nanjing 473,000 Cairo 450,000 Vijayanagar 350,000
1650	Constantinople 700,000 Beijing 600,000 Isfahan 500,000 Edo 500,000 Agra 500,000 Paris 455,000 London 410,000
1750	Beijing 900,000 London 676,000 Constantinople 666,000 Paris 560,000 Edo 509,000
1800	Beijing 1,100,000 London 861,000 Guangzhou 800,000 Constantinople 570,000 Paris 547,000
1850	London 2,320,000 Beijing 1,648,000 Paris 1,314,000 Guangzhou 800,000 Constantinople 785,000
1875	London 4,241,000 Paris 2,250,000 New York 1,900,000 Beijing 1,310,000 Berlin 1,045,000
1900	London 6,480,000 New York 4,242,000 Paris 3,330,000 Berlin 2,424,000 Chicago 1,717,000 Vienna 1,662,000 Tokyo 1,497,000

Adapted from Chandler and Fox (1974, pp.368–369). Figures for London differ from Wrigley (2010), but are retained for comparison unique in size compared to previous epochs, but by 1850 it was well and truly unique as a single contiguous settlement.

By 1875 it was clear that the industrialising economies of Europe and the New World were fostering cities of unprecedented scale. The energy regimes they were part of, as we have seen, allowed them to escape the restrictions of solar-driven cropland and wood as energy sources, and harness the concentrated energy density of coal. Without this the countryside would have been denuded of trees for hundreds of kilometres to feed the energy needs of the city.

No city can exist without a productive surrounding countryside, since the city itself, especially at 19th century densities, grows very little produce. The supply of the city, in energy terms, is not confined to wood for heating and industries like metal-working. It extends to food, building materials and transport, and the productiveness of a region's agriculture is a strong determinant of how large a city located within it can grow. Despite the widespread emergence of the post-solar city in the late 19th century, its reliance on coal made it distinct from the 20th century city. Its railways and factories produced and transported goods, its steamships drew produce from all parts of the world and carried millions of migrants, but for many parts of its functioning, and the agriculture that supported it, the primary sources of power were largely traditional – horses, oxen and people.

How can this be reconciled with the unprecedented growth of cities to 1900? Part of the explanation is that agriculture was not stagnant, and even within solar societies innovation could be richly rewarded. Cities like Beijing, Guangzhou and Tokyo grew in the 19th century within economies that were largely traditionally fuelled and energised. Chinese yields on farmland benefitted from centralised improvements such as elaborate irrigation systems and efficient fertilisation schemes, where human and animal waste were returned to the soil to boost crop yields. The success of these measures is evident in the historically large cities the region sustained over millennia. Smil suggests that the design, execution and maintenance of China's irrigation networks and canals helped constitute and maintain its large bureaucracies. As we have seen, they certainly made possible the shipments of grain that were required to feed large cities (Smil 1994, p.61).

Efficient use of farmland is underpinned by an efficient energy budget, that is a large return of energy in the form of food compared to the energy expended in producing that food. A poor return leads to subsistence farming, where all hands are busy in producing just enough to survive, with little or no surplus for bad times or to support non-productive members of the group. Poor soils, poorly farmed, support very low population densities, as the yield per hectare is low as is the number of people each hectare can support. In highly organised societies practising irrigation and fertilisation, the success of these methods can be indirectly measured in the population density. As yields increase, so does the number of people a given area of land supports. Estimates of population densities for China range from about 2.8 people per cultivated hectare in 1400, to roughly 4.8 in 1600, to over 5 by 1900. This increased density serves as a proxy for gains in agricultural productivity, and presumably also for the surplus required to feed a large urban population (Pomeranz 2000).

The significance of these figures lies in the variability of crop production, which in 1900 was still essentially solar conversion through photosynthesis, even in Europe. Large cities could only grow, and people move into occupations other than farming, if the productivity of farmland increased, or additional areas were brought under cultivation. In the case of England both of these factors came into play. We have seen that the use of coal freed farmland and forest from having to provide fuel in the form of biomass. This enabled the land to be given over to growing crops, providing energy for the urban and labouring population and the vast number of animals that powered so many aspects of English life. And although the area under cultivation was constrained by the size of the British Isles, additional cropland supported English industry through the exercise of colonial power, as in the case of cotton grown in America, India and the Caribbean. Kenneth Pomeranz has characterised this exotically displaced or coal-liberated cropland as "ghost acres", freed up by world linkages and increased mining of coal, a term borrowed from Georg Borgstrom via Eric L. Jones. It was Borgstrom who originally observed that nations can appear to exceed the limits of the food they can produce from their arable land by importing food or fishing. The collective additional nutrition can add up to a substantial portion of the national diet, without which the nation would starve (Pomeranz 2000; Jones 1987; Borgstrom 1965).

Agricultural production in Europe and the New World until 1900 is pertinent to our picture of the energy needed to sustain the modern city because it not only provided food for the city as a non-agricultural entity which produced little of its own, but it did so with limited direct application of fossil fuels. The age of growth of European cities and their related economies took place with the aid of coal, and its industrial extension, steam power. The first industrial steam engines burning coal for heating water emerged in numbers around 1750. These were improvements on Thomas Newcomen's 1712 design, and they lifted water out of deep mines to allow continuous working of the mines. James Watt further improved the efficiency of the fixed steam engine in 1769, and 20 years later he and Matthew Boulton had installed about 500 engines across England. Further improvements through the 19th century, including the use of high-pressure steam, saw the efficiency of engines – the quantity of coal energy converted to useful power – increase tenfold. The effect is hard to overstate: Smil declares

> These advances – combined with the portability of the new engines, their adaptability to many manufacturing, construction, and transportation uses, and their durability – turned the [steam] machine into *the* prime mover of nineteenth-century industrialization … It powered belt drives

in countless factories and revolutionized nineteenth-century land and water transportation. (Smil 1994, pp.164–165)

Yet despite this portability, the steam engine is a large and heavy machine due to the necessity for its coal supply, water supply, boiler and pistons to be close together. It worked extremely well in fixed locations, or in steamships or in locomotives which ran on rails and could harness separate carriages as tenders for water and coal. But the smallest unit was still some tons in weight, and unsuitable for the small-scale motive power required in farming and around the city.

Thus, while the steam engine could improve agricultural efficiency by powering threshing machines and mills, ploughing of fields and transporting of produce were still undertaken using animal power. Yet even here productivity gains were impressive. Replacing oxen with horses aided this, but a host of improvements in the US from 1800 to 1900 saw the number of hours of human labour required to grow one hectare of wheat fall from 162 to 9. Because horses convert the energy in their food into work far more efficiently than people, these improvements represent a significant increase in the energy yielded by the wheat crop in relation to the energy expended in growing and harvesting it. This energy return was about 90 MJ in 1800 – a century later it was around 2400 MJ, or 26 times greater while still relying largely on horse power (Smil 1994).

This growth in agricultural efficiency was crucial for feeding the emergent metropolis, which itself was a vast consumer of feed for its myriad horses that pulled cabs and carts around the city as the lowest level of powered transportation. At the beginning of the 20th century London had around 300,000 horses, needing perhaps 360,000 hectares of cropland to feed them. This, of course, would have to be subtracted from the cropland needed to feed the urban population, an indication of how crucial the land freed up from wood production through the use of coal proved in supplying the grain and hay to keep the urban horses working.

The picture that emerges of the large European or North American city at 1900 is curious because all the attributes of modernity are in place, yet it is not fully modern. The city has grown beyond its historical maximum, and contains a population not directly involved in feeding themselves. Size begets wonder and anonymity, as well as the spectacle of commodities manufactured for consumption, alluringly displayed. Terms in use today to describe the power of the desire they engendered – commodity fetish, luxury goods – originate in this period. So too does the modern image of the ills of the city. The working poor of Manchester and Liverpool inspired social observers and reformers to decry the city as degrading to life compared to the country-side. Indeed, mortality rates in late 19th century English cities were higher than rural mortality rates, and the consequences of urban densities were concentrations of effluent and airborne pollution from fires that rendered parts of these cities grim indeed. Even in affluent areas horse excrement made the best of streets unpleasant for the pedestrian.

After 1900

The liberation from the confines of a solar society had been largely achieved in the modernising world by this stage through burning coal, but two inventions were still required to give the modern city its contemporary form. The first was distributed electricity, and the second the internal combustion engine.

Electricity may have been understood as a phenomenon for decades preceding its widespread adoption, but large compact cities made its adoption particularly attractive. When Thomas Edison opened his first two power plants, in London and New York, in 1882, the intention was to provide bright and convenient lighting to customers. Driven by steam engines, the plants demonstrated both the convenience of the new technology as well as a trend which strengthened over the years – the displacement of the process of actual combustion.

When gas and coal served as the sources of urban light and heat, the energy was liberated by combustion at the point of usage. Thus gas lamps and coal fires delivered their illumination and warmth through being burnt where needed, creating smoke and soot in and above the very interiors that they served. Electricity provides an ideal means of transferring energy from the point of combustion – the power plant – to the domestic or industrial interior where it is needed, without the unwanted products of combustion. This aspect of convenience assured its uptake, but the power plant has a further advantage. It can burn fossil fuel in bulk and with great efficiency, thus increasing the energy available from a fixed quantity of coal. This efficiency is undermined by the invariable losses of energy sustained when it is converted from heat to steam to electricity, but the convenience of delivering coal to one location rather than many, and the benefits of clean energy instantly available at the point of need, made it an attractive form of energy from the 1880s onwards. The city now separated itself by one remove again from the countryside. A rural fireplace may produce inconvenience, but the smoke from thousands of hearths in a large city creates a smog which can be life threatening. With electricity the smoke to produce energy can be confined to a limited number of locations, and with improvements in transmission systems and boiler design many power sources for modern cities are located well away from the city itself.

It is hard to overstate the significance of the adoption of this ubiquitous and exceptionally versatile form of energy. In industry the electric motor displaced the steam pulley and water wheel, again allowing a further subdivision of manufacturing by uncoupling processes that required power from large fixed steam engines and the extensive pulley systems they drove. Electric motors can be diffused throughout industry and households, as long as they can be connected to a power supply. Lights can be placed where needed, again extending the energy network into fine localised branches which steam power and gas simply precluded.

The capacity for electricity to reach into finer and finer networks has been one of its most effective attributes. It has provided the means to mechanise handcraft through appliances and machines. It powers domestic heat and light, and as the primary urban energy distribution network it has allowed the modern city to be a healthier place than the countryside. But it had, at its inception, one major drawback – one had to be connected to the grid. In this it was hardly useful for personal transport, and cities like New York at 1900 had both growing electrical networks for lighting and electric trams, and more horses than ever. The missing technology was one which could extend the power of fossil fuels to a finer network than the railroad, and a smaller engine than the steam locomotive.

It was, of course, the motor car, which effectively mounted and harnessed the internal combustion engine that had been developed in Germany at the end of the 19th century. Production started in earnest from 1902, and the motor car began to rapidly displace horses for urban transportation. The small size and relative power of the petrol engine thus achieved the next stage of penetration of fossil fuels down to the level of personal transport. Individuals did not generally own steam locomotives, but they began to own motor cars.

Electricity may have transformed energy distribution, but until the advent of hydroelectric schemes it was derived from burning coal to create steam. Thus it relied on coal as the primary feedstock, and in that sense is an extension of an industry with roots centuries old. The shift to motor cars is significant because it exploits an energy source that had been untapped until the advent of the car – oil. While still a fossil fuel whose energy content has been compressed and concentrated over millennia, oil has a different distribution pattern globally. The British land mass has an abundance of coal which could be mined in significant quantities, but it has little oil. The US had both in abundance, and rapidly moved to exploit its oil discoveries.

The car indelibly associated with this rise was the Model T Ford, with 15 million manufactured between 1908 and 1927. Its 2.9 litre engine produced about 15 kW. By comparison, the world's cheapest car in 2013, the Tata Nano, produced 28 kW from a 0.6 litre engine. Yet even at this low level of efficiency, the Model T made historically exceptional amounts of energy available to unexceptional households.

At the risk of oversimplifying the issue, the magnitudes involved are startling. The power generated by a single person is low when compared to contemporary power sources – perhaps 50 watts in a sustained manner, with peaks of 100 watts. It would take a gym session of 30 urbanites pedalling intensely on exercise bikes to heat the average kettle. A large working horse is about ten times as powerful as a labourer, with a power output of up to 850 watts. This explains the huge increase in agricultural production achieved using draught horses in the late 19th century, especially when they were harnessed together. The Model T Ford, with its 15,000 watts, has a motive power equivalent to upwards of 180 labourers or 18 powerful draught horses. The Tata Nano almost doubles this again.

This comparison, in short, underlines the significance of the internal combustion engine in diffusing the inter-millennial energy subsidy of fossil fuels across all of society in modernising economies. Even with its innate inefficiencies, with vast amounts of energy dissipated uselessly as heat, the early petrol engine represents a quantum leap in household energy budgets. The effect is to widen the geographic extent of everyday life by making possible the effortless covering of distance. In a rural setting this reduces remoteness and isolation, but in the city the widened ambit of each individual is overlaid with that of others, producing a complexity of interaction with two effects. The first is a vastly expanded range of opportunities, with work, shopping and leisure conceivably kilometres apart. The second is a slow dis-aggregation of the city, with densities dropping and zoning encouraging discrete homogenous areas of housing, industry and retailing.

This process was driven, at first, by expanded public transport systems (Angel 2012). Initially horse-drawn, omnibuses – together with suburban rail and tram networks – soon brought the power benefits of fossil fuels to urban transportation. This drove the first wave of suburban development, when car usage was still relatively low and public transport was the backbone of urban mobility. Electric train services established themselves as particularly suitable due to their lack of local emissions and smooth acceleration. The qualitative change in experience thus engendered also transformed culture and economies. The potential labour market for any job expanded enormously, as did overall mobility. Families could relocate according to opportunity, and communities coalesced around new suburbs and new schools. With the rise in mobility came the potential for even greater anonymity, and the modern detective novel, with its serendipitous connections between individuals and its vast pool of possible suspects, became a cipher for the urban condition.

These effects were most evident in the New World, particularly the US. Its abundance of coal had seen it overtake Britain in sheer steam capacity by 1850, and its technological progress in car production and manufacturing capacity was followed by rapid suburbanisation and population shifts internally. These were mirrored, to a lesser extent, in the British Dominions of Australia, Canada and New Zealand.

How did all this play on the anxieties about the threats to a stable balance between food, fuel and people that emerged in the early modern period? A century after Malthus, the terms under which he framed his thesis of the struggle between population and resources had clearly changed. The sense of the natural limits to resources, especially food production, had altered markedly. The internal combustion engine found its agricultural application in the tractor and combine harvester. Finally the vast energy of fossil fuels could be applied directly to the working of fields, to ploughing and harvesting. But an equally crucial application of energy, perhaps less heralded but no less significant, had been discovered in 1909 by Fritz Haber – the method of synthesising ammonia.

All agricultural products draw nutrients from the soil. In order to prevent specific nutrients being denuded, and the soil rendered sterile, farmers have practised crop rotation and fertilisation. Rotation allows alternating crops to draw and replenish differing nutrients. Legumes, which include peas, beans, lentils and peanuts, have a unique ability to capture nitrogen from the atmosphere and fix it into a form usable by other crops, namely ammonia. This replenishes the crucial nitrogen content of the soil, and determines not only the continued fertility of the soil but also how many grain crops, for example, can be grown within a fixed period. The amount of nitrogen is therefore dependent on successfully growing a legume crop for long enough for it to accomplish its nitrogen-fixing work.

The synthesis of ammonia artificially fixes nitrogen through an industrial process using nitrogen and natural gas, which supplies the hydrogen for the reaction as well as heat and pressure. Although synthetic fertiliser became widespread in the years following the First World War, its contribution to the world's food supply became crucial after 1950. It allowed farmers to circumvent the rate of natural nitrogen fixing, and consequently sped up the rate at which nitrogen-denuding crops such as cereals could be grown. Thus, in addition to mechanisation, synthetic fertilisers stretched the bounds of what Malthus might have regarded as the natural limits to food production by some magnitude.

By 1920 the Malthusian balance had been reshaped, and the threats to civilisation transformed in the collective minds of Europe, and to a lesser extent the US. The unevenness of development across the world had seen almost every country drawn into the cycle of modernity, but with differing concerns. The audacity of German industrialisation in the 19th century had been a necessary precursor to the First World War. Between 1850 and 1870 steam power in Germany increased tenfold, placing the country on a par with Britain in this regard. The reach for colonial "ghost acres" drove ambitious projects in the 1880s to emulate Britain's empire, but with limited results as German colonies in Africa and the Pacific were stripped from her after the defeat of 1918.

Within Europe the abundance of almost everything, delivered by the 19th century, had its horrifying denouement in 1914–18. Yet prior to this other consequences of the population/resource equation produced by industrialisation had become clear. The most evident among these was the rise in agricultural productivity sufficient to support large cities. Concomitant with this, though, was the appearance of the first fertility transition.

The general principle of a fertility transition has been summed up thus: "we see that no population has maintained high levels of fertility for long in the face of increasing well-being and declining mortality" (Livi-Bacci 1992, p.107). As these two factors swept across Western Europe, they set in train the steady decline in the number of children borne by successive generations. The most widely used indicator is the Total Fertility Rate (TFR) – the total number of children born to each woman, on average. This has become a contemporary topic of interest because a decline leads to an ageing population, a development evident in many advanced economies. But the pattern

Table 2.2 Total Fertility Rate (TFR) for selected countries, 1850–1950

	1850	1875	1900	1925	1950
Sweden	4.28	3.51	1.9	2.05	1.98
England and Wales	4.56	3.35	1.96	2.15	2.06
Germany	5.17	3.98	2.08	2.06	1.72
France	3.27	2.6	2.14	2.59	2.11
Italy	4.67	4.5	3.14	2.27	1.88
United States	4.48	3.53	2.48	2.94	1.96
Australia		3.22	2.44	2.98	2.3

Adapted from Livi-Bacci (1992, p.107)

became manifest surprisingly early, in the aftermath of the rapid industrialisation of Western Europe after 1850. Table 2.2 gives the TFR for
selected countries from 1850.

The decline is clear from 1850 – indeed, from earlier where records are
available, with England and Wales peaking at 5.87 in 1775. France is an
interesting anomaly, with its early adoption of birth control in urban and
rural areas leading to a relatively low TFR even before industrialisation.

Malthus had imagined that the primary check on reproduction would be
late marriage. A century later, around 1900, contraception played a large role as
a voluntary check on population growth. The TFR required for a population to
reproduce itself in the following generation varies depending on the number
of children who will die before adulthood, but for low-mortality countries it
is about 2.1, rising to 2.3 in those with high child mortality. If we assume the
higher figure for the countries listed in the table, then in 1875 all were above
replacement level, while 25 years later all bar Italy and the colonial offshoots
of the US and Australia were below this threshold.

The significance of this shift is subtle but profound. The fractious history
of Europe in the first half of the 20th century cannot be blamed on population growth, as it was not at anything like historical highs. However, the
higher rates of 1850 translated into the swelling urban populations of the
1880s. Supported by an agricultural surplus, and subject to the fascination of
the industrial city, new segments of society appeared which were not defined
by their productive capacity. The bohemian underclass, a staple of depictions
of late 19th century urbanity, assumed mythical status in later portrayals of
the origins of modernist art. Puccini's *La Bohème* may depict starving students
and artists, but their very existence is predicated on the city somehow providing the minimum means for their survival without the privileges of family
wealth.

While these developments may be regarded as either affirmation of Malthus'
views, in that the voluntary checks to population succeeded, or refutation in
the breaking of his unforgiving nexus between population and resources,

they did turn some minds to the paradoxes of a world whose productive capacity seemed startling, if not boundless. William Stanley Jevons proved to be an astute historian and analyst of the industrial revolution – perhaps the most astute. An economist in the classical English tradition, his *The Coal Question* was first published in 1865, with a comprehensively revised edition appearing in 1906. Jevons builds upon Malthus' suppositions, but with the observations afforded an observer who had witnessed the tremendous increase in productive capacity in England by the 1860s. Indeed, he is worth quoting at length:

> Malthus, Ricardo, and other economists of the same period, were too much inclined to regard [poverty and superfluity of population] as the normal state of society. Population seemed to them always full to the brim, so that each ship-load taken to the colonies would no more tend to empty the country, than a bucketful of water would tend to empty the ever-running fountain from which it is drawn. They could not bring themselves to imagine such a state of things in this country, that one man should not stand in another's way, and that men, rather than subsistence, should be lacking. (Jevons 1906, pp.222–223)

Jevons, in the 1860s, was well placed to record many aspects of English economic power. He cites, with great care, figures showing the dramatic rise in coal production and consumption over the preceding decades. He is in no doubt as to the central role coal plays in the British economy. His words strike us as modern, if we substitute fossil fuels for coal, as Jevons astutely identifies the role increased energy availability played in 19th century England:

> Coal in truth stands not beside, but entirely above, all other commodities. It is the material source of the energy of the country – the universal aid – the factor in everything we do. With coal almost any feat is possible or easy; without it we are thrown back into the laborious poverty of early times. (Jevons 1906, p.2)

With this insight came another – Jevons reasoned that with exponentially (or geometrically, using a term familiar to Malthus) increasing quantities of coal being used, it was only a matter of time before the resource would be exhausted, or at least mined at such depths as to make its extraction impractical.

Much to Jevons' indignation, this was a matter of contention in 1865, although it is currently a commonplace. For Jevons the happy situation he observed where population and resources seemed in balance was only temporary, given the finite nature of coal reserves:

> And though others have been found to reassure the public, roundly asserting that all anticipations of exhaustion [of coal] are groundless and

absurd and "may be deferred for an indefinite period", yet misgivings have constantly recurred to those really examining the question. (Jevons 1906, p.3)

The modernity of Jevons' observations does not end with his prediction of resource exhaustion. His most subtle observation lay in the dynamic of coal use itself – as technological advances rendered the use of coal more efficient, rather than leading to decreased use this tendency only leads to an increase in overall demand. In Jevons' words:

> Nor will the economical use of coal reduce its consumption. On the contrary, economy renders the employment of coal more profitable, and thus the present demand for coal is increased, and the advantage is more strongly thrown upon the side of those who will in the future have the cheapest supplies. (Jevons 1906, p.8)

Jevons' predictions are framed in patriotic terms – his prediction of the decline of English industry leads, for him, to the decline of the relative position of England as a world leader in manufacturing and its attendant power and prestige. Yet his observations could be applied to any country moving rapidly through modernisation, as its initial advantages in resources or labour are transformed or depleted by the very success they engender.

In many other respects Jevons' work strikes us as remarkably current. He grasps the difference between solar societies and fossil fuel-driven ones with acuity, and in a chapter titled "Of supposed substitutes for coal" he surveys all options with remarkable prescience. Electricity is discussed, and again the conclusion is apt more than a century later: people "treat electricity not only as a marvellous mode of distributing power, they treat it as a source of self-creating power" (Jevons 1906, p.161). In other words they overlook the fact that even today it is largely derived from burning coal, or gas, or fissioning uranium. Petroleum too is considered, but it is classed as essentially the same as oil, a conflation that has contemporary relevance as they are both fossil fuels.

Wind, water and hydrogen are all assessed as part of a sombre survey of energy sources. The tenor of Jevons' work is pessimistic for reasons which accord well with our current situation of conflicted plenitude. In this we may regard Jevons as the commentator *par excellence* on the matter of modern population and resources, in the technical sense. His arguments, framed on classical economic antecedents, reveal that it was not only Marx who had an astute sense of the dialectic, or the pattern of the inversion or super-session of circumstances by which history, in his account, proceeds. For Jevons the situation described by Malthus was in abeyance, but only tem-porarily. The very success of coal would lead to its decline and supersession, in an unforgiving dialectic.

However, as the modern era found its primary energy sources by 1910 in the form of coal and oil, and the subsequent diffusion through electricity and the internal combustion engine, the notion of sustainability, understood as the balance of population and resource, shifted from supply to demand. The forces unleashed by the 19th century played out in the 20th in ways that might have confounded Jevons, with the survival of societies framed in ideological rather than empirical terms. But before considering these issues as framers of the last century, the next chapter will consider in greater detail the shaping of the 20th century city.

Bibliography

Angel, S. (2012). *Planet of cities*. Cambridge, MA: Lincoln Institute of Land Policy.

Berman, M. (1982). *All that is solid melts into air: The experience of modernity*. New York: Simon and Schuster.

Borgstrom, G. (1965). *The hungry planet: The modern world at the edge of famine*. New York: Macmillan.

Chandler, T., & Fox, G. (1974). *3000 years of urban growth*. New York: Academic Press.

Cook, J. (1971). *The explorations of Captain James Cook in the Pacific, as told by selections of his own journals, 1768–1779* (A. Price, Ed.). New York: Dover Publications.

Hobsbawm, E. (1977). *The age of capital, 1848–1875*. London: Abacus.

Jennings, H. (1985). *Pandaemonium: The coming of the machine as seen by contemporary observers, 1660–1886*. New York: Free Press.

Jevons, W. (1906). *The coal question: An inquiry concerning the progress of the Nation, and the probable exhaustion of our coal-mines* (3rd ed.) (A. Flux, Ed.). London: Macmillan.

Jones, E. (1987). *The European miracle: Environments, economies, and geopolitics in the history of Europe and Asia*. Cambridge, UK: Cambridge University Press.

Livi-Bacci, M. (1992). *A concise history of world population*. Cambridge, MA: Blackwell.

Malthus, T. (1959). *Population: The first essay*. Ann Arbor, MI: The University of Michigan Press.

Malthus, T. (1973). *An essay on the principle of population*. London: J.M. Dent.

Marx, K., & Engels, F. (1977). The Communist Manifesto. In D. McLellan (Ed.), *Karl Marx: Selected writings*. Oxford: Oxford University Press.

McNeill, J. (2000). *Something new under the sun: An environmental history of the twentieth-century world*. New York: W.W. Norton & Company.

Panofsky, E. (1955). Et in Arcadia Ego: Poussin and the Elegiac Tradition. In *Meaning in the visual arts: Papers in and on art history*. Chicago: University of Chicago Press.

Pomeranz, K. (2000). *The great divergence: China, Europe, and the making of the modern world economy*. Princeton, NJ: Princeton University Press.

Rosen, W. (2010). *The most powerful idea in the world: A story of steam, industry, and invention*. New York: Random House.

Smil, V. (1994). *Energy in world history*. Boulder, CO: Westview Press.

Winch, D. (1987). *Malthus*. Oxford: Oxford University Press.

Wrigley, E. (2010). *Energy and the English industrial revolution*. Cambridge, UK: Cambridge University Press.

3 The modern city emerges

In terms of sheer numbers, events of the 19th century had shifted the most populous 15 cities in the world to Europe, the Americas and Japan. In 1900 only two cities, Beijing and Kolkata, lay outside these regions, and 25 years later none did. The reason lies not in the relative growth and decline of various cities as previously, but rather in the dramatic growth within industrialised and partly industrialised nations. The largest seven cities in 1925 are particularly instructive: New York and London both have seven and three-quarter million, followed by Tokyo, Paris and Berlin in the four to low five millions, and Chicago, Buenos Aires and Osaka holding two to three and a half million. All the largest 15 cities of the time exceeded 1.7 million.

Size may not have been a consistent indicator of the importance or influence of a city historically, but the list of the largest cities in 1925 is nonetheless testament to the importance of technological innovation, and the harnessing of diverse energy sources, to the growth and functioning of the modern city. The initial period of expansion for all the cities mentioned above is significant for what it tells us about the specific ways that the city grew and incorporated energy innovation.

The pattern for each city is unique, and incorporates both opportunity and cultural constraints. However, there are two aspects of city growth that are useful indicators of urban structure, and serve as starting points for understanding the unique, and the common, aspects of the relationship between energy and urban form. The first, of course, is sheer size. This is tricky to ascertain historically, for two reasons. Population size is often equated with relative importance and the sheer presence of a city as an historical spectacle, and hence there is a tendency to exaggerate city size for effect. For this reason I have relied on Chandler and Fox's seminal work, although it is now 40 years old (Chandler & Fox 1974). The consistency of their methods at least yields comparable results, and their cross-checking of estimates against various factors such as trade or consumption has yielded lower figures than are often found elsewhere. They have also consistently addressed the second reason that urban populations are hard to pin down, and that is the tendency to equate a city's population with that of its region. The problem in this regard is to ascertain where the city as an entity ends and the countryside begins, and it is an issue we will return to a number of times.

The second indicator which is historically useful for understanding urban structure and energy is density. This can be represented in many ways, but the most useful is that which represents the number of inhabitants within a given area, most commonly expressed as people per hectare or per square kilometre. In North America this is sometimes expressed as people per square mile. I have generally used metric conventions. This expression of density is naturally a crude figure. It tells us how many people lived in a given area taken as a whole, but the actual physical form of the city can still vary widely and produce similar density figures. A city with wide roads and parks, and with many apartment buildings, may have the same overall population density as a city composed of narrow streets, no parks but many small individual houses. In general we might say that a city with a high population density has higher buildings, more closely packed, than a city with a low population density, although this can again be distorted by the actual number of people per dwelling unit, be it a house or an apartment.

Urban density has been the subject of considerable interest in recent years as discussion has centred on the desirable directions contemporary cities should take. While this discussion will engage us in the latter parts of this book, in English-speaking countries low-density cities are associated with a greater degree of suburbanisation, and higher-density cities with apartment or terrace house living. This crude distinction has been at the core of much recent urban speculation, with a vast literature extolling the virtues of dense urban areas over the suburb.

Traditional urban densities in pre-industrial cities were a function of how desirable a location was, how much land could be usefully developed, and what cultural and symbolic functions the city accommodated. Technical issues also played a role – bringing water to households has always presented challenges, and sewage, urban refuse, smoke and smells all influence the form buildings take, and how they sit together. Protection for the city as a whole was an important factor for most of settled history, and cities were often defined by their enclosing walls, which expanded if the settlement grew. Chandler and Fox propose a number of rules of thumb in this regard, based on numerous examples. For many pre-industrial cities a gross ratio of 100 people per hectare prevailed. When growing cities were squeezed within old city walls, this ratio would rise to 200 immediately before the city walls were expanded. New walls were built to accommodate future growth, and so they would enclose a population density typically of about 75 people per hectare (Chandler & Fox 1974, p.5).

Why cities traditionally converged towards these figures is a complex question to answer, as individual factors differ from city to city. As we have seen in chapter 1, ancient Rome reached a density of 500 people per hectare, while Chang'an in the 7th century had a figure of about 100. Florence in 1333 had a density of between 88 and 138, depending on which population estimates one accepts, and Venice peaked at about 250 in the mid 16th century. Thus the Roman figure is at the high end, and accords with accounts of the city as noisy, cramped and composed of tens of thousands of apartment blocks. Chang'an benefitted from an orderly layout and wide roads, but the actual accommodation in walled wards within the city was tightly controlled, with access restricted at night. Florence expanded its walls but suffered population decline from plague, and hence it retained a low population density overall through its most influential period, while Venice was always restricted by the cost and effort of reclaiming and stabilising its built up area from its marshy surrounds, and it never had the option of simply expanding city walls to enclose farmland.

These factors account in some measure for differing densities. They also indicate the range of densities prevailing in pre-industrial cities, and enable some observations to be made about how this attribute emerges. Clearly there are countervailing tendencies which both encourage consolidation, and attempt to mitigate the negative effects of having too great a density. Thus the figure of 100 people per hectare represents a median of sorts, while the highest figure of around 600 for Genoa in the Middle Ages shows the effects of extreme geographic constraint for a city wedged between coastal mountains and the Mediterranean.

The factors driving cities to greater density are easy to understand if we consider the practical issues of town building in a world where, at best, less than a quarter of the population was urbanised, and the ratio was often as low as 10%. Before the advent of the nation-state, with its centralised and dominant control of law and order, the city needed to ensure its own security against threats local and distant. This alone encouraged consolidation within city walls, whose extent was determined by the resources available to make them sufficiently massive and secure. The success of the city led to the building of new walls, which entailed a huge investment and a measure of faith in its continued growth. Within these walls, extending the water supply and having some means of disposing of refuse and effluent were crucial, and keeping these separate was a constant challenge. Human waste could either be flushed away into rivers or the sea, or in more finely tuned societies it could be collected and used as fertiliser.

The provision of water and the disposal of waste, if carried out at a communal level, tend to make cities more dense to keep the cost of the public works involved as low as possible. The same is true of street networks, whose surface area determines the cost and effort of construction. The trading and mercantile mentality so crucial to city development also encourages greater density. Not only do goods have less distance to travel as they are exchanged or bought, but the sheer proximity of people – buyers and sellers – fosters myriad interactions and commercial activity. The convenience of living in urban cores, so much a selling point of urban redevelopment in modern cities, has always been a feature of city life. Easy access to the street has been prized through the ages, as has the sheer entertainment value of watching people going about their daily lives.

These rules work for the public domain, that of commerce and civic life. However, within the home, space has always been highly prized. The patrician families of Rome lived within relatively large houses with a central court, not specifically to enjoy privacy in the modern sense but to be able to control their household. Within the house domestic decorum prevailed, evident in an orderliness that was in contrast to the commercial and political affairs that constituted life in the city at large. This dual aspect of urban life has long been sought after: to have access to the most diverse life being lived in the city, and yet to be able to retreat to one's home for security and predictability. Thus large houses or compounds centrally located became an urban ideal, but they remained rare precisely because too many of them would have decreased the density of their locality, and hence their desirability. But their very existence served as a countermeasure to high gross urban density.

Other practical aspects of early city life also worked towards lowering densities. Fire was a constant threat, and its spread in tightly packed cities could be devastating. The avenues of Chang'an served to contain fires within specific wards or blocks. Social control was also more difficult where cities were dense and contiguous, and riots sporadically challenged city rulers. And then there were the issues around what we might term health and amenity, whose net effect was to give city dwellers a shorter life span than rural dwellers for much of the pre-industrial period. Close proximity fostered epidemics, with devastating effects, even though the role of density in spreading infection may not have been understood. But the smells and the smoke, the fetid open sewers and the levels of noise and aggression in many cities would have to be constantly weighed against the irreplaceable feeling of being at the centre of human affairs.

Thus the crude indicator of density hides many factors, but from the point of view of urban history the specific density figure for a city at a point in time represents a balance between the forces that encourage greater urban concentration, and those that impel the components of the city towards separation. This concept is at the core of the argument of this book, since the industrial city has brought enormous and historically unique forces to bear on the terms of this balance. However, the balance prevailing at any point in time also needs to be understood in relation to an overall historical tendency. Cities rarely remain in equilibrium: instead they change in density as people migrate from the country to the city, as urban birth rates fluctuate and as the number of people in each dwelling changes. The prevailing form of development also has an effect, as detached dwellings hold lower population densities than apartments, for example.

Tracking the population density of a city over time can be very difficult, since both building form and population will change at various stages of expansion and contraction. Many European historic city cores have changed very little physically over the past 30 years, yet they have experienced dramatic declines in population density as housing rises in value and large working families are driven out. Venice is perhaps the most dramatic example. While demolition and urban redevelopment has been almost absent in the last 100 years, the resident population of the city itself fell from 121,000 to 62,000 between 1966 and 2006. Thus, with no physical change, the population density of the city halved over 40 years, as residents moved to more affordable housing in Mestre and Marghera.

The issue is also clouded by how urban statistics are presented. Historically city walls gave a good indication of the physical extent of a city, although in the case of Florence, for example, they contained significant open space. Modern figures for city size often refer to administrative areas rather than built up areas, and they may contain areas yet to be developed, or areas with no development such as harbours or national parks. The most accurate indicator of urban density, if we wish to compare types of development, is actual population divided by built up area, and, when considering a city as a whole, merged or contiguous built up area is the measure that is sought.

Nonetheless there have been a number of serious attempts to capture historical change in city form and density using historical maps and modern satellite images. A team under Peter Bosselman produced one such book in 2008, where 41 world cities were mapped at a constant scale using satellite images and software that discriminates between the graphic characteristics of built up areas and those of vegetation or natural features. The exercise produced a fascinating atlas showing the relative size of significant cities when laid on a 50 km square grid, as well as the population densities when correlated against figures for urban populations. Although the method struggles when faced with cities such as Milan, which has a very dispersed structure that extends well beyond its historic core, it yields some interesting comparative densities (Table 3.1, Bosselman 2008).

Table 3.1 Densities of selected cities, 2007

City	Density (people per hectare)
Hong Kong	704
Lagos	692
Istanbul	342
New York	204
Mexico City	184
Tokyo	142
Paris	137
Beijing	105
London	70
Sydney	38

Adapted from Bosselman (2008)

These figures should be taken with some caution, mainly because the statistics for urban populations are difficult to correlate with physical area unless they are checked against specific census maps. While the orders of magnitude seem correct, aberrant figures obtained for Milan (11 people per hectare) underline the technical difficulties of this type of exercise. New York, too, seems to yield a high figure that does not fully take into account the suburbs that are part of its continuous urban area but fall under different administrative jurisdictions.

While the figures obtained for 2008 may seem to correlate loosely with the figures obtained for pre-industrial cities, the overall magnitudes involved make such comparisons superficial. Ancient Rome was clearly very different to modern Hong Kong, despite density figures of 500 and 700 respectively. What is of greater interest is undertaking the exercise over a span of time, so that we might discern overall tendencies in the transition of cities to modern form.

At this stage we will consider urban density as the number of inhabitants accommodated within a continuous built up area. This generally correlates to the experience of the city. One might drive in a line from the city centre, through various rings of urban development, and end up in the furthest suburbs as they shade into rural smallholdings. At some point a distinction needs to be made between city and country, perhaps on the basis of dwelling density or the number of houses per unit area. In many cases local authorities legislate minimum lot sizes at the city fringe, to maintain a rural atmosphere and prevent the haphazard conversion of rural holdings to suburbs. The US Census Bureau sets a specific population density threshold of 3.86 people per hectare for land to be declared urban. In general though we might say that where the suburbs end, the city ends.

This definition underpins the urban maps derived from satellite images. Using software that distinguishes the graphic patterns of suburbia from those of the countryside, at some point a line is drawn that represents the urban boundary, a process that is inherently imprecise but necessary. This delineates the physical extent of the city as perceived and generally understood, but this may correspond only to the city as perceived through driving, for example, and not through economic analysis. An alternative view of a city may be that of a metropolitan labour market, defined by how far people are prepared to travel between home and work on a daily basis. This yields a very different view of the extent of a city, but one that will be familiar to an inhabitant considering their job and housing prospects. In some cases the metropolitan labour market may correspond very closely with the city extents as viewed from space, as in the case of isolated centres like Perth in Western Australia. In other cases the physical city is very different from the labour market that centres on it. Zurich is a good example. Given the excellent public transport in Switzerland, many people who work in Zurich choose to live in distinct villages that can be accessed from the city centre in less than an hour. From space these may look like traditional villages surrounding the city and physically separated from it by farmland, but in reality they are dormitory suburbs that many Zurich workers commute to in the evening. Thus the city itself has about 400,000 residents, and the countryside is easily accessed from the city, but the metropolitan area of Zurich has over 1.8 million people and has an economic presence far greater than the physical size of the city would imply.

This latter case indicates how tricky the issue of density is in the modern city, since its connections can be diffuse and highly technical. However, for issues of historical clarity, let us concern ourselves for the moment with the city as a physical entity – the city which conforms to the impressions of the casual observer. In a similar vein to Bosselman, a team led by Shlomo Angel at the Lincoln Institute of Land Policy undertook a more comprehensive analysis of urban density over the first decade of this century. The results were published in 2012 as *Planet of Cities*, and the findings contain an enormous amount of data and considerations on urban density (Angel 2012).

The study aimed to clarify questions around urban expansion, a phenomenon that all thriving cities have to deal with. In order to inform planning policy, Angel decided to study urban expansion historically, which gave rise to some specific questions, including how compact and dense are cities currently, and how this has changed over time? Within it were folded a number of other questions around city structure and the location of functions within that structure. But the main purpose behind Angel's work is to understand how cities in developing and fast-urbanising countries will meet the demand for additional land, given current trends to limit the physical extent of cities in developed countries for a range of ideological and ecological reasons. The question then, for Angel, is whether the prescriptions for urban development emanating from developed countries are relevant for developing countries, and whether they acknowledge the historical patterns of urban expansion that developed countries themselves passed through. To put it more directly, is the current distaste for urban sprawl in Europe and North America useful for informing urban policies in rapidly growing cities in Asia, Africa and South America?

In order to chart changes in density and city size over an extended period, the group narrowed their sample list to 30 cities for which sufficient data was available from 1800 to 2000. Historical maps were digitised, and correlated with population statistics for the time. This exercise is an excellent starting point for a consideration of a group of world cities which grew and changed through the advent of modernity, and modern energy sources and innovations. The most interesting conclusion regarding urban density found by Angel and his group is that despite two centuries of increasing urbanisation, urban densities are declining almost everywhere, and have been declining for a long time.

This trend has been observed in the US for over a century, but recent availability of digitised census data and maps dating back to 1910 allowed population figures to be measured precisely against their enclosing area. In

Baltimore, for example, Angel calculated the average urban density across the city as declining from 98 people per hectare to 15 between 1910 and 2000. For 20 cities, including New York, Boston, Chicago and Los Angeles, the average density decline over the 90 years was from 69.6 to 14.6 people per hectare. This decline was fastest in the years after the Second World War, and has in fact reversed in a small number of cities in recent decades (Angel 2012).

Applying a similar analysis to a sample of 30 cities worldwide produced a varied picture, from which a limited number of generalisations could be made. In the 19th century this sample group exhibited both increasing and declining densities, but in the 20th century this shifted to predominantly a lowering of urban density, albeit uneven. However, when one looks at the data by region, patterns emerge that tell different stories about economic development, wealth and energy consumption. London peaks in 1830 at about 327, and then shows a steady decline, with a marked acceleration between about 1910 and 1930. Paris enters the 19th century with about 500 people per hectare, and then from 1830 it starts to decline, falling to 125 by the turn of the 20th century. Figure 3.1 shows the relative change in urban density for a small group of cities.

Each one of these lines can be expanded into a telling urban history, since they each encapsulate a series of physical maps, a series of population figures and an unfolding economic and energy story. Correlating the graph with a history of a specific city or cities gives us a good sense of how the physical size of the city grew to accommodate increased population, using the increasing volume of energy available.

Paris seems an apt city to begin with, as it exhibits the most consistent decline in density from 1800. The early period, from 1800 to 1846, saw a doubling of the city's population to over a million. The clear concentric pattern of development enables the tracing of the city from its Medieval core, centred on the twin islands in the Seine, the Île de la Cité and the Île

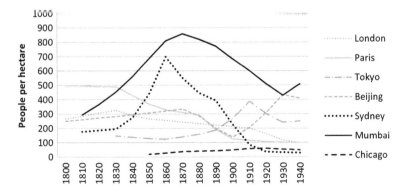

Figure 3.1 Urban densities of selected cities, by decade
Adapted from Angel, Parent, Civco & Blei (2010, Annex iv)

Saint-Louis. The city walls, over time, enclosed increasingly larger areas, aided by the confiscation of church lands following the French Revolution. The traditional pattern of development of the city echoed that of Rome, with proximity to the street the most desired location. This fostered commerce and a general sense of intense urban life, and was ingrained in the form the city took and its attitude to space and class. Since being close to the street was desirable, street frontages to lots were narrow to increase the number of lots per length of street. Lots were often deep as well, and developed as a series of courts accessed through narrow paths and walkways. Social classes were stratified vertically, with larger dwellings just above the ground-level shops, and cramped dwellings housing the working class inserted in the attics. The result was a city structure that encouraged interaction and trade, that valued street frontage though not street width, and that built upwards from the street and back along its narrow lots.

The expansion of the city through the 19th century took the form of *faubourgs*, neighbourhoods which grew from key streets built as extensions of the city core. These were built at lower densities, as the density graph of Paris indicates. Often this was not immediately obvious. Building regulations maintained the practice of building to the street alignment, so the continuous wall of buildings characteristic of the city centre was continued into the newer areas, even if there was little building behind. Whereas this gives the Paris of today a remarkable visual cohesion, in the mid 19th century it masked the differences between pre-1800 Paris and later development. What did emerge over time, though, was a lessening of the mix of shops and workshops, of rich and poor, that had been part of the Medieval urban culture of the city (Loyer 1988).

Other changes emerged as the city population exceeded one million. According to Loyer, this was the point at which the dense network of streets and lanes became too clogged and narrow to accommodate the volume of trade and goods traversing the city. It had reached saturation point. The situation was exacerbated by the traditional Parisian fondness for streets with lots of activity, and a reluctance to spread out. As the city walls became filled in, buildings on individual lots were raised higher as additional storeys were added. But the million mark for population had not stood over time as a natural urban limit without reason. The impetus to densify and build higher could only absorb so much of the population influx. Nineteenth century Paris, when faced with the challenges of population growth, approached these in a distinctive and inventive way that meshed with its fondness for the experience of urbanity.

David Harvey's ode to Paris is titled *Paris, Capital of Modernity*. The book title expresses a sentiment that runs through French literature and many modern reflections of this city as a place where the distinctive urban sensations of the Industrial era could be sampled. In 1875 London and Paris were unrivalled in size anywhere, but the French capital is more closely associated with the new experiences, many unprecedented, that the modern city gave rise to. While the writings of Baudelaire convey these, emphasising the visual spectacles of the city and the thrilling anonymity of the observer, later observers such as Walter Benjamin embedded these experiences in the study of the phenomenon of modernity itself. All of these historical discoveries are implicit in the title of Harvey's book (Harvey 2003).

The phenomenal growth of the city engendered a number of modern urban developments. As the average building height, and hence volume, increased, so did its function. The modern apartment building emerged. Previously houses on several storeys had been subdivided between landlord and tenant internally on an informal basis, like a boarding house; however, the apartment building housed repetitive dwellings entered from a communal staircase, but private from it (Loyer 1988, p.48). As lots were consolidated apartment buildings were built, and the rented apartment became accepted as both a housing type and a form of investment. But the greatest transformation of an overbuilt and sclerotic Paris came under the direction of Baron Haussmann, prefect for the Seine.

As any visitor to the city knows, the grand avenues that give Paris visual coherence and formal structure were constructed by Haussmann in the 1850s and 60s. Under the patronage of Napoleon III, the prefect carved his large avenues through wealthy and poor neighbourhoods alike. While it has been popular to see these as instruments of social control whereby rioters and revolutionary mobs could be suppressed by police and military forces, the intent was much greater. Both the emperor and the prefect had visions of social reform and urban beautification, inspired by the squares and streets of Georgian London. As Loyer asserts, "Rather than repudiate the new socio-economic order or pretend that it did not exist, the city endeavored to tame industrial society by integrating it into a broader cultural vision" (Loyer 1988, p.232).

The project of Haussmann not only made the city understandable to the casual wanderer through the opening up of vistas, it also involved the construction of sewers and water supplies, and the consolidation of the appearance of the city through building regulations and massive redevelopment projects. Moving goods and people across the city also became incomparably easier, aided by the creation of a single omnibus company from many providers. This effectively tripled trade, as the number of passengers carried rose from 36 million in 1855 to 110 million five years later (Harvey 2003, p.113).

Through all this, as the density graph of Paris shows, the city continued to decline in density. The major lesson to draw is that the decline began before the advent of public transport. Thus, although public transport was critical in allowing people to move about the modern city, it did not in itself drive lower densities. The decline in Parisian density precedes the development of mass rail transport in the city. By 1848 Paris had a number of railway stations, but each served as a terminus for services extending from the capital outwards. The circular line of the Petit Ceinture railway was conceived in

1851, but it took nearly 20 years to complete and it may have aided a decrease in density, but could not have helped initiate it.

By 1875 Paris was home to two and a quarter million inhabitants, over four times the number of 1800. It had endured a major insurrection four years earlier in the form of the Paris Commune, but was about to embark on a period of unparalleled cultural and economic flowering that would last until the Second World War. The period of physical reconstruction of the city under Haussmann was over, and France had experienced an immense expansion of industrial and transport capacities. It had moved into the modern era. Paris itself had also expanded substantially in size, and railways and omnibuses were established as the primary means of moving people and goods both into and around the city.

The early omnibus was a horse-drawn vehicle which picked up and set down passengers along a set route, as opposed to stagecoaches which required prior booking. Arguably the first form of urban mass transport, the basic vehicle allowed services to start up with relative ease. The first service commenced in England in 1824, and by 1830 omnibus lines operated in Berlin, Paris and New York. They proved immensely popular, conveying passengers across the burgeoning metropolitan areas and extending the range of daily life and social interaction. Subsequent development of the services illustrates the 19th century approach to meeting one of the principle challenges of land transport – friction.

The advantage that water transport had long held over land-borne goods lay in the volumes that could be carried, and the mechanical advantage of the small resistance offered to barges and ships as they moved through the water compared to the effort required to shift loads in carts or wagons. Two main forces made this hard going – the resistance to the wheels themselves as they sank in mud or traversed rough roads, and the friction operating on the crude wheel bearings rotating around the shaft or axle. Lubrication was difficult with the greases and fats available, and the shafts and simple bearings wore down easily. In early 19th century Sydney vehicles were quickly passed from the wealthy to poorer traders as they wore out, and the second-hand wagons became known as "growlers" from the noise caused by their worn and poorly lubricated bearings. Thus the effects of friction served both to increase the mechanical effort needed to move carts, and to shorten the life of the wheel and axle set.

While improvements were made to wheel technology, the real advance in overcoming the friction on the rotating wheel hub bushings would have to wait until the perfection of mass-produced roller bearings and ball bearings at the end of the 19th century. However, the overcoming of rolling resistance caused by poor road surfaces could be addressed through railroad technology. Steel wheels running on steel rails were well established as having a low rolling resistance, and a high coefficient of friction or grip between the two surfaces. This allowed the rotary motive force transmitted through the locomotive wheels to be translated into forward or backward movement of the train. Since the motive force for omnibuses was supplied by horses, and relied on the friction between their shod hooves and the surface of the road, this factor provided little incentive to run omnibuses on rails. However, the low rolling resistance of rails and steel wheels increased the efficiency of the horses by making the carriages themselves easier to start forward and keep moving, and this alone spurred the laying of rails along omnibus routes. Although steam omnibuses were available in 1833, their huge weight (a modern replica weighs 3.2 tonnes) and steering difficulties allowed the horse-drawn lobby to curtail their use through organised opposition. By the 1860s the omnibus had largely given way to its rail-bound successor, the horse tram.

The horse-drawn public transport lasted into the 20th century in the form of trams. The initial adoption of rails for them to run on took the form of the raised railroad type, which proved a hazard for all other traffic attempting to turn across these urban obstacles. The recessed rail thus became the norm when laid in roads. In many cities the tram network meshed with the two other forms of mass transport that emerged – the suburban railway and the mechanical ferry. The enormous advantage that the omnibus held was its ease of stopping and starting, making it ideal for urban services with closely spaced stops. Ferries suited cities that developed around waterfronts, and had vacant land across a sheltered body of water. Suburban steam trains suffered from the limitations of their technology, which is heavy and relies on keeping up constant steam pressure to operate economically. The mechanical effort of stopping and starting steam locomotives leads to stations that are relatively far apart, and hence suburban trains are useful for moving large numbers of people between fixed locations that serve as transport hubs for more diffuse modes of transport like walking or omnibus riding. Nonetheless their adoption helped bring about the dispersal of families from the city core.

Kenneth Jackson's excellent *Crabgrass Frontier* charts the suburbanisation of American cities, starting with the drawing of Brooklyn into the economic life of New York as a commuter suburb in the early 1800s. A steam ferry service connecting Brooklyn and Manhattan commenced in 1814, and it was this technology that bound the two localities across the East River. By 1854 some 1250 crossing took place daily, and in Jackson's eyes Brooklyn deserves recognition as the first suburb in the modern sense (Jackson 1985). The same technology opened up Sydney's north shore as commuter suburbs for the city well before the opening of the Sydney Harbour Bridge in 1932. However, in cities without natural harbours it was the rail-borne systems of trams and railways that responded to suburbanisation, and helped facilitate its expansion.

As we have seen from the work of Angel *et al.* (2010), major cities such as Paris, London and New York began their decrease in density before the era of mass public transport. The same point is made by Divall and Schmucki, who write that urban transport should be viewed as "being both formed by social context and capable of acting back upon it as a powerful force in urban development" (Divall and Schmucki 2003, p.1). Rather than driving urban development in the first half of the 19th century, new technologies such as railways helped transfer to cities the volume of goods and food needed on a daily basis from great distances. Thus the initial expansion of cities was based on the inter-regional application of new technologies, rather than an intra-urban one. In the same way that American grain yields reached historically high returns on energy using teams of horses before the advent of tractors, cities reached historically high numbers using horse-drawn omnibuses and wagons within their confines. However, once they had attained historically unique sizes, the application of new technologies and energy sources inside cities proceeded quickly.

The impact of urban railway systems is a case in point. As late as 1900 only about 25,000 workers used the cheap fares offered on London's railways. In Berlin at the turn of the 20th century the number was 33,000 (Capuzzo 2003). Compared to the numbers riding omnibuses in Paris in 1855, these are small indeed. The omnibus and the tram remained the dominant form of public transport through the rapid growth period of Paris, London, Berlin and New York as they became multi-million person cities.

As industrial cities grew, the ill effects of density and poor servicing became evident. Haussmann's reforms had propelled Paris to a unique position of having confronted the challenges of the modern city, and having addressed its most urgent shortcomings. The city's density declined dramatically, and by 1900 it had dropped to well below that of London. The impetus was not always the benign quest for open space and air: as rents rose in central Paris for the new apartment buildings, the poor were driven to the edge of the city where rents were lower. The traditional Parisian virtues of urban interaction and excitement were divorced from the egalitarian traditions that allowed all classes to participate. Suburban railways brought the inhabitants of outer Paris into the city centre as day visitors, but they also reinforced the increasing social stratification of the city.

One of the striking features when we compare Paris with London is the latter's lower urban density in 1800. With 265 people per hectare, London at the start of the 19th century is almost half as dense as its French counterpart. Although it still exhibited a steep density gradient, which graphs the decline in density along a line from the city centre to edge of the city, the city as a whole was reasonably dispersed. Bruegmann attributes this partly to the developed English economy of the time, but also to the relative peace and isolation of the city from the threat of invasion. With no defensive walls, the city could spread without the physical and administrative (not to mention psychological) constraint that city walls constitute (Bruegmann 2005, p.25). There may also be a cultural component to this early low density in a country where the lifestyle of the landed gentry remains an object of fascination and emulation for many even into current times. The powerful appeal of a country residence remote from the ills of the city was well established by 1800, and drove many subsequent ideals of suburban development (Fishman 1987). Thus the idealisation of urban life in London had less of a hold on the popular imagination than in Paris, and the city maintained some of the virtues of its Georgian expansion and its symbolic function with large parks and squares built into the fabric of the city itself from at least the 18th century. The Mayfair area is a prime example, laced with Grosvenor, Berkeley and Hanover Squares. The cultural and historical factors shaping London at 1800 were distinct from those operating on Paris, but their ensuing densities through the following century produced differing urban forms within an overall trend of decreasing density.

Also evident through this period is the effect of Pomeranz's "ghost acres", or sources of food and energy beyond the traditional confines of English farmland and woodland. The compression of energy in the form of coal, and the compression of food energy in the form of West Indian sugar, provided two critical means to supplement the crops and wood that had fuelled the city before 1650. French colonies in the Caribbean, North and West Africa and Asia served the same purpose, and produce from the closer colonies was freely available in Paris in the latter 19th century (Pomeranz 2000).

London confronted its failing infrastructure from 1848 with the establishment of the Metropolitan Commission of Sewers and its successor, the Board of Works, whose work was given enormous impetus by the Great Stink of 1858 which was caused by an unfortunate confluence of warm weather and an overtaxed sewage disposal system in the capital. An improved extensive sewerage network was in place by 1875, as well as new roads and parks although on a much smaller scale than that undertaken in Paris. These extensive public works still relied on gravity though, and emptied raw sewage into the Thames until 1900. Filtration of drinking water became compulsory in 1855, and the cholera epidemics that had struck the city periodically were eliminated by 1870.

Hand in hand, then, with the enormous volumes of goods, food and fuel entering these world-leading cities, the infrastructures of London and Paris were expanded to meet the demands of sanitation and water supply for their burgeoning populations. In energy terms the greatest effect of the age was movement of goods into the cities, and the powering of industry and pumping of water by steam engines. Trams had established a mechanical norm in relation to friction, and horse power sufficed to make it viable. Within cities themselves, the 19th century was still wedded to the mass of the steam engine, either in its locomotive form or its stationary one which powered manufacturing in factories, and also threshing in the fields. Gas derived from coal was piped for lighting from the early 1800s, and later supplied to individual houses for heating and cooking. These innovations were enough to break the traditional population thresholds of the city by some margin, but the truly transformative technologies for urban expansion appeared at the end of the century.

The advent of electricity as a means of transferring energy to its point of use presented enormous benefits within the city. Thomas Edison initiated the public supply of electricity in 1882, using direct current (DC) to supply local households and street lights. Within two decades, using the more versatile alternating current (AC), electricity had been put to a range of uses that had traditionally been powered by steam or animals. The development of the electric motor by Frank Sprague in the 1880s saw the technology harnessed to two existing uses – trams and elevators. In both cases the new motors brought radical expansion.

The confluence of large electrical generators, redesigned wires and trolley poles, and efficient electric motors led to the widespread and swift adoption of the electric trolley car. These replaced horse-drawn trams, effectively combining the appeal and utility of the tram with the power and cleanliness of the electric motor. In energy terms, the fleets of horses that powered trams in shifts, and the feed which enabled them to work, were replaced by a different energy source. The former required cropland to provide grains and hay for feed, while the latter used coal to boil water, and the resulting steam to drive turbines and generators. This further freed up cropland with the adoption of a fossil fuel, coal, to help move people around the city.

The enormous advantage of the electric motor was the decoupling of the application of energy supply from the huge machinery needed to convert the primary feedstock, coal, into useful motion. While the generators may have required whole buildings, the small electric motor could be mounted close to the wheel that it drove. It also had the advantage in mechanical terms of easy acceleration and braking, unlike the steam engine. Thus, with minimal fuss and no adjustment of the generator, electric trams could start and stop at close intervals simply by regulating the amount of current fed to their motor. The advantages of this arrangement were compelling, and from the late 1880s electric trams began to replace their horse-drawn predecessors in cities the world over. Using existing or new rails laid in the road surface, they emerged as a quintessential part of the urban experience well into the 20th century. In just six years, from 1887 to 1893, more than 60% of America's 12,000 miles of urban tracks were electrified (Jackson 1985, loc.2224[1]).

The reduced cost of ridership also encouraged urbanites to use the city as a distraction, and to explore for simple pleasure. Trams, or streetcars as they were termed in America, were more heavily used at the weekends than on weekdays from the outset. They not only reduced the apparent size of the city and made its parts accessible on a large scale, they also precipitated the development of enormous amusement parks. These were built at the end of tram lines on city outskirts specifically as destinations for the urban masses. Coney Island may be the best known, but they existed in their hundreds wherever tramlines were installed, and they were generally owned by the tram companies themselves (Jackson 1985, loc.2259). In Sydney the scale of now-demolished theme parks and piers by the sea, built at the suburban tram termini like Coogee Beach, seems astonishing even by contemporary standards.

As Jackson notes, the tram may have expanded the city and brought the masses to its edge for leisure, but the radial form of tram networks also reinforced the primacy of the city centre (Jackson 1985, loc.2277). Most routes led into the city, and the easy access they provided encouraged merchandisers to locate their emporia at the intersection of major lines. Thus the rise of the department store as a mass shopping experience is tied to the rise of the tram networks as the lifelines of urban vitality. Conceived as a practical solution for public transport, the success of the new technology not only enabled people to get to where they wanted to go, but it helped foster a desire to go to places for leisure or entertainment. As a mass phenomenon it leapfrogged its original intent, and helped create a new identity for cities commensurate with their growing scale. They achieved what the train never could – a binding of the dense centre to its surrounding neighbourhoods, and an intricate mechanisation at a scale that blended easily with the walking experience of the traditional city.

The success of the tram system can hardly be underestimated. In Sydney the network reached its peak in the 1930s and 40s, with 405 million passenger journeys made in 1945. With a population of about 1.48 million, this translates to an average of 273 tram rides per person per year. Novels set in the city in the 1930s have trams as integral elements for plot and movement, as they became the conveyances of everyday life. Sydney closed down its system, one of the largest in the world, between 1940 and 1961, but Melbourne retained its network and it remains as testimony to the way trams were interwoven with city structure. The extent of Melbourne's system also demarcates the boundaries of the city in the first half of the century. Trams terminate well before the edge of the current, extended city. Indeed they show where the expanded Victorian city ends, and suburbanisation begins. But before we consider this phase, the second achievement of the electric motor needs to be noted.

Soon after making the electric tram viable, Frank Sprague adapted his motors to the elevator. Previously driven by hydraulic pressure or steam engines, the electric motor made the elevator safer, smaller and more convenient. The same advantages it brought to the tram were useful in vertical transportation – the ability to be attached directly to the drive mechanism, and the fine control over acceleration and braking that allowed the lift car to stop often and accurately. Sprague commercialised his invention with Charles Pratt, and they sold their commercial interest in 1895 to the Otis Elevator Company, which had been using steam and hydraulic technology since the mid 19th century (Jutte n.d.). The ingenuity that attended the installation of lifts before 1892 (including in the Eiffel Tower) allowed buildings to be built with upper floors beyond the reach of stairs alone, but the electric elevator ushered in the era of extensive skyscraper construction. This fostered the intensive development of city centres, and a corresponding increase in land value. Despite the potential for massive increases in city densities, the advent of the skyscraper had little effect on the gradual process of declining densities as cities pushed outwards.

Electric tram networks allowed the late 19th century city to fill out to a specific radius, which was determined by travel times. Due to their numerous stops and need to negotiate street traffic and pedestrians, even modern tram systems can only sustain low average speeds. Melbourne trams, the largest surviving system in the world, average 16 km/hr across the network, and 11 km/hr within the central city (Yarra Trams 2015). Tram routes average about 10.4 km long, with the longest route running for just over 20 km. This gives a travel time of around 40 minutes for the average route, and the journey into the city on the longest route takes over an hour. These times represent the limit of commuting range for trams, as the time taken for longer distances begins to exceed the commuter's willingness to sit on a tram for extended periods. Thus the tram moved slightly quicker than the pace of the walking city, but it was limited to the radius of that same urban pace. For the city to truly extend itself into the surrounding countryside, the faster speed and dedicated corridors of rail were the critical technology.

Given the long history of steam as a driver of transport, the first parts of the city that can be truly regarded as suburban are tied into this technology. Jackson may identify Brooklyn and its steam-powered ferry service to Manhattan as the first example of a suburb, but the rail lines linking the city to the interior were less constrained and could follow the initiatives of early suburban speculators and developers. Fishman has traced the cultural origins of the suburb to the Evangelical community established at Clapham, London, in the mid 1700s (Fishman 1987). For Fishman the critical element in the evolution of the suburb was the creation of a domestic ideal distinct from that of the city itself, one that raised the home to a domestic haven befitting the family whose male head may have wrestled daily with the moral compromises of commerce, but who could return home to the elevated morality and sentimental comforts of a house in the country. Within this house the family subscribed to virtues that rested on a new ideal of marriage, where the wife provided the spiritual guidance and upheld the loftier aspirations within the marital partnership.

Whereas this ideal no doubt helped form the aspiration for suburbia, its emergence as the counterpart to the city relied on the railway. Suburbs initially developed as strings of villages along rail lines, each village being defined by a 15 minute walk from the station (Fishman 1987, p.136). With widely spaced stations, and a much higher average speed, the radius of commuting by rail could be triple that of trams. However, the actual uptake of this form of commuting was often restricted by price. This suited the early American form of suburban development, which in many cases strove to keep suburbs homogenous and restricted to a single class, and thus the cost of travel served as a useful barrier. Fishman details the creation of Chestnut Hill as a suburb of Philadelphia in the 1870s as an example of precisely this type of development: a detached settlement populated by urbanites seeking an elitist refuge from the increasingly polyglot city, and its immigrant groups (Fishman 1987, p.145).

Thus, in the Anglophone world of England, America and Australasia the early suburbs followed a model of urban inversion, where the wealthy sought to pull apart the urban experience and remake it in discrete localities that suited their preferences. Commercial activities – trading and shopping – took place in the city centre, on the site of the old urban core. Leisure and home life occurred in the suburb, where the quietness of a controlled environment fostered an idealised version of domesticity. For those cities that took their cue from Paris, the opposite proved true, as the wealthy retained a preference for the city centre and adjusted to large apartments, while the poor were driven to the urban periphery to escape the high values of the redeveloped core. Vienna, Marseilles and Milan followed this model, and developed a form of urban life distinct from the Anglophone one.

The city in both its forms nonetheless had to confront the issues of service reticulation. The clear failure of traditional methods of effluent disposal and water supply led to improvements from the second half of the 19th century in all major and emerging cites. Mumbai, with a population of 816,000 in 1864, commissioned its first water supply scheme in 1860 on the Mithi River. The first sewage collection scheme was constructed in the same decade, and by 1880 the city area's flow was discharging to an ocean outfall at Worli (Ramanna 2002). London and Paris were also undertaking their first large-scale supply and disposal works. Constructed by hand, these systems generally relied on gravity flow although the London water supply had relied on steam pumps to lift water at least since 1822.

The energy required for water supply varies according to topography. Generally water circulates in urban areas under pressure derived from raised reservoirs, with pressure dependent on the height of the reservoir above the final consumers. In cities close to mountainous areas water supply can be accomplished by gravity alone, but in flat regions or where water is brought long distances, pumping is needed. At the beginning of the 20th century these services used a small but crucial proportion of urban energy, a situation that has changed significantly for some cities, such as Los Angeles, over time (Troy 2012). The most visible uses of energy in major cities at 1900 were the tram network, powered by coal-fired power stations situated within urban areas, and municipal lighting. Industry, located typically in a ring beyond the city but within walking distance of working-class housing, was another significant consumer of power. Household consumption of electricity was still small, and the development of electrical supply was uneven.

The early years of urban electricity supply were marked by an ongoing struggle between the proponents of direct current (DC), who included Thomas Edison, and those who saw the advantages of alternating current (AC). Trams ran on DC, using a supply of around 500 V. Early supply systems were beset by issues of voltage, since DC does not easily lend itself to the stepping up and stepping down, through transformers, that allows electricity to be shunted efficiently around modern networks. Thus separate networks existed at distinct voltages, depending on the final requirements of the consumer. The adoption of AC fostered high voltage transmission networks, which operated with much smaller electrical losses from resistance, which causes power in the lines to dissipate as heat.

The city that best exemplifies the spread of electricity as a means of energy distribution is Berlin. Headquarters to two seminal companies, Siemens and AEG, Berlin manufactured a range of electrical equipment from the 1880s (Hughes 1983, p.178). AEG had become a major player in the development of tram networks, and it used its size and access to capital to finance the conversion of horse-drawn tram networks to electric operation for clients. Together these two companies held major interests in German power generation, and in 1903 AEG partnered with General Electric of the US to divide their spheres of operation and to develop the new generating technology of the steam turbine, which began to displace the reciprocating steam engine for power generation. The latter essentially uses the principle of the steam piston, as in locomotives, to turn a flywheel, whereas the former drives steam under pressure through turbine blades to induce rotation, which is then converted to electricity in a generator via a common connecting shaft.

Having developed quickly from a small base, Berlin's public transport was carefully thought through as an adjunct to efficient mobilisation. Twelve lines radiated from train stations outside the city centre, which were connected by a circular and a transverse line that both fed into a dense tram network that was powered and financed by AEG (Hughes 1983, p.181). AEG also owned the municipal utility BEW, which in 1895 had four power stations producing 9,900 kW DC. By 1905 this had increased to 85,100 kW, with the adoption of multi-phase AC and transformers. There were other dramatic changes over this period, as the power for electric motors rose in proportion to that consumed for municipal lighting. Domestic consumption was small, with only 6.6% of Berlin households connected to the grid in 1914, and only 50% by 1927 despite the sophistication of the power industry. Electricity as a domestic tool remained a luxury for Berliners through the early years of the century. Of the electricity consumed in Berlin in 1900, 28% went to street lighting, 24% to fixed motors used in industry, and the balance, nearly half, to streetcars. By 1911 the fixed motor proportion had risen to 32%, reflecting the relative growth in the number of motors used in manufacturing. To understand what the fixed motors were servicing, a list published by the utility in 1914 has 36,783 motors connected to its supply, including 7,032 used in metalworking, 4,940 in elevators and 1,638 for sewing machines, presumably industrial. A year later BEW was operating six power stations, with a combined output of 155,000 kW, or 155 MW (Hughes 1983, pp.189–191).

The only city with a comparable network was Chicago. Here the energy and vision of Edison's protégé Samuel Insull was key, as he expanded the city's generating capacity with the early adoption of large-capacity turbine generators, and the careful management of the current distribution through transformers and high voltages. He also managed to quarantine the electricity sector from the notorious political structure of the city, which proved beneficial to both the industry and Insull himself. By 1910 significant generating capacity had been installed in all major European and American cities, and Chicago alone had 219.6 MW. Takeup and consumption was uneven depending on the efficiency of local utility companies. London's supply, for example, was fractured and without standardisation, and the city's consumption was constrained. In 1913 it was reported that consumption of electricity in London per capita was 110 kWh, compared to 310 in Chicago and 170 in Berlin. Part of this was due to the anomalous situation in London where transport networks like the London Underground generated their own electricity rather than buying power from a central utility, as in the case of Chicago and Berlin (Hughes 1983, p.228).

Practically all of this power was generated by steam produced through the burning of coal. If we take the figures of households connected to the grid in Berlin as representative of the situation in industrialised economies, then electricity supply to individual houses only becomes widespread on the eve of the Second World War. Public services, high rise building elevators and lighting as well as manufacturing dominate electricity consumption in the first decades of the 20th century. But to regard these as the major manifestations of fossil-fuel usage is to ignore the emergence of the equally transformative technology of the motor car. As noted in chapter 2, the motor car developed as rapidly, and on as large a scale, as electricity generation. With the introduction of the Model T Ford in 1908, a means of transport parallel to the public system of trams and trains emerged that could traverse a practically infinite number of routes using roads and tracks.

The popularity of public trams until the Second World War indicates that the car existed comfortably alongside other forms of mass transport for nearly half a century in many countries. Its adoption as transport for the masses did not occur in Germany until the 1960s. Prior to this production had concentrated on trucks, buses and motorcycles (Wolf 1996). For working-class Europeans, the motor car was hardly within financial reach for most of the 20th century. In general they rode trams to and from work, and used trains for longer distance travel. Their cities retained their compactness, even as overall densities declined through the political use of the tram to relocate working-class families outside of the traditional city core. However, in the US it was a different story, as the motor industry grew into a major manufacturing force for the industrialised north. It embodied many of the attributes of a nation flexing its industrial muscles, and harnessing them to an optimism that included the increased mobility and opportunity that the motor car fostered.

Although the modern car was invented in Germany, the early leader in production was France. In 1900 the country produced 4800 cars, ahead of the 4000 made in America that year. However, it was in America that the car found its natural incubator as a mass-produced product (Bardou 1982). Early cars and their races were the preserve of the wealthy, and they were seen as objects of leisure. Road surfaces were poor: in 1903 the US had less than

200 miles of paved finish (Volti 2004, p.7). Steam cars and electric cars were also in the mix, with the former being powerful but heavy and complex to operate, and the latter restricted due to their rechargeable batteries. In the end the internal combustion engine triumphed due to its simpler requirement of only needing to carry one fuel or supply, gasoline, whose energy content became more impressive as the efficiency of car motors improved. Compulsory registration soon followed, and even in 1907, the year before the introduction of the Model T Ford, Americans had registered over 143,000 cars, to France's 40,000. However, a better comparison is the number of inhabitants per car in each country. In the US there was one car for every 608 people, in France one for 981. Britain also took to the technology, almost matching the American figure with one car per 640 Britons. The rest of Europe lagged well behind. Germany had a ratio of one car per 3824, and Italy one per 5554. At this stage car ownership, even in its biggest markets, was something of a rarity. The growth that followed can be seen in Table 3.2.

On the eve of the First World War US firms were the 12 largest producers of cars worldwide. The thirteenth largest, Peugeot of France, was turning out 5000 units annually. By comparison Ford, the clear leader, made 202,667 cars in 1913.

The advances Ford made in changing cars from hand-made objects to mass-produced ones are part of manufacturing folklore. The effect on price, and hence affordability, is instructive. At the start of the 20th century an American factory worker was earning about $600 per year. When the Model T first went on sale it was priced at $950, or over a year and a half of average wages. By 1915 it sold for $550, and by 1924 the price had dropped to $290 (Volti 2004, p.23). This is a similar, or better, ratio of car price to average wage than pertained in Australia in 2014. It made the car genuinely accessible as a family vehicle. Uptake was particularly keen in rural areas. By 1920 over 30% of American farm households owned a car. This adoption shows the enormous appeal the car had for breaking the isolation of rural families in the vast distances of the American farming landscape, as well as its utility

Table 3.2 Growth in car numbers, 1907–1913

Country	Cars registered 1907	Cars registered 1913	Inhabitants per car 1907	Inhabitants per car 1913
United States	143,200	1,258,000	608	77
Canada	2100	50,600	3053	152
Britain	63,500	250,000	640	165
France	40,000	125,000	981	318
Germany	16,214	70,615	3824	950
Italy	6080	17,000	5554	2070

Adapted from Bardou (1982, Tables 2.1 and 4.2)

as a means of mechanically transporting things around the farm, and between farm and town. Before the advent of the car the social radius of visiting was ten miles (16 km), whereas the car at least doubled this (Kern 1983, p.217).

In the city the effect of cars was more geographically varied. In a city like Berlin the huge investment in trams, and the planning of the city around the transport needs of its workers, made car ownership less appealing for the working class. The same held true for London and Paris, where enormous investments in the London Underground and the Paris Metro in the first decade of the 20th century made travel around the city core and its adjoining suburbs convenient and predictable. Powered by electricity, these systems have sustained mobility within their cities successfully for over a century using networks that were largely in place precisely when car ownership was increasing exponentially. Neither did the car lead to the suburb. The ideal for the suburb had existed in England and America for over half a century before the car became widely available, and early suburbs were built around horse-drawn transport. In addition, before the First World War, suburban houses benefitted little from the city utilities supplying electricity for public lighting and transport. The suburban house existed in 1900 in a form recognisable to future generations, but reliant for its day to day existence on simple technologies much in common with rural households.

Thus in 1913, before the outbreak of war, an observer might have been struck by the overlapping technologies that attached to every facet of life. Within the large city, cars, trucks and trams jostled with horse-drawn carts and pedestrians for road space. The three modes of transport filled particular niches in demand as cities groped their way towards forms and technologies to suit their emergent modernity. The function of the city as a commercial hothouse of trade and exchange remained as potent as ever, with manufacturing added to its traditional suite of activities. The growing skilled working class became a factor in all political equations, stimulating the provision of public works and transport to enable them to travel to and from work, and to spend their excess money on leisure. Despite the plans of Haussmann, the sense of how the city should be was still poorly developed, as cities grew according to demographic demands, and altered in response to new patterns of work and commerce.

Energy had become not so much a determinant of form as a means of fulfilling demands – of infrastructure, of manufacturing, and of transport – as they arose. In doing so it accelerated tendencies already inherent in urban form, but it rarely initiated them. The dual desire in cities, for intense interaction but also occasional solitude and silence, had been evident as an inherent part of the urban experience at least as far back as ancient Rome. What became evident, after the bloodletting of the First World War, was the possibility of summing up the potential and the limitations of cities as they quickly expanded and changed.

It is surely no accident that the age of great urban proposals – the decades from 1910 to 1930 – coincides with the vast application of energy to issues of urban connectivity more than to simple consumption. Frank Lloyd Wright and Le Corbusier are key figures in this story, and they could not have formulated their plans and proposals without profoundly altered ideas to a previous generation of the quanta of energy that could be put to use in the reconfigured city.

These two architects might be regarded as less than representative of visions for how cities should be, given the great array of figures concerned with urban proposals. Ebenezer Howard is regarded by Peter Hall as the seminal figure of urban planning, understood as the idealistic response to the evident ills of the 19th century city. These had been aptly described by Friedrich Engels in his 1845 tract *The Condition of the Working Class in England*, initially published in German and translated into English in 1885 (Engels 2009). By this stage the problems of urban overcrowding had become widely evident, exacerbated by the increase in land value in central cities that encouraged the widespread exploitation of tenants. Families, in order to live close to work and, in many cases, to fellow immigrants, were prepared to live in sublet premises at enormous densities. The actual proportion of the city where these conditions prevailed could vary substantially, but they were influential in fomenting schemes for the rehousing of their inhabitants. In New York the Tenement House Commission of 1894 estimated that three-fifths of the city's population lived in unsatisfactory overcrowding, echoing popular press reports that came to the same conclusion (Hall 1988, p.35). In Sydney these conditions were confined to several blocks in the southern section of the city, but they produced similar reformist sentiments. The practice of maintaining a house beyond the confines of the city, long the preserve of the wealthy, became a driving vision for social betterment in the hands of social reformers. For Ebenezer Howard, the solution lay in directing the poor out of the city to a series of Garden Cities, remote Medieval-sized communities surrounded by land that could be farmed and provide the benefits of clean air and open space that the city dweller had forfeited. These cities would be linked by rail, reducing the isolation of each and reversing the parochial limitations of rural towns.

Howard proposed a density of 32,000 people living in a town of 1000 acres, or 79 people per hectare, which approaches the lower limits of the Medieval city and would constitute a walking city. In itself it is not reliant on new technology, save for the rail connections between cities and the circular rail line around the perimeter. Artesian wells and sewage farms took care of water and effluent, and some provision was made for factories and work-shops. First published in 1898, no doubt Howard had in mind using modern conveniences where necessary, but the basic vision is a moralising reversal of the drift to urban life so characteristic of the age in England. Indeed that country was the most urbanised on earth at the time of publication, with over 30% living in large cities of 100,000 or more, and over 60% in all cities and towns greater than 10,000. The equivalent figures for the US were just over 15% for large cities, and a total urban population of about 27%. Australia, perhaps surprisingly given its landmass, has nearly 30% of its population living in large cities at the start of the 20th century, a greater number than all countries except those of Great Britain (Webber 1899, frontispiece).

The drift to towns and cities was clearly attaining an unmistakeable momentum by 1900. Its unevenness attests to the differences in rural productivity in different countries, and the relative attractiveness of the city for raising both living standards and opportunities. Whereas Howard may have been struck by two factors in late Victorian England – the size of cities and the urban majority countrywide – the second factor was absent in both France and the US. France's urban population just exceeded 25%, and the proportion in large cities was about 12%. Yet it was here that the most comprehensive re-imagining of the city took place two decades later, in the work of a Swiss immigrant to Paris, the architect Le Corbusier. Le Corbusier's visions are remarkable not for their efficacy, for they did not come to fruition in any significant way until the 1950s, but for the sheer invention he displayed in sketching out the possibilities he saw in modern planning and design. Free of any sentimental attachment to the homeliness of pre-industrial life, with its local character and perceived authenticity, Le Corbusier imagined a city structure which would have been inconceivable two decades earlier.

This had not always been Le Corbusier's position. In 1910 he was still wedded to planning as a reversal of the logic of the rational city, and he favoured picturesque roads and views (Passanti 1987). It was on a visit to Athens in 1911 that he saw the Parthenon, and everything changed. It seems curious that an ancient classical Greek temple could inspire some of the most seductive of modernist visions, but this is a recurrent theme among architects who invented and popularised modern architecture. The link between ancient Greece and modernism is rationalism, or the practice of thinking and constructing that places its faith in the capacity for rational thinking to uncover the veiled organisational structures that determine the form of human creations and social structures. The strict geometric purity of ancient Greek buildings, rediscovered from the 18th century onwards as part of a general interest in the classical world, became the references for how architecture might look if it freed itself from the sentimental nostalgia that was the first reaction to the changes wrought by the modern era. Passanti cites Le Corbusier on his impressions of the Parthenon as "a terrible machine" that "grinds and dominates" (Passanti 1987, p.58).

This resolute monument to an abstract ideal of physical beauty came to dominate Le Corbusier's thinking, and combined with his study of planning principles as he understood them in the years of the First World War. Also influential were the views of the architect August Perret, who consistently advocated for the skyscraper as the desirable building type for emergent modern cities. The result was Le Corbusier's scheme for a contemporary city, exhibited in 1922 as the Ville Contemporaine. The plan is founded on abstract symmetrical geometry, with the major axes setting a rectilinear pattern that is intersected by four secondary diagonals. However, it is the re-imagining of contemporary life that is the most striking aspect of the proposal, as the architect absorbed and reconfigured the needs and attributes of the city as he observed them. The most notable aspect is what we might call the dis-aggregation of the traditional city, where the practice of merging classes and functions had long been a source of vitality, as well as congestion.

In Le Corbusier's proposal, functions are separated so each can achieve its individual aesthetic and functional expression. His aesthetic touchstones are not only the buildings of classical Greece, but extend to the technologies that he saw around him. He had a deft feel for the forms that attached to the energy flows of the time. Cars travel on designated boulevards, free of pedestrian crossings. Foot traffic largely circulates separately from cars, and the city contains large swathes of parkland within which the towers of its centre rest. This argument, presented as an urban proposal, has a long way to run in 20th century planning. The proposition is that the modern city has alienated its inhabitants from nature, conceived not as a wilderness but as the idyllic tamed landscape of Claude Lorrain's 17th century paintings. Thus to effect the reconciliation of people and nature, buildings soar upwards and absorb accommodation vertically. This frees up the ground plane for landscaping, as opposed to the pre-industrial city which could only reach a height of seven storeys, the vertical limit for stair access.

In the Ville Contemporaine the towers that form the core of the city hold offices, and are surrounded by lower residential blocks of varying design. These had been the subject of a number of projects in which Le Corbusier had experimented with new configurations of family life. The Parisian experience of building apartments along Haussmann's new boulevards had produced prototypes of how an apartment could accommodate the aspirations of the middle class. Le Corbusier extended his concerns to working-class housing, and in his plans for single dwellings and apartments, widely published but rarely built, Le Corbusier invented new types of spaces and planning. Because the streets became entwined with the large parklands, the apartment blocks are set back from the footpath, in distinction to the Parisian tradition of building to the edge of the property. Within the apartments domestic life has been reorganised to take advantage of new technology. In his seminal work *Towards a New Architecture*, published in French in 1923 and in English four years later, Le Corbusier describes his middle-class maisonettes as being less reliant on servants through the use of mechanical means to provide "constant hot water, central heating, refrigerators, vacuum cleaners, pure water etc.". Servants attend the house for eight hours, "as they would a factory" (Le Corbusier 1986, pp.247–248).

Given the small number of households connected to electricity at the time, these are ambitious proposals. Berlin, for example, only had 11% of households connected in 1922, and the appliances of the time could be primitive. Yet Le Corbusier in the same year had grasped the integration of energy into urban functioning, if not into existing city form. His urban proposals, and the detailed house and apartment designs he undertook alongside these, can almost be reduced to the form that modern energy might take if channelled into a city at the outset. The vertical offices are reliant on the elevator, electric lighting and telephones. The apartments have elevators as well, not only to make life easier for the inhabitants but also for the delivery of meals, which he envisages being supplied either cooked or raw from vast communal kitchens. The whole, in the architect's words, is "rational and sensible, without emphasis in any particular direction" (Le Corbusier 1986, p.249).

The significance of Howard, and subsequently Le Corbusier, as well as the numerous proponents of town planning of the time, was the absorption into their thinking of the tremendous changes they had witnessed. Le Corbusier puts it most clearly, in his reductive view of the city as a pattern of discrete functions, each taking place in a designated zone and, for the first time, reliant on the application of gasoline and electricity for its very functioning. Cognisant of the arguments about the value of labour, and the passing of handcraft in the face of mass production, the spaces Le Corbusier proposes are unadorned and composed of simple planes which nonetheless enclose complex volumes. In his vision luxury is defined by light and space, rather than opulence and the frozen labour that ornamentation embodies. Ideas of the city thus moved from being reactive, and mitigating the evident ills of urban growth, to idealistic visions that attempted to distil the apparently inevitable into its simplest form.

The version of his plan that Le Corbusier produced for a section of Paris, the Plan Voisin, proposed to demolish the 19th century pattern of buildings and streets and replace them with the towers, apartments and parklands he illustrated in the Ville Contemporaine. The plan exists only as a proposal, and Paris remains remarkably intact within its elevated circular freeway, but Le Corbusier's vision has eliminated one of the binding forces of traditional Paris, the intense commercial environment of the street. The city has become a functional zone, dominated by offices and with manufacturing relegated to a satellite industrial area. This version of rationalism has subsequently proven inimical to the dense interactions of commerce, and the messy colour of city street life, and it was mercilessly parodied in Jacques Tati's beautifully underplayed 1958 film *Mon Oncle*.

Nonetheless by the 1930s the practice of speculating how cities should be planned and altered was commonplace. The reality of large cities involved the public utilisation of electricity for trams and lights, with subway lines in the very largest. Regardless of the wholesale visions emerging, the modern city in the 1930s was a unique amalgam of traditional urban virtues such as anonymity, variety and entertainment, and the application of energy to increase the potential exposure of its inhabitants to these. The evening became a time for mass entertainment, as trams ran well into the night. Sporting events grew in size at central locations, newspapers bound cities culturally through shared stories and local concerns, while the spectre of class warfare encouraged urban rehousing schemes in European capitals that built on the rationalist visions outlined in the 1920s not only by Le Corbusier but by more radical architects such as Hannes Meyer and Ludwig Hilberseimer.

It remains a curiosity how New York, London, Paris, Berlin, Sydney, Buenos Aires, Shanghai or Los Angeles of the 1930s could be subject to such extreme desires to reshape them, when their very form and functioning already brimmed with contemporary phenomena. One only has to view movies set in these localities and time, or read novels, to get a sense of life historically unique in its pace and possibilities. Yet this very success engendered the conditions to supersede itself. Social class, for one, attained a sharpness that owed much to both the proximity of various classes in the modern city, and the ability of the city to promise that one's class of birth could be transcended. The Russian Revolution had made the possibility of revolution real, and all governments were aware of its seductive power as an idea, if not a reality. Lenin had famously described communism as composed of "Soviet power plus the electrification of the whole country", a process necessary for the country to achieve real industrial power (Lenin 1920, n.p.). For Lenin, political success may have been achieved by 1920, but economic success awaited industry and electricity.

Aware of the power of class as a political force which gave an identity and a political programme to workers, the city in the years between the wars became the crucible of the new politics that claimed to speak for those who wielded little economic power. While this may seem divorced from the issue of energy, it was in fact the life made possible by abundant energy that fostered this egalitarian mindset. The close contacts of urban commerce, the gathering of workers in large enterprises, the transformative powers of the metropolis, all served to bring into everyday life the power of the new. For conservative reformers the vision of workers acting en masse in their own interests proved disconcerting in the extreme, and they searched for a contending vision that could guarantee social cohesion.

In the US, the issue of class extended to rural areas as well, since historically these had been seen as frontiers full of opportunity, in a way that the closed land tenure system of Europe was not. This impression was dealt a blow by photographs commissioned by the Farm Security Administration in the late 1930s documenting the rural effects of the Great Depression. The photographs of Dorothea Lange and Walker Evans captured the plight of those impoverished by the Depression and seemingly cut off from the benefits of the age. Terry Smith draws attention to these photographs and the national concern for the rural poor they generated, when he asks what exactly makes them "so attractive for the displacement of attention from the plight of industrial labor, even the stressed city?" (Smith 1993, p.298). The point is well made, for many of the results of social concern in the US took the form of energy schemes. The Tennessee Valley Authority, for example, was set up in 1933 to revitalise the valley, as the full extent of its poverty and environmental degradation became apparent. Commencing with Norris and Wheeler Dams, the Authority used the hydroelectric power that its growing number of dams generated to transform rural living and attract industry (Tennessee Valley Authority n.d.). On the other side of the country, Boulder Dam (now Hoover Dam) was completed in 1936 to harness the flow of the Colorado River for electricity generation and water supply.

While these initiatives linked electricity supply to projects for rural expansion and revitalisation, within cities the impetus for social change was channelled into urban reconstruction schemes, and plans to bring the sub-urban vision into reach for all. The former may have had the more compelling logic, but the latter proved the more enduring. One noteworthy vision that garnered much attention was the Broadacre City proposal of Frank Lloyd Wright. First exhibited in 1935, Wright's vision of a city composed of smallholdings, and serviced by arterial trunk systems that combined road and passenger rail traffic, displays a remarkable disregard for economics in the broadest sense. The simple expediency of the density metric to length of service – in other words, how many users can be expected per km of road or rail – is wildly exaggerated in the four square mile model he constructed. The lessons of industrial farming seem to also have gone unappreciated, perhaps overshadowed by the emergence in the Great Depression of the rural poor as the bearers of the American tradition of individualism, com-prehensively let down by the bastardry of urban financiers and politicians. The division of farmland into small units goes against the economics of genuine broadacre farming, where machinery and large fields produce greater yields. Not surprisingly Wright's vision has been built nowhere, given its poor understanding of the effort, in energy and money, that would be required to bring the benefits of modern urban life to so dispersed a population.

Broadacre City requires the decentralisation of almost everything, while the city has a particular genius for matching aspirations and abilities to opportunities through its sheer size. Wright's vision is unashamedly political in this regard, and the proposed arbiter of its construction and fairness is the architect. The reduction of the scope of life is compensated by the control citizens exercise over their lives lived out, in Wright's words, in "little farms, little homes for industry, little factories, little schools, a little university ..." (Wright 2000, pp.346–347). The city, on the contrary, may have undergone dis-aggregation as zoning laws and social stratification caused like to group with like, but this was a result of its central function, not a concerted effort to dismantle it. The suburb, when it emerged as a mass phenomenon that absorbed the bulk of American urban growth in the 1930s in larger cities, bore no relationship to the self-sufficiency that Broadacre City idealised. On the contrary, it was a product of urban specialisation and differentiation. Before the Second World War in America it had a strong class base, allowing the middle class and professionals to create a small world to their taste, while reaping the benefits of the city as a place to make money.

In Europe the relatively low level of car ownership precluded the development of dispersed suburbs except for the wealthy. Social activism in Germany, and the political turmoil of the early 1920s, spurred on experiments in mass working-class housing. Bruno Taut and Ernst May were involved in a series of discrete developments that attempted to combine the benefits of the traditional home with the products of industrialisation. Initially these used picturesque components to imbue some charm, but over time the definition of housing as a social problem, defined through its needs rather than its wants, made the results more modernist in form. The result nonetheless was invariably compact and walkable, so much so that these projects have been included in a recent encyclopaedia of garden suburbs (Stern, Fishman & Tilove 2013). The intent of these developments was to reinforce social stability by giving working-class families private, secure and healthy accommodation, planned around the nuclear family as the basic unit. Collective aspirations were met through shared facilities, and the power of the city street to socialise children into its wiles and ills was neutralised. Accessed by tramlines, these developments reinforced the compact form of European cities when their American counterparts were being transformed in anticipation of what was to come.

Note

1 Refers to location numbers in the Kindle edition.

Bibliography

Angel, S. (2012). *Planet of cities*. Cambridge, MA: Lincoln Institute of Land Policy.

Angel, S., Parent, J., Civco, D., & Blei, A. (2010). *The persistent decline in urban densities: Global and historical evidence of "sprawl"*. Cambridge, MA: Lincoln Institute of Land Policy.

Bardou, J. (1982). *The automobile revolution: The impact of an industry*. Chapel Hill, NC: University of North Carolina Press.

Bosselmann, P. (2008). *Urban transformation: Understanding city design and form*. Washington, DC: Island Press.

Bruegmann, R. (2005). *Sprawl: A compact history*. Chicago: University of Chicago Press.

Capuzzo, P. (2003). Between politics and technology: Transport as a factor of mass suburbanization in Europe, 1890–1939. In C. Divall & W. Bond (Eds), *Suburbanizing the masses: Public transport and urban development in historical perspective*. Aldershot: Ashgate.

Chandler, T., & Fox, G. (1974). *3000 years of urban growth*. New York: Academic Press.

Divall, C. & Schmucki, B. (2003). Technology, (sub)urban development and the social construction of urban transport. In C. Divall & W. Bond (Eds), *Suburbanizing the masses: Public transport and urban development in historical perspective*. Aldershot: Ashgate.

Engels, F. (2009). *The condition of the working class in England* (D. McClellan, Ed.). Oxford: Oxford University Press.

Fishman, R. (1987). *Bourgeois utopias: The rise and fall of suburbia.* New York: Basic Books.

Hall, P. (1988). *Cities of tomorrow: An intellectual history of urban planning and design in the twentieth century.* Oxford: Blackwell.

Harvey, D. (2003). *Paris, capital of modernity.* New York: Routledge.

Hughes, T. (1983). *Networks of power: Electrification in Western society, 1880–1930.* Baltimore, MD: Johns Hopkins University Press.

Jackson, K. (1985). *Crabgrass frontier: The suburbanization of the United States.* New York: Oxford University Press. Kindle edition.

Jutte, E. (n.d.). *Frank J. Sprague.* Retrieved July 28, 2015, from www.theelevatorm useum.org/e/e-1.htm

Kern, S. (1983). *The culture of time and space 1880–1918.* Cambridge, MA: Harvard University Press.

Le Corbusier (1986). *Towards a new architecture* (F. Etchells, Ed.). New York: Dover.

Lenin, V. (1920). *Our foreign and domestic position and party tasks.* Retrieved August 17, 2015, from www.marxists.org/archive/lenin/works/1920/nov/21.htm

Loyer, F. (1988). *Paris nineteenth century: Architecture and urbanism.* New York: Abbeville Press.

Passanti, F. (1987). The skyscrapers of the Ville Contemporaine. *Assemblage, 4,* 53–65. doi:10.2307/3171035

Pomeranz, K. (2000). *The great divergence: China, Europe, and the making of the modern world economy.* Princeton, NJ: Princeton University Press.

Ramanna, M. (2002). *Western medicine and public health in colonial Bombay, 1845–1895.* New Delhi: Orient Longman.

Smith, T. (1993). *Making the modern: Industry, art, and design in America.* Chicago: University of Chicago Press.

Stern, R., Fishman, D., & Tilove, J. (2013). *Paradise planned: The garden suburb and the modern city.* New York: The Monacelli Press.

Tennessee Valley Authority (n.d.). *From the New Deal to a new century.* Retrieved July 29, 2015, from www.tva.com/abouttva/history.htm

Troy, A. (2012). *The very hungry city: Urban energy efficiency and the economic fate of cities.* New Haven, CT: Yale University Press.

Volti, R. (2004). *Cars and culture. The life story of a technology.* Westport, CT: Greenwood Press.

Webber, A. (1899). *The growth of cities in nineteenth century America: A study in statistics.* New York: Macmillan.

Wolf, W. (1996). *Car mania: A critical history of transport.* London: Pluto Press.

Wright, F. (2000). Broadacre City: A new community plan. In R. LeGates & F. Stout (Eds), *The city reader* (2nd ed.). London: Routledge.

Yarra Trams (2015). *Facts & figures.* Retrieved July 29, 2015, from www.yarratrams. com.au/about-us/who-we-are/facts-figures

4　20th century transformers

Wars, suburbs, commodities

By the 1930s, a number of the key dynamics that marked the growth of cities, and the technologies that accompanied this, were becoming clearer. Perhaps the most dramatic of these was the decanting of cities according to social class. The adoption of the car, and the advent of suburbs, allowed the abrasions between classes that had long been a feature of city life to be circumvented. Rose and Clark note how, from about 1880, the wealthier residents of Kansas found refuge from the "increasingly unpalatable smells, dialects and sights of an industrializing city" in the new suburban developments fostered by Jesse C. Nichols (Rose & Clark 1979, p.348). These were not unusual sentiments, although they were not always displayed in the same way. The catalyst seems to be the very possibility, new in the 19th century, that the city could sustain a separation of social classes through the physical development of new areas that were homogenous, and linked to the city by convenient transport. The suburban village on a train line is one manifestation of this, and middle class and professional life sought to make these in their own image in America and England. In mainland Europe the pattern was inverted, and high rents and land values encouraged the relocation of working-class families to the urban periphery.

Physical separation was not the only proposed solution to anxiety about the intentions and abilities of people from different classes. In an age increasingly confident of its rationalist credentials, and the related ability to determine and solve the underlying conditions that manifested in modern cities, proponents of eugenics advocated for the forced sterilisation of the apparently socially hopeless. Whereas earlier cities had fostered an indifference to their plight as all classes contended with the inconveniences of urban life, the 20th century city enabled planning to address class anxiety at its core, through the gradual elimination of those seen as congenitally poor. This movement had its counterpart in proponents of city planning – often their advocates were the same. The logic was that city planning, especially the rehousing of slum-dwellers, was in the interests of national development. The ills of the Victorian city could be counteracted by building new housing schemes either in the city where the slums existed, or further out away from pernicious influences. However, a certain portion of slum dwellers were deemed to be beyond reform, due to genetic defects. Thus reforming of the most blighted classes could not succeed for that defective fraction, who needed to be prevented from reproducing.

This shift from remediation, as in the case of Haussmann's Paris where the plan was imposed on the city as it had come to be, to comprehensive planning based on rationalist visions of how the city would evolve, is a notable transformation in several ways. First, it could only happen once urban growth had been observed for some period, and its tendencies summarised. Second, it relied on a confident and unsentimental rationalism, allied with the means and power to give effect to city plans. Third, it needed the reach and cohesion of the modern state to place the city and its role in the context of national development. Thus the slums of English industrial cities were not only offensive to anyone with a measure of empathy, they also produced physically smaller men less able to serve in the military. The skewing of urban concerns towards social reform thus reflects both the modern state and modern commerce, no longer reliant on the bustle of the city for its exchange and vitality.

Both Le Corbusier and Frank Lloyd Wright tried to encapsulate this change in their urban proposals, if we regard them more as manifestos than blueprints for cities. Each drifted to a political notion that sanitised class relations within the city through idealised forms and prescriptions for everyday life, Le Corbusier using collective ideas and Wright those that rested on possession and farming of a portion of land, however small. Le Corbusier's may have proven the more economical, but Wright held so fast to a belief in the boundless promise of technology that his architecture came increasingly to look like the speculative futurism of the 1920s. His last major work, the Marin County Center completed in 1966, is shot through with futurist and popular science-fiction details and conceptions of space. Wright's appointment for this project was marred by accusations that he was a Communist sympathiser, as he had been listed as one in 1951 by the House Un-American Activities Committee. Wright had been on record for criticising both the Committee and the portrayal in the US of the Soviet Union as the major threat to world peace (Twombly 1987, p.370).

Thus American and European cities on the eve of the Second World War were all deeply influenced by the capacity of modern sources of energy to reconfigure their forms in ways that displayed idealised solutions, through urban planning, of the tensions that existed within them (Tafuri 1976). Within a single city there might exist parts organised for efficiency, parts organised as social remedy and parts that were comprehensive embodiments of an ideal of family living. The uptake of the car made this last part feasible for the individual. The car extends the privacy of the house all the way to the driver's destination. This cocooning of life is an integral part of how the city developed after 1940 in those parts of the world affluent enough to pursue abstract urban ideals. The formulation of these ideals, and the political tendencies and interpretations that they embody, tells much of the story of urban development after the Second World War.

The lesson for energy of this story is that the vast increase in energy use did not, in itself, create these ideals. All futuristic visions picture a reconciliation of tensions evident in the here and now. All technologies are harnessed to social needs, and in the process transform those needs. To regard technology as having the capacity to determine its own direction of development is a prospect only to be canvassed in science fiction, yet the pace of change within the modern period often leads to this illusion. The same holds true for energy. Its increased usage is powerfully transformative, but it acts on institutions and relations already existing.

War is a stark reminder of this. The First World War coincided with the maturing of many technological advances. Tanks and aeroplanes were used for the first time, both propelled by internal combustion engines whose production was barely two decades old. Artillery pieces and rifles were manufactured in their thousands and millions, as were shells and bullets. This occurred on both sides, but the manufacturing advances that made industrial war possible did not determine the alliances of the combatants. When the US entered the war in 1917 its contribution was decisive, as it brought its industrial might to bear on the conflict. Yet this might was not developed in anticipation of war, but as a consequence of its own social and productive history.

A corollary of this is that technology often migrates from its initial use to another area of need. This is a commonplace of energy history, where inventions appear and die for lack of application, only to recur in another context and become key. The reciprocating steam engine is one example, where its refinement as a means of lifting water out of coal mines made it efficient enough to be transferred to rails as a self-propelling entity. The bicycle was the means of perfecting the ball bearing, which then became a staple of mechanical engineering in reducing friction in cars and motor-driven devices that use rotary motion. In this respect the bicycle was a key invention for overcoming friction in many applications, but it was initially intended purely for personal transportation, where it proved wildly popular before the advent of the car (Dowson & Hamrock 1981).

Modern war provides perhaps the most instances of technology migration. The First World War is remembered for its machinery, but it may be its chemistry that was more decisive. The story attached to the Haber–Bosch process for synthesising ammonia is as dramatic as it is significant, despite being largely unacknowledged outside the history of modern chemistry and its applications. The process is named after Fritz Haber and Carl Bosch, the former an experimental chemist and academic and the latter a chemical engineer, although this job description would have been new when he commenced his career.

As outlined in chapter 2, the rate at which nitrogen can be fixed in the soil by legumes such as peas, chick-peas or soybeans determines the productivity of soil. Grain crops denude the soil of nitrogen: legumes replenish it due to their hosting of specialised bacteria capable of fixing atmospheric nitrogen in a form that can be taken up by the plant, and released into the soil when it dies. In the oceans different bacteria also convert atmospheric nitrogen into usable form. Terrestrial plants absorb the nitrogen in the form of either ammonium or nitrate, and this process is essential to growth. Thus the yield from farmland newly converted from forest or grassland will slowly decline unless some form of replenishment, like crop rotation or the application of nitrogen compounds, is undertaken. Compounds containing nitrogen are not only critical for crops, they are also the basis for explosives such as gunpowder, nitroglycerine and TNT or trinitrotoluene, which needs nitric acid in its preparation. Both these uses of nitrogen compounds were well known in the 19th century, but the natural rate at which bacteria fixed atmospheric nitrogen, or the known methods of producing potassium nitrate for gunpowder, were slow and limited the crop yields of farms and the volume of explosive armaments (and fireworks) that could be made.

For millennia human and animal excrement had been used as fertiliser, often with great efficiency. The discovery of large masses of guano or weathered bird excrement on islands off Peru and Chile in the early 1800s sparked a boom in its export for use as fertiliser, since it is rich not only in nitrogen but in potassium and phosphate. When applied to farms the results were deemed almost miraculous, as yields from depleted soils leapt after fertilisation. The trade in guano was fierce, and within decades most islands had been stripped of their deposits. Attention then turned to the Atacama Desert, which contains huge quantities of sodium nitrate as mineral deposits. At the start of the 20th century German farming and armament manufacturing were dependent on this source, and the country was importing over 800,000 tonnes from South America by 1912 (Hager 2008, p.51). Given this reliance on a salt shipped half-way around the world, German industry was motivated to find a way of making these crucial compounds from elements available in Germany.

Atmospheric nitrogen is effectively inert, bound up as two atoms and inclined to break apart only under extreme conditions. Lightning or electric arcing can induce it to split, but the first is capricious and the second uses vast amounts of energy. The goal for German chemists was to create ammonia, a liquid compound of nitrogen and hydrogen that is a useful precursor to a range of chemicals used for farming and explosives. In the first years of the 20th century Fritz Haber experimented with feeding the two gases into a small chamber where they were subject to great heat and pressure, and in the presence of a catalyst he succeeded in demonstrating the viability of the process to produce ammonia. In partnership with the chemical company BASF and its remarkable employee Carl Bosch, Haber embarked on a mission to scale up the nascent technology. The technical challenges were enormous, and it was Bosch who harnessed the ingenuity of a talented team, and his own excellent grasp of engineering principles, to make the first ammonia plants. These operated continuously at pressures in excess of 150 atmospheres, and temperatures of over 300°C. The two were eventually awarded Nobel prizes for their work on the process, despite

Haber being an avid proponent for, and developer of, gas warfare during the First World War.

The major impact of this achievement was initially to produce fertiliser, since ammonia is not easily converted to the nitric acid essential for explosive production. By 1915 the inventive Bosch had succeeded in converting the ammonia into sodium nitrate in industrial quantities, and this in turn could be easily used for arms and explosives. In 1917 Bosch oversaw the commissioning of a truly gigantic chemical complex at Leuna, far from the fighting on the Western Front. His intent was to make Germany self-sufficient in its prosecution of war, with the capacity to produce explosives limited only by the plant's output. By 1918 Leuna was producing 145,000 tonnes of sodium nitrate annually, and it almost certainly extended the war's duration (Hager 2008, p.168; Smil 2006, p.9).

The inputs for the process depended on separating hydrogen from oxygen as one of the feedstock gases, together with purified nitrogen. The latter was achieved through continuous cyclical refrigeration that lowered the temperature enough for the air to become liquid, with the different gasses in the liquid air separated by boiling them off at different temperatures. Coal was needed to raise the temperature inside the Haber–Bosch conversion chambers themselves, and pumps were refined to create the high internal pressure. The process of making ammonia produces its own heat, so once underway it is considerably more efficient than at startup. Collectively these inputs achieved, in the most effective way, what had previously been the domain of bacteria and the slow weathering of rock – the production of industrially and agriculturally useful nitrogen compounds. The results, on a worldwide scale, were the scaling up of food production and an enormous increase in military destruction.

At the outset there were a number of competing synthetic processes for making ammonia, but the superiority of the Haber–Bosch method saw it come to dominate the industry. In 1920 the process accounted for 20% of world production, but by 1940 this had reached 69%. Since 1990 almost all production worldwide has been by the Haber–Bosch method. However, these figures alone give little idea of the widespread adoption of the process, as in 1940 total ammonia production amounted to only 3.2 million tonnes of nitrogen, whereas by 2013 this had reached 140 million tonnes (Smil 2011; International Fertilizer Industry Association n.d.). In the interwar years most of this was used in making fertiliser, and almost all production in the years after 1945 has been used in agriculture. Crudely put, the net effect was to guarantee the food surpluses necessary to support the increasing number, and proportion, of people living in cities.

The uptake of fertiliser had been small but critical before 1940, and was confined to countries which had the industrial capacity to either develop their own processes, as happened in the US and Britain, or to copy the Haber–Bosch method. This was not easy, since the technical and metallurgical challenges of feeding gasses continuously into large diameter steel tubes under great pressure had taken Bosch and his team thousands of man-hours to solve. In the aftermath of the First World War, Bosch licensed his technology to France, and then proceeded to get production underway again at his home plants. The close nexus of the productive and destructive capabilities of synthetic nitrogen fixing were brought home when a fertiliser storage silo at Oppau, containing ammonium sulphate with some proportion of sodium nitrate, exploded in a catastrophic industrial accident in 1921. A total of 561 workers were killed, and large parts of the complex, with its workers' housing, were levelled. The incident deeply affected Bosch, who was running the entire BASF company at this stage. He nonetheless persisted with the application of industrial chemistry to economic problems, championing the extraction of petrol and diesel from Germany's large coal resources in a bid to make the country independent of imported oil. Haber continued to court official recognition after the award of his Nobel Prize in Chemistry in 1919, and occupied himself with an ambitious scheme to extract gold from seawater to assist Germany to pay the onerous reparations imposed by the Treaty of Versailles. When this proved pointless he encouraged research in chemistry through the Kaiser Wilhelm Society. Compelled to flee Germany in 1933 by the Nazi push to remove Jews from positions of influence, he died in Switzerland while seeking opportunities to find a new intellectual home (Hager 2008).

As Germany lurched through the politically chaotic and socially unstable 1920s with state-sponsored industrial initiatives, the US was experiencing a boom in car numbers and the suburbanisation of its cities. Jackson (1985, loc.3477[1]) notes how US car registrations grew by 150% between 1920 and 1930, and at the same time the suburbs of 96 of the largest cities grew twice as fast as the urban areas. He also points out the general effect on urban structure. Whereas the railroad suburb encouraged development along suburban lines like the spread fingers of a hand, the car allowed the areas between the fingers, distant from public transport lines, to be developed. This pattern also assumed a class character, with the takeup of cars predictably skewed towards professional and managerial families. In Pittsburgh in 1934 20.3% of wage earners drove their cars to work, with 48.8% still using the tram (streetcar) system (Jackson 1985, locs.3592–3614).

Jackson also draws attention to the role of the truck in decentralising industry. This trend became evident by 1930, when the number of trucks on US roads reached 3.5 million, and factories relocated from the urban core to the periphery where land was cheaper. This occurred in every major city in the US in the 1920s. The number of horses in service declined dramatically as well, their haulage methods unable to compete with trucks in distance, efficiency or load size. The trends sustained by both the car and truck were similar – the privatisation of modes of transport for both goods and commuters, and the increasing independence of the urban location of housing and work from the dominance of the city centre, with its convergence of tram and rail lines. The result was a clear decline in population density in developing subdivisions, as well as in inner-city areas such as New York where the subway system made living close to work less important.

The advent of the Great Depression, triggered in 1929 by a massive decline in share values and the ensuing withdrawal of capital from new investment, reversed some of these trends. Car manufacturing fell dramatically in France, Italy and the US, and by 1938 none of these countries had returned to the production levels of 1929 (Bardou 1982, p.140). Of the major manufacturing countries, only Britain and Germany expanded production over this period. The Depression years also created a strong public sentiment for aiding those who suffered most. This is perhaps the prevailing ideological shift of the era in a number of industrially developed countries, and it manifested in a variety of ways.

In the US, the New Deal not only set up initiatives like the Tennessee Valley Authority to bring the benefits of industrialisation to rural areas, but the rehousing of urban dwellers who lived in substandard housing also became a national goal. Indeed rehousing the poor became the prevailing idealistic concern for architects across Europe, the US and Australasia, although results generally fell short of expectations or intentions. In part this was because the building industry in many countries had suffered badly from the economic downturn, and volumes of construction were slow to recover. In Australia the amount of building undertaken in 1929 was only matched again on the eve of the Second World War. More important, though, was the emergence in the 1930s of a professional concern with urban development and form that had as a basic principle equality of opportunity regardless of social class, or perhaps in practice precisely because of social class.

The decanting of social classes in cities, initially determined by rail fares, house prices and access to cars, tended to leave behind the urban poor in the centre of cities while the suburbs were the domain of the middle and upper classes. This occurred mainly in English-speaking countries, where the cultural value of a residence outside of the city underpinned the desirability of suburbs that seemed village-like in atmosphere. Simultaneously the decline of inner-city areas due to lack of investment created eyesores of dilapidated dwellings that were reaching the end of their useful lives. These urban slums were centrally located, visible and affronting to those living in the new suburbs, with their houses in good repair and enjoying relative class homogeneity. As the historic urban condition of mixed classes declined, the contrast in living conditions between the urban core and the suburbs spawned a reform movement which had a powerful agenda for remaking cities in a fairer way, often through rehousing programmes. The relative paucity of dwellings built before 1945 under these rehousing initiatives should not be taken as a sign of indifference: the Depression and subsequent war diminished productive capacity or diverted it to military needs.

While the First World War saw the massive mobilisation of the key inventions of the preceding decades, including the internal combustion engine, the aeroplane and the synthesis of ammonia and nitrogen salts, the

Second World War saw the industrial genesis of at least two technologies that played a significant role in subsequent energy generation and utilisation. The first, nuclear power, announced its arrival with the devastating demonstration of the power of the atomic bomb, while the second, the jet engine, was less influential but could have proven decisive had the war lasted any longer.

The events leading to the first atomic bomb are well summarised by Smil (2006). From a theoretical possibility entertained by Einstein, the potential energy of nuclear fission was surmised by Lise Meitner and Otto Frisch in 1939. Meitner's erstwhile colleague Leó Szilárd had in fact taken out a patent in 1934 on the nuclear chain reaction, but he made little practical progress on the idea until 1939 when he, Walter Zinn and Enrico Fermi observed in a laboratory at Columbia University the small flashes signifying neutron multiplication in uranium. He was moved to draft the Einstein–Szilárd letter to President Roosevelt describing the possibility of nuclear weapons, which led to the establishment of the project to build the first atomic weapon. In December 1944 Szilárd and Fermi applied for the patent on the nuclear reactor, or "neutronic reactor" as described in the patent (Szilárd & Fermi 1944). Thus the genesis of atomic, or nuclear, weapons and the process of using nuclear fission to generate electricity lay in the same series of insights, and were the work of a common group of physicists.

The jet engine, a development of turbine technology that includes stationary gas turbine engines, made its debut in the form of the British Gloster Meteor and German Messerschmitt Me-262, two planes which appeared for opposing Air Forces in July 1944. Their development had been parallel, in Britain at the hands of Frank Whittle, and in Germany under the guidance of Hans-Joachim Pabst von Ohain (Smil 2006, p.67). The range, speed and efficiency of planes powered by these engines as they were developed by the major manufacturers eventually led to the phenomenon of mass air travel, and the subsequent fraction of global energy it consumes. A further branch of turbine technology produced the stationary gas turbine, a powerful engine that can be harnessed to generators or any other large demand for rotary power with great efficiency.

Significant as these developments are, the earlier prime movers invented in the 1880s, the internal combustion engine, the electric motor and the steam turbine, continued to dominate energy conversions. Following the Second World War their technology and uptake "shaped both the economic possibilities of nations and the conduct of everyday lives" (Smil 2006, p.67). In urban terms the period from 1945 onwards saw the enormous unfolding of the social possibilities engendered by these machines. Their basic functions remained the same. The steam turbine provided baseload power for electricity generation, mainly through the burning of coal to produce steam, which was then fed at pressure through the turbine to induce rotation and drive an attached generator. In a modern power station the actual generators are relatively small, as most of the facility is devoted to pulverising the coal, burning it in large furnaces, and the circulation of water and pressurised steam through the turbine cycle. The process of conversion means invariably that energy is lost, and the inefficiency of early turbines and generators meant that less than 4% of the energy available from coal was actually converted to electricity. By 1950 this had climbed to about a quarter, and in the 1960s conversion rates plateaued at 40% for the most advanced generators (Smil 2006, p.38).

The takeup of domestic electrification also happened gradually and unevenly. In 1919 about half of urban dwellings in the US were connected to an electrical supply, while in Berlin the figure was less than 10% (Hughes 1983, p.190). On the eve of the Second World War electricity in the home was confined to lighting and a small number of appliances. In the US these were generally vacuum cleaners, refrigerators and washing machines. Actual takeup rates for all US dwellings for selected appliances chart the domestication of electrical energy for household use (Figure 4.1).

These rates reflect both the adoption of the technology within households, as well as the increasing rate of household electrification. The significance of the figures lies not so much in the overall energy these appliances consumed, but rather in the home becoming a place where appliances were continually replacing hand labour, and eventually providing entertainment as well. Whereas in the early years of the century electricity was destined largely for trams, lighting and industrial motors, by the end of the century domestic consumption claimed a significant proportion of electricity generated.

Ronald Tobey (1996) has made a spirited argument for social and political factors as the drivers behind domestic electrification in the US. He argues that the change in domestic values that appears to be linked to the uptake of appliances in the interwar years was not modernisation in the broad sense. Rather they could be just as easily linked to the reinforcement of conservative family values, which simply adopted electrical technology with little effect on social habits and aspirations. The New Deal, which sought to counter rural backwardness with dams and power stations, had its urban counterpart in

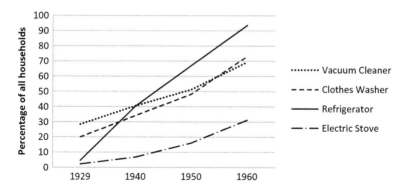

Figure 4.1 Domestic appliance takeup (US), 1929–1960
Adapted from Tobey (1996, Table 1.1)

President Roosevelt's view of electricity as a force for "social revolution" (Tobey 1996, p.97). In 1935, for example, refrigerator ownership was subsidised nationally through the National Housing Act of the previous year, which insured credit providers against any losses incurred in providing finance "for the purpose of financing alterations, repairs, and improvements upon real property" (United States Congress 1934). This trend was initiated in the Depression years, but the broad aims of the project were only fully realised in the 1950s.

The story Tobey tells is part of a wider pattern evident in Western Europe, the US and the British Dominions of Canada, Australia and New Zealand, where the social idealism of the 1930s was held in abeyance by the war years, only to resurface in a range of programmes in the post-war decades. These programmes, more than technology itself, determined the form of post-war cities as they expanded. Major manifestations were the New Towns movement in the UK, Post-War Reconstruction initiatives in Australia and the completion of the New Deal in the US. All these programmes had been bolstered by the war experience, when a sense of national unity had been consciously fostered as the demands on industrial production, and young lives, disrupted living and working norms in fundamental ways. Since the efforts and sacrifices of war had been shared across society, the rewards of peace were expected to be shared equally too.

The forms of housing and suburbs that emerged in the 1950s varied enormously according to prevailing views and aspirations. In Australia a Commonwealth Housing Commission had been convened in 1943, and it travelled throughout the country inspecting housing conditions and hearing witnesses on the prevailing state of housing supply and conditions. The Commission found that there was indeed an acute housing shortage in all major cities (estimated to rise to 300,000 dwellings by 1945), and by 1944 the Commonwealth (national) government anticipated providing 30,000 new houses in the first post-war year (Troy 2012, p.52). The Commission marked the entry of the Commonwealth into housing provision, alongside the efforts of individuals who set about building their own houses in the post-war years. The immediate concern in both sectors was to correct the deficiencies of the 1930s and early 1940s, when too few houses and apartments had been constructed to deal with new households that were forming through marriage. In its draft report the Commission had calculated what it per-ceived to be an annual economic rent of 6.5% of the cost of the dwelling, which equated to about 22% of the basic wage. Thus the provision of housing became an issue of political calculation, and benchmarks of afford-ability were set that reflected this calculation, rather than leaving rents to the market.

In the 1950s both ways of providing housing – government financed and privately built – operated side by side. In Sydney the early work of the New South Wales Housing Commission took the form of small cottages inter-spersed with three storey flats and groups of shops, all with modest plans but solidly built (Troy 2012). At the same time large parts of the city were developed by owner-builders on subdivided land which was supplied with water and electricity, but was often lacking reticulated sewage. Septic tanks dealt with effluent, and where this method was used the size of housing lots was determined by the area needed for the dispersal trenches or drain field which returns the treated water to the ground. Many urban areas in Australia retained this form of sewage disposal into the 1970s, when a national programme replaced septic tanks with an expanded urban sewerage system.

The basic urban form of these new houses was the low-density suburb, its economics underpinned by the provision of roads and services by local authorities and regional utilities. The buildings themselves, if owner built, used the timber balloon frame that had evolved in the US in the 19th century. The frame substitutes many smaller framing members for the large posts and beams of traditional construction, and can thus be made on site and erected by hand due to its relatively light weight. A modest home could be built with basic construction skills and hand tools, using the frame for structure and enclosing it with sheet cladding internally and externally. Most houses in these quickly developed suburbs were externally sheathed in asbestos-cement sheets, which use asbestos fibres to bind the cement and can be produced in sheets as thin as 6 mm. These could be cut and nailed, and proved remarkably enduring. The material was eventually banned due to the carcinogenic properties of asbestos fibres, which were released when the sheets were sawn or drilled. The legacy of the period is vast suburbs across Australia still composed of the modest houses of the post-war era, now nearing the end of their useful lives and presenting a disposal problem of some magnitude.

Building materials also assumed class characteristics. A superior dwelling was one built of solid brick and roofed in terra-cotta tiles, while weather-board, asbestos-cement and corrugated metal roof sheeting were regarded as inferior. Also regarded with suspicion were the Victorian-era terrace houses, many entering their seventh decade of service in the 1950s. These made up the urban slums, and they were the target of housing renewal programmes that aimed to replace them with new blocks of apartments that were modern and sanitary. In this Australia followed the lead of Britain, which instituted a wide-scale programme of urban rehousing that saw swathes of inner cities demolished and replaced with tower blocks. The sentiment for this programme was evident in the early 1940s, when a secret report titled *Post-War Housing Policy* envisaged the need for nearly 1.5 million houses after the war (Troy 2012, p.67). The mathematics of this endeavour were sobering, and the County of London Plan produced by Abercrombie and Forshaw in 1943 proposed a density for inner London of 336 people per hectare, with about one-third in houses and the rest in eight to ten storey flats. The implementation of these ideas was spurred by the enclosure of London by a green belt, an area that prohibited development and was intended to contain the city and keep a clear distinction between the urban and the rural zones. Coupled with a growing birth rate in the 1950s, the result was the wave of tower building for housing in London through the 1950s and 60s (Hall 1988, pp.220–225).

In the US the push for public housing had found legal form in the Wagner–Steagall Act of 1937. The Act provided the mechanism for the United States Housing Authority to construct housing projects, but the stipulation that these should arise from local initiatives meant that the location of public housing was highly selective. In addition, such housing needed to replace slums, so areas with good housing stock were not eligible for funding assistance. Nonetheless by 1962 roughly half a million units had been built in the wake of the 1937 initiative, although relative to Western European programmes this represents a very small proportion of the total US housing market.

From the outset, too, slum clearance and affordable housing for the poor in the US were tied up in the complex legal and financial arrangements of the various Federal Housing Acts. The alliance of urban renewal advocates, who lobbied for investment in the city to aid commercial redevelopment, and proponents of public housing was always tenuous. According to Hall (1988) this grouping was susceptible to resistance from urban residents and small business, who often thwarted their ambitions. Nonetheless public housing projects emerged in major cities as a means of housing the poor, who struggled to meet market rents. The end result was the demolition or abandonment of poor areas within the old urban core. Jackson (1985) has argued that suburbia was effectively subsidised through this period by Federal mortgages that were directed away from city centres and mixed neighbourhoods by lending criteria that preferred homogenous, suburban tracts. Again, this hastened the demise of well-located urban housing as suburban development became the dominant housing choice for almost all middle-class families.

Shutting down tram lines also had an effect. The continuity of the old lines from the urban periphery, through the various historic rings of urban development and into the city centre, had maintained the sense of urban cohesion as passengers traversed these areas at slow speeds and were familiar with the street life they saw, and the passengers that rode within these inner suburbs. The motor car effectively cocoons its occupants from their surroundings. With the advent of freeways the inner-city neighbourhoods were bypassed, and the dis-aggregation of the city by class and experience became more pronounced. The freeway itself began to define urban form and experience in US cities in the wake of the Federal-Aid Highway Act of 1956, which provided Federal funding for 90% of the cost of the proposed 66,000 km network. The system not only encompassed inter-city freeways, it also included beltways and sections to speed car travel within urban areas. The freeway system counteracted the tendency of earlier transport systems to adopt a radial structure, with the city core as a hub. Beltways, bypasses and orbital roads reroute traffic around, above or in recent years below the city street network, as a solution to the crippling congestion that car ownership brought to these streets in the years of initial growth (Rae 1971, p.307).

As we have seen, the freeway neither initiated nor promoted suburbia in itself. The desire to own a home where family life could play out in a homogenous environment had gathered momentum through the 20th century. For major cities in the US the trend had been evident for some time. Figure 4.2 shows the percentage of population growth in urban areas absorbed by the city core and the outer suburban rings from 1900. The apparent reversal for the decade 1941–1950 encompasses the war years – by 1956 the city cores were absorbing just 16% of the population increase.

These figures need to be read against a backdrop of increasing urbanisation, so population increase was caused by natural increase (births) as well as migration from the country to the city, and migration from outside the US. Between 1900 and 1960 the urban population of the US rose from 39.7% of the total to 67.1% (Rae 1971, p.201).

Suburbia as a phenomenon not only became the housing form of choice, it also developed its distinctive version of architectural idealism. Many architects had imbibed the social idealism of the 1930s across all industrialised nations, and the public housing schemes of the 1950s and 60s were a sought-after outlet for this idealism. Others turned to the free-standing domestic house as a worthy problem, a path trodden by Frank Lloyd Wright when he designed a series of modest houses, the Usonian series, that were aimed at families of modest means. The most influential group of buildings, though, were the Case Study Houses sponsored by John Entenza and his Los Angeles based magazine *Arts and Architecture*. The intention was to influence the building boom anticipated to occur after the end of the Second World War. The houses were part of a proselytising tendency in modern architecture, which sought to convey to the average houseowner the advantages of modern thinking. Principles included convenience, the adoption of modern appliances to reduce household labour, and creating a series of spaces around the house that encouraged outdoor leisure and what later came to be called lifestyle. The suburban house now became not only shelter but also a place of leisure, and in the process the urban leisure sites of the

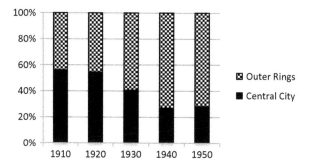

Figure 4.2 Percentage of population growth in the preceding decade – outer and inner city
Adapted from Rae (1971, Table 10.1)

1930s, the downtown movies and amusement parks that linked to the tram networks, were neglected for the convenience and social predictability of the home and its private garden.

The Case Study Houses programme attracted many bright young architects, including Charles and Ray Eames who built a widely described house in Pacific Palisades in 1948–1949 as Case Study House number 8. The building is an iconic one for domestic architecture, since it combines the industrial aesthetic of steel framing and off-the-shelf components with an egalitarian intent to bring a low-cost, yet architecturally distinguished house to the market. Indeed Esther McCoy places the precedents for the whole pro-gramme in the 1927 Weissenhof dwellings built in Stuttgart, and the Werk-bund Exhibition of 1930 in Vienna (McCoy 1989). Both had attempted to demonstrate the efficacy and appeal of well-designed modernist houses and flats. The appeal of the Case Study Houses was also aided by their location. As the qualities that made the East Coast cities of America urbane and desirable – their history, vitality and public amusements and attractions – diminished in the face of urban dis-aggregation and suburban distractions, Los Angeles emerged as the newly desirable city with its combination of glamour and benign weather. The Californian garden was usable the year round, and the suburban house could also incorporate a pool as the focus of relaxation. Together with the ubiquitous refrigerator, and the quick adop-tion of air conditioning, the house could cater for a range of entertainments and leisure pursuits.

All these attributes were magnified and refined in the Case Study Houses. Julius Shulman photographed them in the most alluring manner: his images of Pierre Koenig's house number 22, cantilevering over greater Los Angeles, are amongst the city's most iconic. The aspirations they evoke are telling. The old urban aspiration of being close enough to participate in the economic and social opportunities of the city, yet being able to retreat when desired, have been given a new scale by the car. In the example of Case Study House 22 the physical separation from the city appears complete, as does the incorporation of the lights and view of the metropolis as a backdrop to everyday living raised to a glamorous pitch, with the house free from over-looking neighbours, leaving its transparency uncompromised. The car also allowed a new sense of urbanity to emerge, where the physical distance of work, shopping and leisure is understood in terms of travel time rather than proximity. An abstract perception of urban connectedness thus emerges, based on a selective collection of well-used destinations.

If the Case Study Houses represent the ideal of suburban life, the reality of suburban development in the 1950s and 60s took in a vast range of development tracts, with few matching the Californian prototypes. In the popular history of suburbia Levittown is the most representative, named for the family firm headed by Abraham Levitt and his sons William and Alfred. During the war years the firm had built large estates for war workers, and had perfected their building techniques to mass-produce individual homes on concrete slabs using pre-made frames. In 1946 they bought a 1600 hectare site on Long Island, and proceeded to roll out houses at a peak rate of 30 per day. The process itself was highly mechanised. Bulldozers prepared the building sites, all the complex assembly was done offsite, and hand power tools decreased the time taken to erect each house. The development was highly successful, but bore the imprint of the mortgage insurance guidelines of the Federal Housing Administration, which encouraged racially and socially homogenous neighbourhoods. The suburb housed many Second World War veterans for whom it presented an attractive financial proposition, but as the market broadened it became synonymous with the post-war boom in children, and the ability of average wage earners to afford new houses. Two additional developments followed, one in Pennsylvania and one in New Jersey. The first housed many of the workers at the United States Steel plant at Fairless Hills, the second served as a dormitory suburb for Philadelphia (Jackson 1985, loc.4698).

While Levittown may have been architecturally undistinguished, it provided detached houses and the self-contained suburban life to a broadening market of buyers. This lifestyle was powered not only by the motor car, but also by the electricity needed for the television sets or the Bendix washers that were added to the house packages as inducements. Levittown was the New York equivalent of the post-war housing tracts sprouting at the edge of Australian cities, containing within them the middle-class aspirations of a population flushed with post-war optimism. As car ownership continued to climb, the tenor of everyday life altered to suit the new mobility. Shopping, previously centred on the urban core and served by the tram lines which brought shoppers in from surrounding neighbourhoods, was now independent of its traditional urban locations. Indeed the congestion of the city centre encouraged the development of suburban shopping, and the combination of carpark and shops fostered the ubiquitous mall.

Suburbanisation, and its associated decline in urban density, was most pronounced in the older industrial cities of America's Eastern states. The steepest inner-city declines occurred from 1950, with Baltimore, Philadelphia, New York, Detroit and Chicago all experiencing dramatic drops in overall population density. Between 1950 and 1990 these cities saw density halve, but at a decreasing rate. The centrifugal force of suburbanisation declined over the decades, as urban areas tended towards a stasis or, in many cases, a small rise in density. These trends were different in the newer cities of the West Coast and Southern states. Los Angeles showed a rise in density for the period, as did Miami. Despite the growth in freeways, Los Angeles was constrained by other infrastructure issues, and its early loose physical spread was gradually filled in by a growing population (Bruegmann 2005, pp.62–63).

By 1960 the early assumption of theorists that the American city would maintain its concentric form was under some question. In 1925 Park and Burgess, using Chicago as a case study, proposed a generic diagram of the city which showed an urban business core surrounded by a degraded ring of transition areas housing poor and immigrant communities, followed by a working-class zone which, in turn, was encircled by a middle-class residential zone (Park, Burgess & McKenzie 1967). The diagram recognised the urban trend towards class separation, as well as the preference of middle-class families for the spaces of the outer suburbs. Despite its poor representation of the city as an economic entity, or its over-simplification of homogenous urban rings, it nonetheless functioned as an aspirational figure that assumed that relocation to the city edge was the aim of families who could afford the means to make it happen. The rise of the suburb in the 1950s showed that these aspirations were still strong, but the dominance of the centre also weakened as jobs shifted to locations at the urban edge. As shopping followed this trend, many families saw no reason to enter the city centre on a regular basis.

The drift was clearly enabled by the vast numbers of cars produced and sold. Yet the suburb *per se* was not a technical inevitability. Its rise in the US, and in Australia, can be attributed both to a cultural aspiration and to the manufacturing capacity that produced the cars and appliances that drew on existing energy sources, and created huge demand for the expansion and diversification of those sources. In Europe the reality was different. Post-war aspirations were manifest through state intervention in planning and housing provision, and the limited space and energy available in European countries restricted their options. Repairing war damage absorbed enormous resources immediately after the war, and considerable national discipline was exercised in allocating materials. The results were mixed, but not universally in the direction of lower density. London displayed a downward trend from 83 persons/hectare in 1950 to 68 in 1960, but Paris showed almost no decline (99 to 97 p/ha). Warsaw, on the other hand, almost halved its density over the decade, as a result of state subsidised pre-fabricated housing estates being built following the launch of a national housing policy in 1956 (Tasan 1999).

The US, by contrast, could boast not only undamaged cities and industry, but also a country straddling several climatic zones, with few physical limits on space for urban expansion. In addition it contained oil and coal to fuel the post-war boom. The simple arithmetic of car ownership graphically illustrates the difference (Table 4.1).

The degree of suburbanisation possible for a society relies on a proportion of car ownership sufficient to meet the transport needs of everyday life. The enormous imbalance in motor transport between the US and the rest of the world can also be gleaned from the crude oil consumption figures of 1951. Approximately 540 million tonnes of crude were extracted that year, with US wells producing half the volume. Consumption in millions of tonnes was estimated as shown in Table 4.2, using coarse geographic groupings and excluding the former USSR.

The figures help explain the dominance of US suburban growth in the urban histories of the 1950s. Its size was unmatched, as was its demand for energy. Installed generating capacity tells its own story. Figure 4.3 shows the

Table 4.1 Motor vehicles per 1000 inhabitants

	1950	1960	1970
United States	260	240	430
France	40	110	240
West Germany	40	90	230
Britain	50	110	210
Italy	15	30	190
Japan		5	80

Adapted from Bardou (1982, p.197)

Table 4.2 Crude oil consumption by region, 1951

United States	311 million tonnes
Rest of Western Hemisphere	64 million tonnes
Western Europe	65 million tonnes
Rest of Eastern Hemisphere	62 million tonnes

Adapted from BP Oil Review (1951)

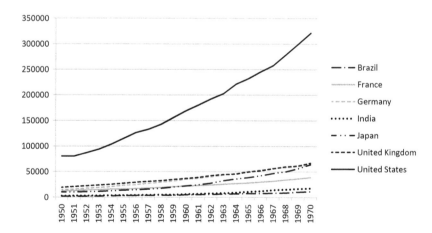

Figure 4.3 Installed generating capacity (MW), selected countries, 1950–1970
Adapted from Canning (2007)

total generating capacity for selected countries for the period 1950–1970. The US not only enters the 1950s with the largest capacity of any country, it continues to add generators at a rate that dwarfs other industrialised and partly industrialised nations.

Thus the image of the American post-war suburb is, in world terms, an anomaly, yet it dominated visions of domestic life, underpinned by the energy available through oil and electricity. The latter continued to be fuelled primarily by coal, with contributions from hydroelectric schemes.

Two other factors played a significant role in shaping the form of cities both in the US and elsewhere in the industrialised world. These involved food and population growth, and the list of the world's largest cities in 1950 shows the continuing development of the traditional trade and industrial centres: New York, London, Tokyo, Paris, Shanghai, Moscow, Chicago, the Ruhr (Chandler & Fox 1974, p.371). Yet for all these cities except Shanghai, the future was already sketched out in the national and regional demographics. The effect of the change in the rate of population increase has been noted in chapter 2, but by 1960 the profound effects of the demographic transition in Western countries was evident.

The concept of the demographic transition is simple but powerful. In countries entering the transition, which is a function of modernisation, the rate of death declines, followed by a drop in the birth rate. Critically there is a lag between the two, and this is the period when population will increase dramatically. The fall in the death rate reflects better medical care, improved sanitation, declines in violent death and better nutrition, but the fall in the birth rate is a more complex change, and is not specifically tied to modern contraception. France is the defining case of a gradual and long transition, with death and birth rates declining almost in parallel over 185 years. Through this period the French population increased more slowly than its neighbours, and the Total Fertility Rate (TFR) of French women in 1960 was 2.09. This is the number of children on average that each woman would bear through her reproductive years, and it is a useful metric because it quickly indicates whether the population is growing or shrinking. For countries with low death rates the TFR required for a stable population, or the replacement TFR, is about 2.1. Thus by 1960 the French TFR indicated a society about to enter slow demographic decline, with marginally fewer babies born than in the preceding generation. Germany was even lower, at 1.65, and no Western European country was at or above replacement TFR. Even the US, with its enormous material advantage, had a TFR of 2.01 (Livi-Bacci 1992, p.106).

It should be noted that national TFR encompasses the entire population, and indicates the rate of natural increase or decrease for the country as a whole. Countries with policies that encouraged immigration continued to grow in population, even with TFRs at or below replacement. The US had long taken in substantial migrant numbers, and Canada and Australia were also popular post-war destinations. Argentina had benefitted in the interwar years, and its share of European migrants declined as it entered a turbulent political phase. Nonetheless Argentina's share of earlier immigrants, and its agricultural productivity, saw Buenos Aires grow to a major metropolis of 4.6 million by 1950, with internal migration almost doubling that figure by 1970. Countries with below-replacement levels nationally can still see their major cities grow, as people move from the country to the city for a range of reasons. However, when this trend ceases, and without immigration from other countries, cities will stabilise in size if the national TFR is around 2.1, and will shrink if it is lower.

These trends were clear by the 1960s, but they were soon overwhelmed by the magnitude of the transition occurring outside of the industrialised countries. A major stimulant of this broader transition was the diffusion of the Haber–Bosch process and its products. The range of nitrogen-bearing products used as fertiliser changed the productive capacity of farmland the world over, with developed countries using some 9.5 million tonnes in 1960 and the developing world applying 2.3 million tonnes. A decade later these figures had grown to 24.37 and 8.8 million tonnes respectively (IFA n.d., 2015). The implications have been enormous. Smil estimates that without fertiliser the volume of world crop production in 2000 would have required four times as much farmland. The amount of corn produced per hectare in the US averaged 1.6 tonnes per hectare in 1900. A century later the figure stood at 8.5 tonnes. In 1900 in Japan a sophisticated agricultural system was growing 2.2 tonnes of rice per hectare: fertilisers and improved rice cultivars increased this to highs of around 6.5 tonnes by 1980 (Smil 2011).

Increased yields translated into a multiplying volume of food available, with triple the traditional yield not uncommon. At a minimum these relative surpluses made cities more viable for a greater proportion of the population. Chinese figures bear witness to this phenomenon. In 1970 China produced about 1.2 million tonnes of nitrogenous fertiliser, or 3.7% of the world total. After ordering and installing 13 large Haber–Bosch factories, output rose to 10 million tonnes in 1980, or 15.9% of global production. The 1970s took China from the brink of catastrophic famine, as experienced in the early 1960s, to the food sufficiency evident in contemporary Chinese cities (Hager 2008, p.269). These surpluses, and the broadacre farming methods used to maximise yield and reduce labour, provide the backdrop for the massive shifts to the city of Chinese farmers and peasants in subsequent decades.

For Smil (2011) the acceleration of the nitrogen cycle through industrial conversion of the atmospheric form of the gas into fertiliser is perhaps more significant in its proportional effects than the more widely discussed carbon cycle. For the growth of cities it is also underappreciated, since agricultural surplus has always been a pre-requisite for urban growth. As with most applications of technology, the age where cities transcended the historical maxima of 1–1.2 million inhabitants occurred well and truly before the advent of synthetic fertiliser. But the synthetic process made it available everywhere, regardless of local natural deposits, as long as its energy source and feedstock, in the form of coal and natural gas, were available. Energy thus becomes a range of resources in the abstract, since it can be applied to create substitutes for a variety of naturally occurring and useful deposits. A derivation of the Haber–Bosch process can extract oil from coal, for example, and was used to fuel much of Germany's military transport in the Second World War.

The combination of demographic transition, food sufficiency and the driving back of the colonial conquests and ambitions of the European powers set in train the major shifts that characterised the second half of the 20th century. With the demography of much of Europe static, the changes in European urban form came as a consequence of increasing emulation of American modes of consumption. By 1979 car ownership in France, Germany and Italy was over half the American figure, and averaging about one vehicle per three inhabitants. The compact European city, with its dense network of public transport and state-sponsored worker's housing, was slowly adding a ring of aspirant suburbs, or suburbanising villages, to its metropolitan area. The shift to cities in mainland Europe occurred later, in general, than in Britain, and much of Europe retains its rural character. In France, for example, the area of Paris and its immediate surrounds harboured a disproportionate share of France's modernisation. In the early 1960s this region of Île-de-France, comprising just 2% of national land area, held 19% of the French population and 29% of industrial jobs. This exceeded the industrial jobs for the entire Western half of the country. Paris has since continued its dominance of the French economy, and its size, in comparison to other Western European cities, is anomalously large. Much of the population growth has been taken up in a group of peripheral new towns, which absorbed almost all population growth in the region between 1977 and 1982 (Hall & Tewdwr-Jones 2011, pp.182–187).

A more typical pattern was a levelling off of city growth as internal migration accomplished its shift of populations from rural to urban areas, as the demographic decline became manifest, and as policies of decentralisation encouraged the establishment of subsidised industry in traditionally poorer areas such as southern Italy. At the same time the historic cores of cities such as Milan were slowly reducing in density, as birth rates declined and working-class families were driven out by high land values reflecting the continued desirability of urban living fostered by the Parisian model. As car ownership increased so did locational choices, and the appeal of the free-standing villa became both an ideal and a burgeoning reality. The population of central Milan peaked in 1973 at 1.74 million, and has since declined by a quarter as the suburban population has continued to increase. At the same time the city's urban area has expanded to functionally encompass about four million inhabitants, although some definitions of its sphere of influence run as high as eight million (OECD 2006).

The experience of the US, Europe and countries like Australia, New Zealand and Canada, as well as parts of Africa and South America where wealthy elites could choose their dwelling location in relation to the city, is varied but subject to some general observations. The advent of the car has indeed had a profound effect on urban density and on urban expansion patterns, and is evident in declines in tract density for all major US cities since at least 1920 (Angel 2012, loc.2684). However, the car is not the only driver of this. Angel (2012) has documented declining densities the world over commencing at the end of the 19th century. There have been notable exceptions over this period – Mumbai and Tokyo fluctuate in density but begin their modern decline in 1950, and Shanghai varies wildly in response to prevailing political uncertainties in China before 1948, and the particular vision of modern life that the city cultivated and embodied. It, too, declines from a modern high of 567 people per hectare in 1950 to a figure of 103 in 2000. Sub-Saharan African cities and those of South America enter the 20th century with relatively low densities, probably because of their colonial legacies that favoured the separation of class and race from the outset. This encouraged physical spreading, and the adoption of the separate dwelling as the preferred housing form. Migration to the city emulated this preference, even in poor circumstances, and cities like Lagos or Johannesburg assumed very low densities from their founding.

Suburbanisation as the dominant form of post-war urban expansion in the US, and its later adoption in Europe, embodies not only a profound shift in transportation modes, but also an economic transformation. The industrialisation of Western Europe, North America and Australasia dramatically altered the composition and distribution of national wealth. Piketty has summarised this trend succinctly in a series of graphs showing the composition and value of national capital, which he defines as the sum of farmland, housing, other domestic capital such as commercial buildings and infrastructure, plus net foreign capital. The change from 1700 to 2010 is dramatic for Britain, France and Germany. Before the Industrial Revolution in Britain, agricultural land made up over 50% of national capital. By 2010 its value was negligible, and almost the entire value of national capital was composed of housing and domestic capital. Not only had the wealth of the nation moved from the countryside to the city, but the form of that capital had transformed into the very fabric of cities themselves. The building of housing, by both the state and private developers, appears as a distinct turnaround in Piketty's graphs, commencing at about 1950 in Britain, France and Germany. From mid-century the value of the national stock of housing continues to rise, and in each case by 2010 it makes up the largest component of national capital (Piketty 2014, Figs 3.1, 3.2, 4.1). Thus the boom in housing construction that commenced in 1950, and continued with the suburbanisation of European cities, is evident in the proportion of national wealth embodied in housing and urban infrastructure.

For the US the relevant graphs are different, because of the existence of the moving frontier of colonisation into the late 19th century. Since land was so widely available, its value relative to national income was less than in Europe. Housing increased its share of national capital noticeably from about 1920, reflecting the early takeup of suburban housing around major cities. However, other forms of domestic capital have a greater value in the US than housing in 2010. National investment in roads, factories and offices is greater than in housing, which shows remarkable variation in price across American jurisdictions. In some areas the abundance of land has made detached housing cheap, and in others control of land releases has raised the price of housing allotments. Thus the emergence of the mass suburb in the US continued the tradition of private ownership of housing that had developed as part of the nation's inherent social mobility, as opposed to the more concentrated ownership of housing stock and capital in Europe at the start of the 20th century (Piketty 2014, Figs 4.6, 4.11).

These trends may sound abstract, but their importance lies in the sheer volume of national wealth embodied in housing in advanced economies, and the critical role low-density housing has played in creating and distributing this wealth. The Levittown model brought individual home ownership to working-class urban Americans in a way that the interwar suburb had not (United States Census Bureau n.d.). The managerial class and professionals may have bene-fitted from early suburbanisation, but the car and mass-produced houses created grades of suburbs for all income groups. This was true of post-war Australia and Canada as well, but Europe had to wait until the social mobi-lity of the 1960s and 70s created a later wave of suburbanisation. In France the 1980s was the decade of change, with the proportion of homeowners jumping from 46% to 54% (Meron & Courgeau 2004, p.61). Nonetheless the fondness for detached housing is now visible all over Italy, France and Spain.

The significance of this form of housing development can be seen in Figures 4.4 and 4.5 showing home ownership rates in the US from 1900, and Australia from 1947. The surge in rates after the Second World War is marked, and is largely a consequence of the Levittown phenomenon and Australian owner-builders.

It should be emphasised that home ownership rates in themselves can be indicative of a range of economic developments. In the English-speaking world percentages have stabilised in the high 60s, with a remarkable degree of convergence. Western European countries have lower rates, with France and Germany in the mid-50s and Switzerland below 50%. The very highest current rates are in the ex-Soviet-bloc countries of Eastern Europe, under-lining that rates of ownership do not necessarily correlate with national wealth or productivity. What they do reflect, though, is the distribution of

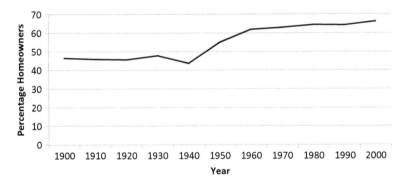

Figure 4.4 US Homeownership Rates 1900–2000
Source: US Census Bureau, Historical Census of Housing Tables

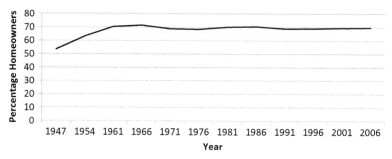

Figure 4.5 Australian home ownership rates, 1947–2006
Source: Kryger (2009, Table 1)

wealth in advanced economies where housing stock makes up perhaps half of national capital.

As a broad principle, energy has thus played a role in the distribution of wealth in advanced economies by enabling the conversion of land around cities to housing. The advent of the car increased the radius of land within commuting distance of the city, and this abundance led to greater land affordability in the post-Second-World-War decades. Houses are often a family's most valuable asset, and in those decades they became the primary way for many families to accumulate some capital. The greater the degree of home ownership, the greater the spread of capital in the form of the house and its land as a private asset. And as long as cities were growing, the relative value of the asset continued to climb due to its better location when compared to newer developments.

Along with suburban tracts came a slew of unique cultural forms and entertainments, including those associated with cars and the institutions that arose from cheap land and mobility – the mall, the drive-in, and the vacation house. The physical proximity that cities traditionally offered for commercial and cultural opportunities gave way to a complex and often multi-centred urban experience. The concentration of firms and individuals that the city centre still fostered remained attractive for service and financial industries, since they did not rely on the transport of bulky items. Manufacturing and warehousing jobs often moved to the edge of cities, and the car allowed enormous latitude in where workers could live. The car overcame, to a large degree, the concentric pattern of public transport which tended to converge on the city centre.

However, the largest effect arguably was the levelling of class differences through the privatisation of transport and the increased energy availability for average households. It is hard to overstate the significance of energy availability for what we might call lifestyle, but which can be qualified in terms of the life that is being lived by various social groupings and strata. The limited sources of motive power in pre-industrial cities gave the wealthy and the nobility, who were often one and the same, command of physical power that exceeded that of the average person by orders of magnitude. This comparison has been often made, but an example taken from pre-modern Japan will make the point. A household staff numbering 2000 serving a daimyo or regional lord in Edo in the Tokugawa period represents some 140 kW of physical power, based on an average of 70 watts per person. Horses provide between 500 and 850 watts each, so a stable of 200 horses makes another 135 kW of motive power available. If we exclude heating and cooking, and assume that these horses and servants are not engaged in agricultural production, then the daimyo has perhaps 375 kW available to himself and his family for daily tasks and transport. This is a fairly large retinue: there were many that were smaller. By way of comparison, for the average Australian household with two medium size cars there is about 240 kW of transport power available, in crude terms about two-thirds of that serving our Japanese noble. If we assume that his staff work for a third of the day, then they contribute 46.2 kilowatt hours (kWh) to his comfort and well-being, around two and a half times the 18 kWh that the average Australian household consumes. Thus with a staff of 2000 and with 200 horses our daimyo has at his disposal roughly twice the power of the average Western family of modern times.

These comparisons have obvious flaws, mainly in the relative efficiencies of the people and horses of the daimyo, and the inclusion of heating, cooling and cooking in modern household consumption. Nonetheless they indicate the sheer volumes of energy underpinning modern domestic life, and the comparison would be more startling (but considerably more complex) if we included food production and distribution. This will be broached in later chapters, but the levelling effects of fossil fuel power in the modern world should be at least obvious. The end result is that, in modern industrialised economies, the lives of the rich and the poor are more alike than at any time in history. Whether this balance is shifting is a matter of debate, but the modern city achieves, through reticulated electricity, gas, water and wide car ownership, a compression of class distinction insofar as living standards are concerned. Rich and poor alike use washing machines, computers, televisions, electric and gas stoves, kettles and air conditioning. They share the roads, and have similar mobility in general terms, although fuel costs and road tolls may determine in practice who travels more.

This relative equality of technology is critical to understanding not only the form of the modern city, and its commuting and travel patterns, but also the class politics of energy that have emerged in recent years. This will be addressed in a later chapter, but the effect of energy abundance in mitigating class differences in the late 20th century has been poorly acknowledged in the literature that deals with energy policy and a move to low-carbon energy sources. The electrification of households and the shift to private cars have remade the modern city with each house a castle in the resources at its disposal, and production, servicing and shopping in the city have arranged themselves to serve these bastions of private consumption.

The advantages of these developments should also be acknowledged, no matter how we may judge them in terms of subjective morality. Crude indicators like life expectancy and literacy correlate well with wealthy cities, as does innovation. Living standards may vary within a city, but not as widely as between wealthy and poor cities. However, these claims need a measure of unpacking, and a consideration of the critical viewpoints that the very success of the modern city has engendered. These will be the subject of the next chapter.

Note

1 Refers to location numbers in the Kindle edition.

Bibliography

Angel, S. (2012). *Planet of cities*. Cambridge, MA: Lincoln Institute of Land Policy. Kindle edition.

Bardou, J. (1982). *The automobile revolution: The impact of an industry*. Chapel Hill, NC: University of North Carolina Press.

BP Oil Review (1951). Retrieved August 18, 2015, from www.bp.com/content/dam/bp/pdf/energy-economics/statistical-review-2015/bp-statistical-review-1951.pdf

Bruegmann, R. (2005). *Sprawl: A compact history*. Chicago: University of Chicago Press.

Canning, D. (2007). *A database of world stocks of infrastructure*. Retrieved August 4, 2015, from www.hsph.harvard.edu/david-canning/data-sets

Chandler, T., & Fox, G. (1974). *3000 years of urban growth*. New York: Academic Press.

Dowson, D., & Hamrock, B. (1981). *History of ball bearings*. Cleveland: NASA Lewis Research Center.

Hager, T. (2008). *The alchemy of air: A Jewish genius, a doomed tycoon, and the scientific discovery that fed the world but fueled the rise of Hitler*. New York: Harmony Books.

Hall, P. (1988). *Cities of tomorrow: An intellectual history of urban planning and design in the twentieth century*. Oxford: Blackwell.

Hall, P., & Tewdwr-Jones, M. (2011). *Urban and regional planning* (5th ed.). London: Routledge.

Hughes, T. (1983). *Networks of power: Electrification in Western society, 1880–1930*. Baltimore, MD: Johns Hopkins University Press.

IFA (International Fertilizer Industry Association) (n.d.). *IFADATA*. Retrieved July 29, 2015, from http://ifadata.fertilizer.org/ucSearch.aspx

IFA (International Fertilizer Industry Association) (2015). *World NH$_3$ Statistics by Region*. Retrieved August 18, 2015, from www.fertilizer.org//En/Statistics/PIT_Excel_Files.aspx

Jackson, K. (1985). *Crabgrass frontier: The suburbanization of the United States*. New York: Oxford University Press. Kindle edition.

Kryger, T. (2009, February 11). *Home ownership in Australia – data and trends*. Retrieved August 4, 2015, from www.aph.gov.au/library

Livi-Bacci, M. (1992). *A concise history of world population*. Cambridge, MA: Blackwell.

McCoy, E. (1989). Arts and architecture case study houses. In E. Smith (Ed.), *Blueprints for modern living: History and legacy of the case study houses*. Los Angeles: Museum of Contemporary Art.

Meron, M., & Courgeau, D. (2004). Home ownership and social inequality in France. In K. Kurz & H. Blossfeld (Eds), *Home ownership and social inequality in comparative perspective*. Stanford: Stanford University Press.

OECD (2006). *OECD territorial reviews: Milan*. Paris: OECD Publications.

Park, R., Burgess, E., & McKenzie, R. (1967). *The City*. Chicago: University of Chicago Press.

Piketty, T. (2014). *Capital in the twenty-first century* (A. Goldhammer, Ed.). Cambridge, MA: Belknap Press.

Rae, J. (1971). *The road and the car in American life*. Cambridge, MA: MIT Press.

Rose, M., & Clark, J. (1979). Light, heat, and power: energy choices in Kansas City, Wichita, and Denver, 1900–1935. *Journal of Urban History*, 5(3), 340–364.

Smil, V. (2006). *Transforming the twentieth century: Technical innovations and their consequences*. Oxford: Oxford University Press.

Smil, V. (2011). Nitrogen cycle and world food production. *World Agriculture*, 2(1), 9–13. Retrieved July 29, 2015, from www.world-agriculture.net/issue/3/World-Agriculture-Vol2-No1-Spring-2011

Szilárd, L., & Fermi, E. (1944). Patent US2708656 – Neutronic reactor. Retrieved August 18, 2015, from www.google.com/patents/US2708656

Tafuri, M. (1976). *Architecture and utopia: Design and capitalist development*. Cambridge, MA: MIT Press.

Tasan, T. (1999). Warsaw under transformation: New tendencies in the housing market. *GeoJournal*, 49(1), 91–103. Retrieved July 29, 2015, from www.jstor.org/stable/41147403

Tobey, R. (1996). *Technology as freedom: The New Deal and the electrical modernization of the American home*. Berkeley: University of California Press.

Troy, P. (2012). *Accommodating Australians: Commonwealth government involvement in housing*. Annandale, NSW: Federation Press.

Twombly, R. (1987). *Frank Lloyd Wright, his life and his architecture*. New York: Wiley.

United States Census Bureau (n.d.). *Historical census of housing tables*. Retrieved August 18, 2015, from www.census.gov/hhes/www/housing/census/historic/owner.html

United States Congress (1934). Public Law 73–479, 73d Congress, H.R. 9620, National Housing Act of 1934. Retrieved August 18, 2015, from https://fraser.stlouisfed.org/scribd/?item_id=457156&filepath=/docs/historical/martin/54_01_19340627.pdf

5 Critiques of progress and ideas of sustainability

The phenomenon of urbanisation – the concentration of population in cities and towns – occurred in markedly different places over the course of the 20th century. In 1925 large cities were almost exclusively located in Western Europe, North America and Japan. A notable exception was Buenos Aires, where European immigration had swelled the city to the seventh largest in the world. By 1950 Shanghai, Calcutta (Kolkata), Mexico City and Cairo had joined the list of the 15 largest cities, but the phenomenon of the growing Asian or South American megalopolis was still some years away (Chandler & Fox 1974, p.371). Yet the ensuing decades revealed two profound trends. The first was the phenomenon of urban growth in countries only partly, or marginally, industrialised. While the older metropolises grew relatively slowly between 1925 and 1968 – neither Paris nor London quite doubled in population, and Berlin declined – a host of cities embarked on dramatic growth seemingly unrelated to national wealth. In Mexico, India, China and Brazil cities with enormous populations emerged, setting the pattern for a deep-seated anxiety about the future for their vast impoverished masses and seemingly haphazard forms of growth.

By the mid-1960s a Malthusian disquiet emerged which blended the vast demographic transition underway in Asia, South America and Africa with a broader Western disillusion with the fruits of industrialisation. The decolonisation of large parts of the globe, under the aegis of local elites and political idealists, propelled many countries to be historical actors in their own right. The years following the Second World War had seen the independence of key countries such as India (1947), Indonesia (declared 1945), the Philippines (1946) and Morocco (1946). By 1960 France and Belgium had lost a swathe of colonial possessions in Africa, and when Algeria became independent in 1962 European acceptance of a shift in colonial relations, and the inevitability of total decolonisation, was complete. The political unification of China under Communist rule in 1949 also created an historical actor of immense size and influence.

The uneven development evident even among industrialised countries in the 1960s led to the second trend: expressions of disillusionment and counter-cultural attitudes that varied from country to country, and issue to issue. The most visible emerged from the US, where post-war affluence had created the conditions for increased numbers of students and the prospect, if not always the reality, of alternative lifestyles. In Europe the earnest efforts of post-war reconstruction had reinforced conservative values, but large numbers of disillusioned youth sought to break from these values and pursue alternative agendas, with a corresponding attack on the symbols of class privilege.

The catalyst for many of these ideas was a resurgent Marxism that called into question not only the prevailing class structure, but also the phenomenon of neo-colonialism that appeared to be perpetuating the subservience of former colonies through economic means rather than through direct political control. The intellectual climate was further complicated by the Cold War division into Eastern and Western Blocs, where Western intellectuals sought to distance themselves from the realities of Communist rule yet continued to tap into the rich vein of the Marxist tradition and its critique of capitalist production.

The result was a shaded spectrum of almost infinite critical variability, arrayed by the transformative powers of the modern era. While the British post-war experience was marked by a precocious puncturing of class pretensions as thousands of working-class returned servicemen gained university degrees and access to professional life, in the US the moral imperative of liberating black Americans from the entrenched strictures of racial segregation generated waves of idealism through all levels of society. Alongside the understanding that the world had to change was the reality that the world was indeed changing quickly, with results that seemed at times shocking. The demographic transition in poorer countries was becoming clearer as organisations such the United Nations began to publish statistics from all regions, and the environmental effects of large-scale industrial processes and chemically aided agriculture garnered growing attention. Two books in particular galvanised opinion on change in America, and more widely, and they remain among the defining works of the modern era. The first was Jane Jacobs' (1961) *The Death and Life of Great American Cities*, and the second was Rachel Carson's *Silent Spring* (Carson 1962)

Carson's book was initially tangential to discussions on urban form and development, as it dealt with the widespread use of pesticides and their potential to accumulate in the food chain, and to accelerate the formation of pesticide-resistant insect populations through natural selection. However, it tapped into a general unease about chemical control of insects and the vulnerability of natural processes to synthetic pesticides. Jacobs' book, however, struck at the very core of US urban planning and development in the 1960s.

In essence, Jacobs was an advocate for the urban life that had emerged in large American cities in the early part of the 20th century. Her concerns were driven by the large changes wrought in the guise of the rational solving of urban problems, especially those aimed at poor communities and the degraded housing stock they occupied. Alongside the massive construction of freeways and the difficulty of getting loans to buy housing in any areas other than middle-class suburbs, the centres of American cities and their surrounding inner-city precincts were declining in vitality and desirability. Jacobs' main targets were the tenets of urban reconstruction as taught and practised in the post-war years. As in Europe, working-class areas were targeted for their lack of upkeep, poor sanitary conditions and in some cases high crime rates. The momentum of conventional thinking was behind demolition of these areas and their replacement with large public housing schemes, or the construction of freeways that fed the city core with commuters who then decamped to the suburbs after work, leaving the centres bereft of life. For Jacobs these solutions were infinitely worse than the problems they purported to solve – in her words "This is not the rebuilding of cities. This is the sacking of cities" (Jacobs 1961, p.5).

Jacobs' book marks a turning against the wide acceptance that urban populations drift towards class homogeneity, and against the effects of planning in reinforcing this tendency through zoning, so that the city developed as a series of defined areas where similar classes and uses clustered. The lower the degree of car ownership, the closer workers tended to live to their work. In the interwar city this was facilitated by trams, but cars of course allowed workers greater latitude as to where they might live, as long as their commuting time remained reasonable. Jacobs revived the vision of urban life that had prevailed in early Paris, for example, where the very proximity of living and working created commerce and exchange. While rationalist planning, based on an abstract idea of how cities should be transformed to solve functional and class problems, leaned towards centralised solutions and large investment projects, Jacobs championed a dense and highly animated city with a myriad of interactions and small investments. She was unusual in her embrace of commerce and small business as key elements of urban life, in an era when planning struggled to come to terms with profitability as a motivating force.

Jacobs devolved her ideas into four basic principles, based on her personal experience of urban vitality in New York's Greenwich Village, and in other parts of American cities where social cohesion was undervalued. She understood well the factors driving families to the suburbs. The first specific issue she deals with in her book is titled "The uses of sidewalks: safety". What follows is her musings on the complex factors that affect safety for those using sidewalks, including the observation that some of New York's safest streets may exist in poor or ethnically diverse neighbourhoods, and some of its most dangerous would fit roughly the same description. The difference lies in the factors that exert social control over the street – the degree to which the street is watched and considered an extension of the interests of those who live along it, and the cohesion of the community that provides the impetus and confidence to enforce civil standards in the public realm. This is doubtless a simplification of Jacobs' more developed argument, but her basic claim is that the same aspects of urban life, such as density and close living, that appear to create urban problems, also contain the subtle means to control those problems.

The argument is then extended through the four principles that Jacobs extracts from successful cities. The first is that of mixed primary uses, that is the existence side by side of uses that attract different people at differing times of the day. The more facets of life an area accommodates, the greater the chance of people using sidewalks through the day and evening, providing the social matrix and physical presence of people that deters crime and vandalism. In describing her own street, with its restaurants and coffee shops frequented by workers from surrounding small industries, she identifies a symbiosis whereby the social matrix of the inhabitants provides variety and stability to the area to a greater extent than if it were purely commercial, and the visiting workers create more economic activity than if the area were only residential.

Her second planning principle is physical – the stipulation that urban blocks should be small, with frequent opportunities to turn corners and take a variety of routes to one's destination. This, she argues, counters the isolation of specific streets that occurs when blocks are long and thus eliminate short cuts or impose a time penalty on alternative routes. A corollary of this is that short blocks and cross streets create more physical length of street frontage within a given area, as well as more complex urban views. In this she is arguing against the economic tendency to reduce the length of street frontage per occupied square metre in new buildings, which encourages the planning of super blocks with few cross streets or lanes because it is cheaper.

Jacobs' third tenet is also grounded in the embrace of an historical feature of cities. This is the need to have buildings at various stages of their useful lives, which includes many old ones. The principle here is to preserve the gradient of economic opportunity that buildings of different ages and stages of repair present. In an area of new buildings, the rents they demand are generally similar in order to garner a reasonable return on investment. This attracts similar tenants: high-turnover chains that provide a generic shopping or retail experience, rather than the risk-taking or niche shops and restaurants that can survive only in the low-rent older buildings before they undergo costly upgrading. Implicit in this principle is the recognition that commerce thrives on unevenness, where a range of possible cost structures allows the startup business to gain a foothold in an old building, and possibly to graduate to something more expensive once its specific business model has been proved and refined. Jacobs' vision thus argues for small-scale enterprises and against the homogenising effects of large capital investments, rather than being inimical to commerce as such.

Her fourth principle she describes as the need for concentration, but essentially it is a call for density. This is argued as a necessary condition for the diversity and vitality of city life, and is perhaps the message from Jacobs' book that has proved most enduring. In support of her argument Jacobs points out that urban areas across America that have experienced revitalisation without extensive rebuilding ("unslummed themselves", in her words) have all had high densities as expressed as dwelling units per acre (Jacobs 1961, p.202). It is probable that in the process densities dropped when expressed as residents per acre, as gentrification generally leads to lower numbers of inhabitants per unit. Nonetheless the contribution of density to urban life is compellingly argued, all the more so as it appeared to go against planning orthodoxies of the time. Jacobs even proposes an optimum net figure of about 200 dwellings per acre, which converts to about 500 dwellings per hectare. With the addition of a dense street network and parks this figure could halve for a particular precinct, but this would still represent an historically high gross figure of 250 dwellings per hectare, or some 750 inhabitants at an average of three people per dwelling.

While these figures exceed those attainable in pre-industrial cities, they are viable if they occur in a city that is heavily serviced by elevators and an underground public transport system. They can also only be attained in the form of apartment buildings. If we assume that a typical building only occupies half of its urban site to allow for setbacks, sun and amenities, then each hectare would yield only about 50 average apartments if built to a single storey. Thus what Jacobs is describing in terms of dwellings per acre would require a neighbourhood of ten storey apartment buildings built to the street alignment or sidewalk. This is a thoroughly urban vision, as opposed to suburban or villa development, but more than that it is a modern urban vision. Indeed she cites the figure of 100 dwellings per acre as the threshold at which urban vitality declines.

One of the curiosities of Jacobs' book is that it takes to task the figureheads of the American reform planning movement, including Lewis Mumford. Despite his professed love of cities, she describes *The Culture of Cities* as "a morbid and biased catalog of ills" (Jacobs 1961, p.20). This divergence is symptomatic of the two significant strands of the dominant critique of the post-war city – those, like Jacobs, who saw in progress the destruction of the early modern city and its unique density and vitality, and those like Mumford who seemed to have a profound nostalgia for the pre-industrial city. These are two very different models, predicated, as we have seen, on very different sustaining quantities and forms of energy. Despite her seductive descriptions of the daily cycle of street life she witnessed in Manhattan, Jacobs' vision was at odds with a prevailing critical view of modern life that hankered for a pre-industrial simplicity, and was suspicious of commerce in general. The counter-culture of the 1960s was less interested in reform and more in transcendence. It would take some time before the city became attractive as a unique space for self-fulfilment in the popular imagination.

In the decades of counter-cultural protest – the 1960s and 70s – urban life fostered its own forms of dissent through the anonymity of large cities, where people could gravitate to distinctive sub-cultures and re-invent themselves through lifestyle choices. This ran counter to Jacobs' view of the unseen matrix of informal social control that constituted the civilising force within urban life, which held conservative overtones. What was of interest to urban analysts, though, was the clear manifestation of class structure in the modern city. For the radical Left the city not only gave form to class differences, it perpetuated them. This discussion was given impetus by David Harvey's *Social Justice and the City*, which appeared in 1973 (Harvey 1973), and the work of Henri Lefebvre in France (Lefebvre 1971). These writers led a re-engagement with the city as a complex phenomenon that shapes and is shaped by modern life, and its processes of production and consumption. But they were more concerned with developing an analysis than presenting solutions, and when these arose they seemed hardly more sophisticated than the slum clearance movement of mid-century.

The political issues around urban development are a subset of the broader modern questions around useful political action. The tendency of the city to decant according to class is difficult to characterise historically, since only the modern city seems to have provided the means for it to be pursued to a high degree of physical separation. No pre-modern city was of sufficient scale to create local illusions of class homogeneity. In Berlin of the 1920s and 30s, for example, workers' housing was located as part of the orderly expansion of the city and its industrial base, and the neatness with which it was done was not intended to be an expression of class antagonism but rather a consequence of pragmatic attention to workers' needs as an antidote to radicalisation. Thus the city physically embodied class differences, but not necessarily as a consequence of crude class interests, although these clearly played a role. Physically reversing class separation does also not necessarily fix the problem. Social justice may imply that the poor should be moved to the wealthy neighbourhoods to enjoy the advantages they provide, but a more radical analysis suggests that over time the principles of capitalist real estate will simply re-assert the original separation for a host of reasons.

Jacobs' book is relatively indifferent to class as a determinant of urban experience. Rather she sees the city as an experience that binds classes through its unique attributes as a social phenomenon. The history of cities and their blend of commerce, culture and socialising, for her, transcends the specific critiques levelled at the modern capitalist city. Indeed she views attempts to alleviate urban ills through large planning interventions as more destructive than the ills of social disparity. However, for geographers like Manuel Castells, who attempted a radical redefinition of the city in Marxist terms in *The Urban Question*, the a priori need to understand the city in an abstract way made its simple pleasures somewhat superfluous (Castells 1977).

While the insights that Marxism brought to cities reinvigorated urban planning as an instrument of social progress, the concentration on the power relations that helped shape them rendered the sophistication of their underlying infrastructure almost invisible. The indolence of much of the popular counter-culture of the 1960s and 70s can be seen as a consequence of the sheer abundance of money and goods brought by the boom of the post-war years, and its critiques of progress centred on existential issues such as the loss of authentic experiences in the face of mass production. Since progress seemed entrenched as the defining experience of the times, its consequences rather than its perpetuation begged consideration. Marxism claimed an analytical monopoly in this, while experiential schools of thought contemplated the loss not only of authenticity but also the prevailing sense of alienation that Marx had raised a century earlier.

The variegated strands of 1970s critiques of contemporary society are nonetheless as fascinating as they are intertwined. Writers and thinkers such as Christopher Lasch and Richard Sennett used their historical and political perspectives to examine the sociology of everyday life, as lived experience rather than abstract categories. For Lasch the age of late capitalism, a description of the post-war international economy popularised by the Marxist economist Ernest Mandel, could be categorised not only by its economic features but also by its prevailing psychological tendencies (Mandel 1975). Lasch's book, *The Culture of Narcissism*, described the narcissist as the personality type most aligned with the features of late capitalism. In an age when so few real opportunities existed for the individual to reshape their world, all that was left was for them to reshape their personality (Lasch 1978). Sennett's argument was perhaps more broadly about cities. His most influential work, *The Fall of Public Man*, argued that modern life has effaced the distinction between public and private life and identity. Previously the public persona was constructed, as it were, to fulfil the conventions of living in the public purview. Contemporary public life has undermined this with the conflation of public and private acts in the expectation that there must be a consistency between the two (Sennett 1978).

Lasch's critique rested on the work and, probably more importantly, the sentiments of the school of cultural criticism known as the Frankfurt School. Founded by scholars who were radical by conviction rather than inclination, they concerned themselves with the kind of culture that emerged and flourished under advanced capitalism. The key figure was Theodor Adorno, who fled Nazi Germany for America in the years before the Second World War. Although he returned to Germany after the war, his experience in the US gave him a feel for the dual lessons it provided. On the one hand it was trenchantly democratic in public life, and effectively saved Adorno's life from the barbarism that had arisen in one of the most cultured nations on earth. On the other American cultural life had been so shaped by its commercial matrix that the popular forms it assumed dismayed Adorno, with his extensive musical and philosophical training and accomplishment. He admired America for its freedom, but disliked it for its tendency to reduce everything to monetary value.

The key point here is that critiques of capitalism could, and did, take two major forms in the 1960s and 70s. The first was economic and politically radical, and sought transformation of society along the lines propagated by Marx and his successors. It viewed capitalism as a total system, and understanding the system allowed one to identify the key aspects that needed to be transformed in order to effect a wider transformation. This was the basis for revolutionary Marxist politics, and its models were the revolutions of Eastern Europe and China. However, in a society that was delivering the material rewards of modernisation to the extent that America was, the level of discontent that was needed to effect a total revolution was very limited, particularly among those who best understood Marxism. Its critique of capitalism might have been compelling, but the revolutionary politics that flowed from the conviction that socialism would be a better alternative presented a much trickier proposition. For many it seemed more constructive, and more attainable, to channel discontent with the status quo into movements for reform, or into pointing out the cultural debasement that capitalism brought. This latter form was widespread and manifest in many ways, and it influenced the politics of activism in many spheres of public life, including city planning.

Thus the work of Lasch and Sennett may have been grounded in their observations of the culturally destructive effects of capitalism, but the end result is a form of conservatism that values the decorum and earnest morality of the 19th century above the showboating of the 20th. Lasch and Sennett were by no means the only thinkers to take this view. A raft of academic Marxist thinkers were extending the tenets of Marxism's founders to encompass all aspects of literature, painting, architecture and psychoanalysis, while moving further away from the political action on the ground that had been the focus of its early history. Thinkers of a conservative bent like Martin Heidegger were making similar arguments about the loss of authenticity in modern life, a cry taken up by many proponents of the counter-culture dedicated to restoring a sense of roots, or of reconnecting with craft and driving back the creeping alienation inherent in modern forms of work and living (Heidegger 1962).

The effect of this convergence was as sweeping as it was profound. The modernism of Le Corbusier, and the plans to remake the city into orderly apartment blocks to rehouse its inhabitants in sanitary conditions while providing cultural facilities for their betterment, collapsed in the face of its poor grasp of the many conditions that determined the quality of urban life. By 1970 the rehousing schemes in Britain and the US left no doubt about how the Corbusian vision looked when built, and it was hardly seductive. Jacobs' work had been sidelined as the more radical critiques of the city played themselves out, but by the late 1970s sentiment had shifted away from intellectual excavation and back to concrete notions of civic urban life that could be quantified and implemented.

Before considering the changing views of urbanism as a field of study informing good cities, it is worth reviewing other views of progress that emerged in the 1960s and 70s. The industrial transformation of the post-war years, and urban growth, had left a discernible mark on the pre-industrial landscape. The conversion of farmland to housing tracts was a common feature, and the location of industry on the edge of cities destroyed pre-existing views and natural features. The scale of change fostered doubts about the benefits of progress as a movement, doubts that had existed for as long as industrial and demographic change had been visible as engines of modernity. Despite the term "baby boom" when referring to the fertility spike of the post-war years, in Europe and the US the demographic transition was effectively complete by 1970 (Livi-Bacci 1992, p.93). This was not the case in Asia and Latin America, where the population was growing at rates indicative of a transition in mid-phase. This can be illustrated in a number of ways, but perhaps the simplest indicator is the Total Fertility Rate (TFR) for various regions. This only reveals half of the picture – the other half is the declining death rate that accompanies a transition, leading to a dramatic increase in population over a short period. Nonetheless it is useful for understanding the concern, indeed hysteria, with which population in developing countries came to be viewed. Figure 5.1 gives the TFR for selected countries and regions averaged over two five-year periods, 1950–1955 and 1995–2000.

The figure clearly shows the differences in TFR between Europe and North America, on the one hand, and developing countries on the other in the 1950s. It also shows that the high TFRs for developing regions outside of Africa were nonetheless linked to a demographic transition that was largely completed by the turn of the 21st century. However, the raw data, in the 1960s, was widely interpreted as a potentially uncontained Malthusian disaster. The concept of runaway population growth beyond the industrialised world, and possibly within it, dominated the popular imagination, and indeed the scientific one: in 1968 biologist Paul Ehrlich published his widely influential book *The Population Bomb* (Ehrlich 1968).

The spectre of Malthus was thus re-invoked, and the new computer technology which allowed a set of rules to run through thousands of iterations was used to extrapolate the consequences of exponential population growth. This approach was used in a set of exercises commissioned by the Club of Rome, a private think-tank founded by industrialists and scientists in 1968

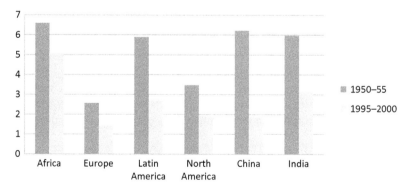

Figure 5.1 Total Fertility Rates, selected regions
Adapted from Livi-Bacci (1992, Table 5.2)

to ask and attempt to answer questions around the future of humanity. The first notable product of this vast remit, using computers, was the 1972 report titled *The Limits to Growth: a Report for the Club of Rome's Project on the Predicament of Mankind*, authored by a team led by Donella and Dennis Meadows of MIT. The book was based on computer simulations of the interaction of five variables: "population, agricultural production, natural resources, industrial production, and pollution" (Meadows, Meadows, Randers & Behrens 1972, pp.11–12). The introduction quotes UN Secretary General U Thant, who states that the world has perhaps ten years (from 1972) to address the most pressing problems of humanity, which includes "the population explosion" (Meadows *et al.* 1972, p.17).

The book is a fascinating document of an integrated model of world development based on assumptions around each of the five variables. The method is historical, that is the authors attempted to model the rate of growth of each of the variables based on historical data from 1900 to 1970, and to use a compounding model of growth to extrapolate future trends. These are then combined into a global model, based on assumed interactions between the rates of growth of all variables. When run on a business-as-usual scenario, the model predicted rapid growth in all variables, but with population eventually decreasing rapidly due to lack of food and medical services. The report firmly established in the popular Western imagination the principle of compounding growth and its exponential effects, and the prospect of crises developing as these effects exhausted available resources.

The argument itself, based as it is on an historically derived model, makes few claims to insight into factors that could alter the predicted outcomes. Despite this qualification, it fed into the prevailing disillusionment with progress that had taken hold in advanced economies. Rachel Carson's book also has an echo, as the accumulation of the insecticide DDT in fish and soil is modelled according to rates of application. The most notable aspect of the book is its assumption that the rates of growth observed historically could not change without the application of specific policies. Without committing to a specific political model to determine policies, the tenor of the book relies on coercive measures to reduce population growth, or industrial growth, to desired levels. As a counter to the prospect of economic and population collapse, the authors play with scenarios for stabilised growth rates that would postpone or eliminate their modelled disasters, at least to the limits of their time horizon. Along with a TFR at replacement level, capital stability – where investment equals depreciation and capital only replaces plant and equipment as it wears out – is a key factor in their model of global equilibrium. However, this still entails slow resource depletion and no economic growth, so taking steps towards technical efficiency becomes important for increasing yields and decreasing the rate at which minerals and fuels are used.

The Limits to Growth both embodied a distinct form of rationalist thinking using mathematical modelling, and gave impetus to this approach in speculations about economic and social policies. The models, as the authors admit, are accurate only within the limits of their understanding of the processes they represent. The view of humanity they rest on is crude, and the exercise underlines why Malthus devoted so much time to understanding the many ways that people instituted their own checks against population growth which exceeded the food supply in pre-industrial times. Humanity as a whole, in *The Limits to Growth*, seems blind, fecund and stupid.

In the study the components of a demographic transition are poorly understood, although the initial condition of declining death rates is a driver of the population modelling. Birth control is perhaps the most widely modelled intervention, although the European demographic transition which preceded the book occurred without modern contraception or coercive measures. The power of cultural factors is paid lip service, but the book entrenches a view of expert guidance on significant matters using key metrics as the authors interpret them.

The conflation of metrics or indicators with the processes they represent has become a hallmark of futurist speculation, for cities as much as for anything else. Although *The Limits to Growth* charts the shift from countryside to towns and cities worldwide, the book does not distinguish between urban and rural issues, nor between those affecting advanced economies and those affecting developing ones. Also absent is the recognition that capitalism is, by its nature, technologically progressive, and advanced economies require less energy per unit of GDP over time. This important trend is illustrated in Figure 5.2.

Because energy is an input in all modern production, there is a continuing incentive to use less in order to increase the efficiency, and profitability, of production. This does not necessarily translate into less overall, just into less per unit produced. If the whole sector expands, it may be more efficient over time in making a single widget, but if the total number of widgets increases then the total energy consumption may rise.

This trend is gentle but pronounced over time, and in the case of Germany, for example, Total Primary Energy Consumption has declined between 1991 and 2012 (EIA n.d.). We shall return to this trend in more detail later, but

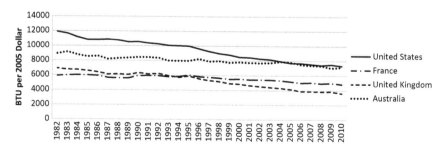

Figure 5.2 Energy intensity per dollar GDP, selected countries
Source: EIA (n.d., International Energy Statistics)

the point here is that the simple models that underpinned the scenarios in *The Limits to Growth* were deficient in key respects. However, the sentiments within the book remained widely influential, and summed up the tenor of the times. As crime rates in US cities soared through the 1970s, the promised cornucopia of benefits implied in economic growth seemed to be transforming into a collection of ills that called into question the very premises of progress.

Dystopic urban life seemed the fate not only of America, but of rapidly urbanising societies across the world. Mexico City, Bombay (Mumbai), Rio de Janeiro or Lagos became ciphers for the alienation that accompanied modern life as millions drifted or were driven off agricultural land into cities. The role of cities in effecting the transition from traditional to modern life was hardly acknowledged, but the widespread poverty that seemed endemic to emerging cities confirmed Western prejudices about the inherent healthiness of rural life, its precariousness notwithstanding.

Within the academic environment of the US and Europe, the loss of faith in progress and the poor prospects for the kind of effective revolution that had animated modern Marxism produced a curious intellectual dead end. Fostering the new and using shock as a means of jolting society forward ceased to be a progressive activity in itself. The imperative to criticise that is a necessary condition for intellectual life took an increasingly nostalgic turn, as aspects of the past that had been swept away suddenly seemed to contain a simplicity and immediacy absent from modern life. In this atmosphere the works of Jacobs, the Frankfurt School and critical trends that did not imply revolutionary action, such as Structuralism, took on a topical sheen (Anderson 1983).

The dilemmas they represented were real enough. The modern city had moved far enough from its interwar incarnation by 1970 to make even that period a source of nostalgia. The animated streets and public events of the streetcar city seemed to hold a vitality that the diffuse suburban city could not match. In the US the decline of inner cities seemed particularly cruel since it went further than in Europe, and in cities that had been harbingers of urbanity. A century after Chicago fostered so many of the technical advances that made the modern city a reality, the great experiment seemed to have run its course.

Architecture and city planning gave form to these prevailing views and sentiments. The welfare state, a post-war phenomenon of class reconciliation based on progressive taxation, provided the means for financing public housing schemes that aimed to house those whom the market failed. This had been an ideal of planners and architects since the 1930s, but the large rehousing schemes of the post-war years hardly altered modernism's reputation as charmless. It was not only the physical appearance of the projects that seemed unappealing: the destruction of street life was equally dismaying. Jacobs' critique of modern urban life took on an increasing potency, and by 1970 the reputation of building and city design was at an historically low ebb.

The counter movement that emerged was perhaps inevitable in the form it took, but its contradictions and ideals remain extremely influential into the present. In architecture the initial reaction was termed Post-Modernism, a clear sign that it defined itself against the tenets of high modernism. Its mode of thinking was different too. Modernism had placed a high premium on abstraction, whereby the problem at hand is analysed beyond its immediate appearance to uncover processes and tendencies that need to be reconciled. Hence its relative indifference to charm and nostalgia, since neither aided the radical rethinking of contemporary problems using rationalism as a tool to see beyond surface appearance. Post-Modernism sought to recover a measure of comfort through making buildings that copied historical details and forms, and looked to the traditional European city for its models.

No practitioner was more skilled at this than Leon Krier, a Luxembourg native who started his career in the late 1960s, initially experimenting with modernist architectural forms to produce building designs that restored symbolic power and interest to civic places and individual buildings. Krier built almost nothing, but his polemical skills were unparalleled. By 1970 he was making skilful drawings of proposals that drew on the charm of pre-modern towns and construction methods, and the design movement based on the traditional European city as a source of building types and streetscapes gathered momentum. In his drawings lay all the allure of an idealised city environment of vistas, elegant streets and places that were personalised and understandable in traditional terms. The accusation levelled against modernism was that it was incomprehensible. Charles Jencks made fun of the modernist master Mies van der Rohe by describing his IIT chapel as appearing to be a factory (Jencks 2002). Following on the efforts of Gordon Cullen to make urban places distinctive and memorable, Krier made the city understandable with avenues and spires, squares and porticoes (Cullen 1961).

Whereas Jacobs had advocated for cities with distinctly modern densities, Krier advocated for cities that took their scale from Medieval towns. His ideal urban quarter was self-contained, and numbered 10,000 people in 33 hectares. This density of about 300 people per hectare is less than half that advocated by Jacobs, and shows Krier's reluctance to rely on modern urban infrastructure. His disquiet is explicit in his charter for the reconstruction of the European city, developed from 1978 onwards. It states

> Industrial forms of production – the extreme development of productive means and forces – in less than 200 years have destroyed cultures and traditions, landscapes and cities, which are the culmination of centuries of human work and thought, of skill and intelligence; they now erode resources and fundamental values without which humanity cannot live. (Krier 1992, p.16)

This statement sums up the motivation for Krier's work, stoked by the transformation of his home city of Luxembourg in the 1980s. It is emblematic of the popular critique of architecture and planning, and gives voice to the concerns embedded in the designs Krier produced. These were widely published and attracted the attention not only of architects but of all designers and planners working with cities.

Krier's fundamental position was the rejection of zoning, which divided up modern cities accorded to function. The basic premise of zoning is that functions such as shopping, living and manufacturing are incompatible when mixed together, and they need to be separated physically into homogenous zones. For heavy manufacturing this made evident sense, as the processes produced smoke and noise that made life unpleasant and indeed unhealthy in adjoining houses. However, it also outlawed the traditional urban form of street shopfronts, residential apartments and small-scale workshops that made up the fabric of pre-industrial Paris, for example. Krier's vision of superseding the industrial city relies on returning to its pre-industrial forms. Ironically it was only the demise of heavy manufacturing in advanced economies that made this a possibility.

It was in the fields of planning and urban design that Krier's visions achieved lasting influence. In 1993 architect Andres Duany convened a meeting of city and building designers in Alexandria, Virginia, to formalise the prescriptions of Krier and like-minded urbanists. The result was the Congress for the New Urbanism (CNU), which published the first edition of its Charter in 1999 (Barnett 2011, p.103). This is a comprehensive set of rules and guidelines to re-humanise the modern city, in particular the modern American city. The historical moment that the CNU attempted to seize was the evident decline in many US cities as their heavy industry either shut down due to the advent of more efficient processes, or the work was sent overseas to countries with lower labour costs.

The CNU was perhaps the most concrete response to the challenges of the post-industrial city as they appeared at the time of its founding, but its vision is not restricted to the simple restoration of a pre-modern civility to cities. It may not have prescriptions for the post-industrial economy as a whole, but certain assumptions are implicit in its programme. The first is the alignment of city and town design with environmentalist concerns for "climate change mitigation, pollution control, natural resource preservation" in addition to the more conventional concerns of "economic development, housing and transportation" (Talen 2013, p.15). The environmental concerns reflect a distinctly millenarian mix which combines the assumptions of Meadows *et al.* of increasing pollution and resource depletion with the widespread concern about the degree to which increasing carbon dioxide in the atmosphere would raise terrestrial and ocean temperatures.

This confluence of concerns is by now widely known, but it is worth separating its components and their lineages. The founding of the US Environmental Protection Agency in 1970 gave legislative clout for controlling and reducing industrial pollution. The widespread perception of declining air and water quality due to industrial effluents and gasses was backed up with scientific testing, and the ability to fine industries who exceeded specific standards of acceptability. These initiatives were not new: what was significant was the creation of a single national body, the EPA, which brought together existing departments from a host of separate arms of Federal administration. The hearings held by the House Government Operations Subcommittee in 1970 were thus on the topic of reorganisation to create a single administrative body rather than the need for environmental controls *per se*. In the Senate subcommittee hearings Senator Jacob Javits spoke in favour of the

> very strong and overdue effort to arrest and prevent the erosion of the priceless resources of all mankind and also to preserve that most priceless asset, the human being himself, who, in a singularly polluted atmosphere, may find it impossible to exist. (EPA 1992)

The motor car was perhaps the most visible polluter, at least in terms of numbers. Its negative effects were well noted by 1970, alongside the recent success of pollution control legislation. The total volume of hydrocarbon emissions from cars in Los Angeles declined from 1965 to 1969 due to mandatory controls, as did carbon monoxide volumes (Rae 1971, p.343). The car was also a major determinant of urban form, and the simple convenience of the car seemed to have set cities on an inexorable path to auto dependence. The two economic shocks precipitated by massive increases in oil prices in 1973 and 1979 underlined the strategic vulnerability of non-oil-producing nations to variations in supply and cost. Since cities depended on cars, and cars depended largely on imported oil, the functioning of cities was inherently tied to the vicissitudes of distant oil politics and geological accidents of history.

By 1982 a leading motoring historian could document the effects of cars on urban health through the noise and emissions they produced, the congestion they caused, and the injuries and deaths they caused through accidents (Chanaron 1982). Absent from this list was the prospect of climate change through accumulation of carbon dioxide in the atmosphere. Global warming and climate change emerged as issues in the 1990s, but the problems of car travel were well recognised before then. However, as new cars replaced old, major cities saw dramatic improvements in air quality. Tetraethyl lead had been added to fuel since the 1920s to boost octane ratings and allow greater compression, and to reduce valve wear. It has now been phased out in all advanced economies, and is almost universally illegal due to concerns about accumulation in human tissue, with toxic effects. The fitting of catalytic converters to cars since the 1970s has had a major impact on air quality, as these devices convert poisonous carbon monoxide and unburned fuel to carbon dioxide and water. Modern devices also reduce nitrous oxide emissions. The effects of these technological improvements on air quality in Los Angeles can be seen in three decades of EPA indicators of air quality shown in Table 5.1. The first figure is the second highest average eight hour measure of carbon monoxide for the year in parts per million (PPM), and the second

Table 5.1 Car related pollutants in Los Angeles, 1980–2010

Year	Carbon monoxide (PPM)	Nitrogen dioxide (PPB)
1980	24.9	350
1990	15.9	240
2000	9.9	129
2010	3.6	73

Source: EPA (n.d.-b, Airdata Reports)

figure shows the 98th percentile of the daily maximum one hour measurement of nitrogen dioxide in parts per billion (PPB). These measurements are designed for consistent comparison of actual pollution levels.

Thus the technology built into modern motor cars has made considerable inroads into air pollution, but the cleaner burning engines tend to produce greater volumes of carbon dioxide. This is not a pollutant in the traditional sense of being an industrially produced irritant or poison: it is produced by all air-breathing animals, and is essential to the photosynthesis of plant matter. The major concern with carbon dioxide is its effect at rising concentrations in the atmosphere, where it absorbs solar radiation that has been re-radiated from the earth's surface at specific wavelengths. This process has entered the popular imagination as the greenhouse effect.

Thus the early assumption of toxic pollution as an inevitable and increasing consequence of industrialisation has given way to the more specific concern of atmospheric greenhouse gasses accumulating and causing regional and global climate change. It is an important distinction to make, because the idea of the city as an emitter of pollution through industrial processes renders its image fundamentally unappealing, and the city becomes the source of its own demise. The issue of climate change is different. Since atmospheric carbon dioxide is diffuse, its effects occur at regional scales and not at the point of release. The autonomous rural house that was viewed as an ideal antidote to city life in the 1970s and 80s has lost its potency as the concerns about the toxicity of pollution have waned. Instead the prospect of the city as a possible solution to rising carbon dioxide levels has gained currency.

The combination of the New Urbanism with proposals for reducing carbon dioxide emissions has proven potent. Since the New Urbanism is antithetical to industrial production, and draws heavily on an idealised artisanal vision for making things, it proposes to reintegrate all the components of the pre-industrial city into a compact form that reduces the need for private car use. From the outset this has been a core principle of New Urbanism, and walkability, or the reduction of car use for everyday purposes has been one of its defining characteristics. Its concerns are "the placelessness of modern suburbs, the decline of central cities, the growing separation in communities by race and income, and the environmental damage brought on by auto-dependent development" (Talen 2013, p.xiii).

This attack on the dominant form of post-war development in the US, Australia, New Zealand and increasingly parts of Europe and Asia is predicated on a bias against suburbs as causes of profligacy, particularly in energy use. The establishment of the Intergovernmental Panel on Climate Change (IPCC) in 1988 made carbon dioxide emissions reduction an international aim of various arms of the United Nations, in a programme which has subsequently been embraced by governments to varying degrees across the world. Thus the imperative to reduce car usage is driven not only by a desire to return to the walkable pre-industrial town or urban quarter, but also by the rational exigency, supported at international level, of reducing carbon dioxide emissions.

Two points need to be made here. The first is that there is a vast natural flux of carbon dioxide annually, driven by ocean absorption and release, as well as the spring growth and fall shedding of trees and shrubs in the northern hemisphere, among other things. The natural addition and subtraction of carbon dioxide from the atmosphere is many times greater than human, or anthropogenic, emissions. However, the quantity of carbon dioxide released through the burning of fossil fuels is at an historical high, and this adds to the annual carbon cycle. Thus all discussion about reducing emissions relies on estimates of the surcharge imposed on the natural cycle by gases released through human activity. According to the EPA, carbon dioxide makes up 77% of heat-trapping atmospheric gases produced by humanity, with the rest comprising mainly methane and nitrous oxide. About three-quarters of anthropogenic carbon dioxide is emitted through the burning of fossil fuels to release their energy, with the remainder coming from changes in land use such as removing forests and releasing the carbon stored in trees.

The EPA also provides a good summary of the global sources of greenhouse gasses by sector and activity. The largest proportion, 26%, comes from burning fossil fuels to create electricity and heat. Industry produces 19% to fuel its processes, excluding electricity production. Cars, trucks, trains, planes and ships release another 13%. Buildings produce about 8%, mainly from heating systems and gas stoves, but exclusive of electricity. The rest comes from agriculture and forestry operations, but again excluding any associated transportation or electricity use (EPA n.d.-a). Thus the second point derives from the breakdown above. While the car may be the most visible source of carbon dioxide in everyday life, it is by no means the dominant one worldwide. The implications of the various sources of greenhouse gasses for urban form will be taken up in the last chapter, but the focus on the car as the major threat to urban life has a qualitative aspect as well as a quantitative one. One may dislike what the car does to cities irrespective of what comes out of its tailpipe. But disliking both is a powerful driver of urban policy.

The focus on cars is better understood if we look at the breakdown of US sources of carbon dioxide. According to the EPA, electricity generation in the US accounts for 38% of carbon dioxide emissions, and transport 32%. Within transport, the breakdown by fuel type is given in Figure 5.3.

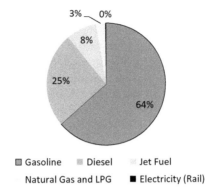

3% — 0%

8%

25%

64%

☐ Gasoline   ▨ Diesel   ▨ Jet Fuel

Natural Gas and LPG   ■ Electricity (Rail)

Figure 5.3 Carbon dioxide emissions by fuel type in transportation, US 2012
Adapted from EPA (2014, Table 3-12)

The breakdown by fuel reveals the type of vehicle producing the carbon dioxide. Gasoline is overwhelmingly the dominant fuel in cars and light trucks, while diesel is used for heavy trucks and to a lesser extent (about 13%) rail and buses. A small fleet of light vehicles use natural gas and LPG, and the electricity used by rail is effectively negligible. As one of the most car-dependent societies on earth, these figures represent one extreme of carbon dioxide emission sources. The figures also reveal a trend within some advanced economies, where the total of CO_2 emissions is in decline. In the US this reduction amounted to about 12% between 2005 and 2012.

The differences in fossil fuel usage by sector between the US and the world as a whole underlines the problem of assuming that the issues of an advanced economy are mirrored elsewhere. The push to reduce car usage emanates from countries like the US, which have had very high rates of ownership for some decades. The net effect of this has been the spread of cities because the energy required to sustain this on a day to day basis has been available and affordable. It has also provided working-class Americans with unprecedented mobility, and made internal travel possible for almost anyone. This in turn has created exceptional fluidity in the American labour market, with a population willing and able to relocate to distant regions as opportunities become available. The effect of this mobility cannot be underestimated, as it enlarges the pool of possible applicants for full-time jobs by orders of magnitude compared to previous eras.

In the tram age, employment, housing and shopping developed in a largely radial pattern, with lines converging on the city centre. The motor car has leapfrogged this structure, which is still evident in most cities that expanded before 1950. Private car ownership has allowed enormous latitude for owners to decide where to live and where to work, whose locations increasingly bear little resemblance to the radial structure of public transport. In practice this is limited by the time and expense of driving, but people are surprisingly hardy in how much of either they will tolerate. Despite this, the notion of the city as distinct quarters or neighbourhoods has taken hold of planning and urban design ideals since the formulations of New Urbanism were set down.

The logic is easy to follow. If car use is to decline, then the more aspects of everyday life that lie within walking distance the better. This would make cars unnecessary except for journeys outside of the urban quarter or neighbourhood. Two conditions are needed for this. One is the reversal of zoning, so that all functions of daily life, including work, retail and entertainment, can physically exist together. The second is an increase in density of dwellings by building higher and closer together, as this increases the number of customers per length of urban street for retail and entertainment, and increases the potential number of establishments within walking distance of each dwelling. In effect this seems mutually beneficial if the city is viewed primarily as a place of consumption and social exchange.

This, in sum, is how the modern Western, and increasingly Eastern, city is regarded. The shift in thinking needed both the critique of progress that emerged in the 1960s and the transformation of manufacturing in the subsequent decades. Few Western cities retain heavy industry, and the red glow of cooling steel furnaces at night has disappeared from their visual lexicon. Inner-city power stations have shut down or been converted to other uses, as electricity generation takes place well outside city limits near coalfields or cooling water sources. These modern plants achieve energy conversion rates of up to 40% for coal, compared to about 15% in 1925. They are not only efficient, but they also require a staff numbering in the tens to oversee regular operations, making them relatively small employers. Most visible markers of the industrial age have gone from historical city precincts in Western societies, either displaced to the edge or into rural zones, or sent overseas. At the same time the efficiency of modern agriculture has reduced the number of people involved in farming to historic lows. With the bulk of modern populations working in service industries, the energy underpinning all of modern urban life has become all but invisible apart from personal transportation.

It is salient to note the shifts in employment over the past century. In Australia these figures are particularly instructive, since the country moved from a largely agricultural base to a service economy over this time. It is still a major exporter of wheat, wool, cotton and meat, but this employs such a small proportion of the workforce that their experience and interests struggle to be visible on the national agenda. Equally prominent in export dollars are the extractive industries, especially iron ore and coal, but again these operations are rarely visible in everyday life. A full breakdown by sector is useful as a snapshot of an advanced economy that not only feeds itself, but exports food and minerals in significant quantities (Figure 5.4).

The figures show the number of workers, and their proportion to the overall workforce, who staff the various areas of productive life. These numbers underline the enormous shift away from primary production and extraction, towards the service sector generally. The figures for basic utilities, agriculture and mining – the sectors that feed, water and power everyday

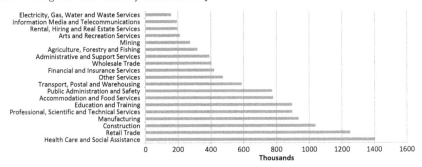

Figure 5.4 Australian employment by sector, 2013
Adapted from Vandenbroek (2014)

life – are surprisingly small, numbering 157,000 for utilities, 319,000 for
agriculture and its branches and about 275,000 for mining (which includes
coal extraction). Collectively this makes up 751,000 people out of a working
population of 11.646 million, or 6.45%. Manufacturing and construction
make up another 1.972 million jobs, or 16.9% of the total workforce. The
remainder, over three-quarters of all jobs and professions, are concerned
with the distribution and delivery of goods and services.

Taken as a proportion of the total population, which still has to be fed,
powered and watered, the figures are at absolute historical lows. For mining,
agriculture and utilities it represents some 3.25% of the Australian population. Another way of looking at the figures is to use the broad breakdown as
presented by the CIA *World Factbook* (CIA n.d.). While there are problems
in comparing these figures due to differing ways statistics are collected, they
nevertheless provide a snapshot of the degree of transition taken by countries towards modern service-dominated economies. Percentages are given in
the *Factbook* for the proportion of the labour force involved in agriculture,
industry and services. A sample is presented in Table 5.2.

Table 5.2 Percentage employment by sector, selected countries

	Agriculture %	Industry %	Services %
Brazil	15.7	13.3	51
Cambodia	55.8	16.9	27.3
China	33.6	30.3	36.1
Ethiopia	85	5	10
Nigeria	70	10	20
Poland	12.9	30.2	57
Singapore	1.3	18.6	80.1
United States	0.7	20.3	79

Adapted from CIA (n.d.). US figures consolidated

The extremes for agriculture, in countries with substantial land area, range from 85% in Ethiopia to 0.7% in the US, dramatically illustrating the substitution of labour power by mechanised farming in modern agribusiness. This reduction is powered almost entirely by fossil fuels. The volume of coal and iron ore extracted by a modern workforce is also staggering. The largest mining haul trucks can carry loads of over 400 tonnes at speeds in excess of 50 kilometres per hour. Machine loaded and unloaded to rail and then to ships, they mechanically magnify the effectiveness of a single driver by a factor of 100,000 compared to hand haulage.

The broader point is the transformed labour structure of modern societies, and its effect on the perception of how everyday life is sustained. In the case of modern cities, the overwhelming predominance of services and retail creates the illusion that these are the essential components of economic activity. The largest consumers of fossil fuels, electricity generators, are all but hidden on a daily basis. Agriculture, too, remains outside the urban purview, its products subject to ever-increasing sophistication as they are marketed as if they come from small-scale traditional farms. The reality of modern agribusiness, its volumes and efficiency, belie this sleight of hand.

In modern cities the net effect has been to conflate consumption with urban life. The modern concept of urban vitality is predicated on the city as a place of eating, entertainment, social interaction and a set of experiences that relies on fine-grained choices made possible by the anonymity and diversity of urban populations. The demise of the suburb is not so much a result of the compelling argument for doing away with cars. Rather it is that the old urban middle- and working-class notion of the city as the site for the production and reproduction of the nuclear family is in retreat, carrying with it the magnified anxieties of class, security and stability that attend family life. The result is an urban cool, glossing over these old anxieties not because it is so generous in spirit but because it has minimal emotional investment. It is not defensive because it has nothing to defend.

The push to reduce car usage has extended beyond the twin arguments of reducing carbon dioxide emissions, and restoring density and vitality to urban centres. The former carries a compelling logic that attempts to stave off the consequences of car usage as understood rationally. The latter is a preference that describes what cities might be as places of consumption and entertainment. To these another dimension has been added in recent years, that of the dense city as a therapeutic place. The transition to service economies has changed the physical characteristics of modern populations. They are taller and longer lived, but generally fatter and undertake less exercise. The relationship between these factors is complex, and they often coexist in the same population. Body Mass Index is a crude measure of the ratio of weight to height, and is widely used to determine how overweight a population is. Rising BMIs in developed service-oriented economies have led to calls for urban forms that force people to walk more by increasing public transport usage through denser urban development. This meshes with other arguments for increased density in cities, and is a consequence of the over-availability of food energy through modern farming methods and food processing.

The cultural extension of this trend has seen the vilification of weight gain in popular culture. In ancient times a symbol of affluence, body fat has become associated with poor self-control and indolence. The distinction between the medically obese and the merely overweight has been smudged, and compact city form has been dragooned into the service of the assault on fat. Frumkin, Frank and Jackson laid out the tenets of this connection in their 2004 book *Urban Sprawl and Public Health: Designing, Planning and Building for Healthy Communities*. Despite concluding that "Not only are environmental interventions only one part of the solution to physical inactivity, but in most studies their impact is relatively modest" the authors press for more walkable cities as part of the solution to lack of exercise (Frumkin, Frank & Jackson 2004, p.106).

The book also raises older health concerns such as air quality, motor accidents, water quality and mental health, despite indices for the first three showing consistent improvement for developed cities, and connections between urban sprawl and mental health proving spurious at best. Nonetheless the book is indicative of the alignment of health concerns behind the general trend to denser cities and less car use.

Proponents for suburban development have been hard to find in the current intellectual climate, despite suburbia continuing to be the dominant form of housing development in developed economies, and in many developing ones. The declining urban densities charted by Angel (2012) show that reversal occurs only when urban densities reach very low thresholds. Many developing cities record dramatic declines in overall density as they modernise, often from the very dense form associated with poverty and overcrowding. The concentric rings of Beijing's expansion, for example, show enormous declines in density for each phase. Wendell Cox divides the city into an Inner Core, First Ring Suburbs (within the Fifth Ring Road) and Second Ring Suburbs. He estimates the population density for these urban areas, which grew outwards over time, as 235, 75 and 8 people per hectare respectively, although the last includes considerable tracts that are still rural (Cox 2011a).

A similar pattern prevails in Mumbai, where the inner-city population experienced a small increase from 1961, but declined between 2001 and 2010. After 1961 the bulk of growth occurred in suburban areas, but these too became saturated in the new millennium, when growth moved to the neighbouring district of Thane. Despite an overall decline in density since a modern peak in 1950, the prevalence of slums has kept the average urban density high at about 324 people per hectare. By comparison, Singapore overall has 109 per hectare, and Sydney 20 (Demographia 2015).

These declines are not absolute, according to Cox. After years of losing inhabitants to the suburbs, and gentrification reducing the average number of inhabitants per dwelling, the core of Milan has seen a rise in population in recent years due to immigrants, often poor, from outside Italy who are drawn to the opportunities of the city. However, the suburbs of Milan continue to account for the bulk of population growth in the region, a pattern characteristic of most Western European cities. Despite the widespread critique of car-dominated cities, the arguments for reversing declines in density have had little effect on development patterns across major metropolises. The same is true for US cities. While international migrants are drawn to inner-city areas, internal domestic migration shows little evidence of a return to the traditional city core (Demographia 2011; Cox 2011b).

Two major trends thus mark attitudes to urban development in the influential centres of Western thinking. The first is the negative reaction, now over four decades old, to the modern city, especially its suburban dimension. The argument against the car as the means by which cities exist in dispersed form has traversed air quality, safety, diminished neighbourhood cohesion, an anodyne urban experience, climate change and the health effects of less walking. The tenets of the New Urbanism are now widely followed in urban design and planning. Urban Growth Boundaries have been implemented in a number of cities, most notably Portland, Oregon, to contain the physical size of cities and force growth upwards rather than outwards.

The second trend is the extrapolation of these conclusions to the centres of urbanisation in developing economies. This is highly problematic, as these cities find themselves at different points in the trajectory of national or regional development compared to cities in advanced economies. The particular demographics, labour markets, industrial bases and energy sources of developing cities that prevail give a different developmental form and logic to each. Many have very different job profiles to advanced economies, and their class structure may also be profoundly different. For any coherent strategy to be advanced for these cities, both in terms of physical development and energy, they need to be placed within the developmental cycles that shape their form and thrust.

Bibliography

Anderson, P. (1983). *In the tracks of historical materialism*. London: Verso.

Angel, S. (2012). *Planet of cities*. Cambridge, MA: Lincoln Institute of Land Policy.

Barnett, J. (2011). *City design: Modernist, traditional, green, and systems perspectives*. Abingdon, Oxon: Routledge.

Carson, R. (1962). *Silent spring*. Boston: Houghton Mifflin.

Castells, M. (1977). *The urban question: A Marxist approach*. Cambridge, MA: MIT Press.

Chanaron, J. (1982). The automobile under fire. In J. Bardou (Ed.), *The automobile revolution: The impact of an industry*. Chapel Hill, NC: University of North Carolina Press.

Chandler, T., & Fox, G. (1974). *3000 years of urban growth*. New York: Academic Press.

CIA (Central Intelligence Agency) (n.d.). *The World Factbook: Labor Force – by occupation*. Retrieved September 7, 2015, from www.cia.gov/library/publications/the-world-factbook/fields/2048.html

Cox, W. (2011a, August 29). The evolving urban form: Beijing. *NewGeography*. Retrieved July 30, 2015, from www.newgeography.com/content/002406-the-evolving-urban-form-beijing

Cox, W. (2011b, September 14). The evolving urban form: Milan. *NewGeography*. Retrieved July 30, 2015, from www.newgeography.com/content/002441-the-evolving-urban-form-milan

Cullen, G. (1961). *The concise townscape*. London: Architectural Press.

Demographia (2011). *Migration: Metropolitan regions in Western Europe*. Retrieved July 30, 2015, from www.demographia.com/db-eurcitymigra.pdf

Demographia (2015). *Demographia world urban areas* (11th ed.). Belleville, IL: Demographia.

Ehrlich, P. (1968). *The population bomb*. New York: Ballantine Books.

EIA (Energy Information Administration) (n.d.). U.S. Energy Information Administration – EIA – Independent statistics and analysis. Retrieved September 7, 2015, from www.eia.gov

EPA (Environmental Protection Agency) (1992). *The Guardian*: Origins of the EPA. Retrieved September 7, 2015, from www2.epa.gov/aboutepa/guardian-origins-epa

EPA (Environmental Protection Agency) (n.d.-a). *Global emissions*. Retrieved September 7, 2015, from www.epa.gov/climatechange/ghgemissions/global.html

EPA (Environmental Protection Agency) (n.d.-b). Retrieved September 7, 2015, from www.epa.gov/airdata/ad_rep_con.html

EPA (Environmental Protection Agency) (2014). Inventory of US greenhouse gas emissions and sinks. Retrieved September 7, 2015, from www.epa.gov/climatechange/Downloads/ghgemissions/US-GHG-Inventory-2014-Chapter-3-Energy.pdf

Frumkin, H., Frank, L., & Jackson, R. (2004). *Urban sprawl and public health: Designing, planning, and building for healthy communities*. Washington, DC: Island Press.

Harvey, D. (1973). *Social justice and the city*. Baltimore: The Johns Hopkins University Press.

Heidegger, M. (1962). *Being and time*. New York: Harper.

Jacobs, J. (1961). *The death and life of great American cities*. New York: Random House.

Jencks, C. (2002). *The new paradigm in architecture: The language of post-modern architecture* (7th ed.). New Haven: Yale University Press.

Krier, L. (1992). *Leon Krier: Architecture and urban design, 1967–1992* (D. Porphyrios, Ed.). London: Academy Editions.

Lasch, C. (1978). *The culture of narcissism: American life in an age of diminishing expectations*. New York: Norton.

Lefebvre, H. (1971). *Everyday life in the modern world*. New York: Harper & Row.

Livi-Bacci, M. (1992). *A concise history of world population*. Cambridge, MA: Blackwell.

Mandel, E. (1975). *Late capitalism* (rev. ed.). London: NLB.

Meadows, D., Meadows, D., Randers, J., & Behrens III, W. (1972). *The limits to growth: A report for the Club of Rome's project on the predicament of mankind*. New York: Universe Books.

Rae, J. (1971). *The road and the car in American life*. Cambridge, MA: MIT Press.

Sennett, R. (1978). *The fall of public man*. New York: Vintage Books.

Talen, E. (Ed.). (2013). *Charter of the new urbanism: Congress for the new urbanism* (2nd ed.). New York: McGraw Hill.

Vandenbroek, P. (2014, February 14). *Snapshot of employment by industry, 2012 to 2013.* Retrieved September 7, 2015, from www.aph.gov.au/About_Parliament/Parliam entary_Departments/Parliamentary_Library/FlagPost/2014/February/Employm ent-by-industry-2012-13

6 Shifting production and consumption
Developing economies

As we approach the third decade of the 21st century, the issues of urban development appear to devolve into two broad groups of cities – those that have evolved over the first wave of industrialisation, mainly in Europe and North America, and those in emerging economies in Asia, South America and Africa. While there is a great deal of common ground between these cities, there are also distinct differences that reflect the differing circumstances and periods of growth for each city.

This chapter is devoted to the emerging city – those urban areas that are experiencing rapid, and in many cases uncontrolled, growth in countries that are transforming and seeing a large shift in population from country to city or town. The dramatic statement that more than half of the world's population is now urbanised hides a significant qualifying fact. Of the global urban dwellers, over half live in cities and towns of less than 500,000 inhabitants, while about 12% live in mega-cities of 10 million or more. The cities growing most rapidly are those with between half a million and a million inhabitants, although the number of mega-cities will rise over the next 15 years from 28 to 41 (United Nations Population Division 2014).

Thus the picture of the modern urban dweller is not necessarily someone living in the opulent parts of Mumbai, or in its teeming slums. It is equally likely to be a Brazilian in a small regional town, or a suburbanite in Raleigh, NC. The characteristic that links all these people is that they are connected to modernity in a way that rural people traditionally have not been. They will have better access to clean water, electricity, education and health services. They are also more likely to be transformed in their beliefs and aspirations, and have a better chance of finding work that suits these aspirations, as well as moving up the class structure. They will probably work in the service sector, or in manufacturing (Yap 2012, p.15). Urbanisation is now widely seen as desirable for the opportunities it opens up, and for the changes it brings to populations.

Before considering these changes, it is worth revisiting the seemingly obvious question: what drives urbanisation? The three factors long cited have been naturally increasing urban populations as life expectancy grows, rural to urban migration and the incorporation of surrounding villages and towns into a growing city. Each one of these, however, is not fixed but fluctuates as countries change in their economic structure, demographic makeup and urban aspirations. The role played by natural increase in the existing urban population, for example, has become negligible for many cities across the globe because urbanites have lower fertility rates than rural dwellers. This is obviously true for countries like Australia and Spain, where the overall Total Fertility Rate (TFR) is below replacement level nationally. However, even in Asian countries where the national TFR might be above 2.1, the urban rate tends to be significantly lower than the rural rate. In the Philippines the 2003 urban TFR was 3, while the rural rate was 4.3. In 2007 Indonesia the corresponding urban/rural figures were 2.3 and 2.8 respectively. In major cities the figures are lower again (Yap 2012, p.17).

The consolidation of surrounding areas into cities has been a feature of urban expansion historically, and it serves as a driver of urbanisation by physically increasing city size, and expanding its administrative and tax base. In China, for example, there are financial advantages to incorporation. As Hu explains: "Since China's urban land ownership belongs to the state, private property developers need to purchase the land use rights from the local governments, which work as the agents of the true land owners, the state" (Hu 2013, p.170). Thus incorporation of surrounding farmland which is sold on to developers is an attractive source of funds to pay for new infrastructure, and to gain recognition from state authorities for subsidies and aid. The creation of a property market in stages from 1978 also encouraged urban development, a process greatly accelerated in 1998 by the establishment of the Ministry of Land and Resources to oversee land use.

However, these reforms took place against a background of continuous and massive rural to urban migration, the most persistent and far-reaching of the drivers of urban expansion. It is a process that has been intimately tied up with economic and political changes, and in many ways charts those changes. My own experience has made me familiar with its dynamic, having spent the first 26 years of my life to 1984 growing up in Cape Town, South Africa.

Life in South Africa in the 1970s was a fascinating but brutal intersection of modernisation, settler-colonial aspirations, racism and political idealism. The urban development of Cape Town since the 1960s had been marked by the movement of large segments of the population into racially homogenous zones as a physical consequence of Apartheid and its system of racial classification. The legislation that set this in train was the Group Areas Act of 1950 and its successor acts. However, these laws did not alone determine the growth of South African cities. Apartheid was many things, but in its crudest form it was a system of labour control. Industry and manufacturing were encouraged in existing cities, and in strategic cases large industrial plants were located in selected growth areas. In a system where ownership of land and businesses was racially circumscribed by law, the Apartheid regime attempted to control the influx of people from rural areas to cities. Since the rise of an indigenous or mixed-race middle class was not a goal of the system, residency rights in cities were strictly controlled through permits. In an effort to further restrict internal migration, parts of the country were designated as preferential labour areas by race. Xhosa, Sotho and other tribal workers were prevented from moving to Cape Town as it was reserved for mixed-race workers, who held a separate racial classification.

By the 1970s this system was breaking down, and shanty towns sprang up along the main highway linking Cape Town to the interior. The shacks were periodically demolished in a bid to enforce planning controls, but they were soon rebuilt. The official attitude was that rural workers should maintain their connection with their home villages, and their status was effectively one of guest workers in urban areas. This strategy, not confined to Apartheid era South Africa, relies on the home villages to raise children and bear the associated effort of health and education. Once their productive working lives in the city were over, workers were expected to return to their villages and again relieve the city of the responsibility of old-age care.

This system works when an unskilled workforce is required, since it does not invest in education and training beyond a basic level. It has the economic disadvantage of a constant supply of cheap labour. This may seem like an oxymoron, but cheap labour provides little incentive for an economy to become capital intensive to reduce labour costs. Over time this lack of innovation becomes counterproductive, as any rise in labour costs leaves labour-intensive industries with little means to improve competitiveness against more progressive enterprises.

Rural areas, too, are transformed by commercial agriculture. Subsistence farming was the bedrock of the Apartheid assumption of rural residency as the default status of migrant city workers, from which they came and to which they would return. This was supplemented by wages remitted from the city to the countryside, supplementing home-grown produce. Traditional villages and their fields were separated from commercial white-owned farms, but the system broke down in the 1980s as more and more subsistence farmers moved onto these neighbouring farms as squatters rather than subsistence tenants.

Thus the vision of urban development under Apartheid, and one that is repeated in various forms wherever significant industrial and rural transformations are taking shape, is predicated on a controlled stasis, or a slow osmosis, between city and country. Ideally the flow of workers to new enterprises can be controlled so that they can be accommodated in planned dormitory developments, with a vast reserve army of workers still available in rural conditions to keep urban wages low, while the cost to the state of maintaining the villages is minimal due to their lack of infrastructure and services. In reality the process is hard to control, as the compulsion to move to the city has proved powerful indeed. China is struggling with this process currently, having instituted a residency permit (*hukou*) system that gives those dwelling legally in cities access to services and residential tenure. For those who move illegally to the cities in search of opportunities, daily life is very different as they inhabit a shadow economy with only basic services, and their security is at the whim of local officials.

Where this has happened and the state has not had the resources to provide housing and services, or the market has seen no advantage to providing housing because of the lack of a secure system of land ownership that allows property to be traded, slums inevitably result. Within slums informal systems arise for determining who has the right to live in a specific dwelling, but without title to the dwelling all improvements are made for convenience, not for profit. Services appear but are often provided by the black, unregulated market, at a price. Electricity in many places is stolen through illegal connections to the power supply. The slum, by its presence and characteristics, is the inverse of the state's interest in orderly urban development. It falls outside of the land title system, it pays little to utilities for services and it is often poorly policed or effectively out of the control of the law. The famous favelas of Brazil are a case in point. As part of the consolidation of state control in recent years, a campaign of pacification has been undertaken by the police in Rio de Janeiro since 2008. This involves quasi-military assaults on the gangs which control the slums, with the intention of bringing them under state control. Observers note that with control come better services, as well as increased municipal rates (Wells 2014).

Whatever the appearance of slums might suggest, they represent a more secure existence at the most basic level than rural subsistence farming. The water reticulation system of the modern city provides enough drinking water for the vast bulk of urban inhabitants. In Southeast Asia, which includes Indonesia, the Philippines and Thailand and their combined slum populations of about 60 million, some 19% of rural dwellings have piped water to the building, as opposed to 34% of the urban poor. However, when access to water from shared taps is included, about 92% of the region's urban population has treated water available, although it may not be under the most convenient conditions. Nonetheless it is better than the contaminated and seasonal water sources often used by the rural poor (Yap 2012, pp.41–42).

In energy terms, too, the city is a more stable and diverse provider than traditional rural life. Indeed, the larger the city the greater the access to opportunities and energy for the urban poor (Pachauri 2012). For all developing countries, about 59% of the rural population has access to electricity, as opposed to about 90% in urban areas. The use this is put to may vary, since poor households are very sensitive to the costs of energy. Thus electricity may power lighting, a TV and a fridge, but cooking would use wood, coal, charcoal or gas depending on price and availability. For countries with some advanced capacity for generation, electricity is almost ubiquitous in cities and towns, even if the supply may be intermittent. In Latin America, India, China, Pakistan, Egypt and Indonesia, over 95% of urban households have access to electricity. In Pakistan, for example, even among the poorest city dwellers 80% use electricity to some degree (Pachauri 2012, loc.2218[1]).

However, in areas of sub-Saharan Africa a majority of urban households rely extensively on biomass fuels such as wood, charcoal and dung for cooking, although this is a pattern that is clearly in transition.

When energy sources are looked at more closely, the difference between rural and urban dwellers becomes more evident. Pachauri and Jiang (2008) have examined these patterns in India and China, two countries experiencing massive shifts in population from the rural to the urban. Rural households in India derive over 90% of their energy needs from biomass, and less than 10% from modern fuels. In urban India the proportion is starkly different, with energy sources split almost evenly between biomass and modern fuels like electricity, gas and kerosene. However, when the figures are broken down again between all urban areas and the largest cities, a further trend is visible. In general urbanites in India use about a third biomass, a third electricity and a third a mixture of coal, LPG and kerosene for energy. In larger cities, however, the main sources are electricity and LPG, with a small amount of kerosene. Biomass and coal use is negligible.

A similar pattern is evident in China, where the dominance of coal in small towns gives way to a mix of electricity, coal and natural gas in larger cities. Thus the energy source mix undergoes change as the city grows, a not unexpected result as the distribution networks lean towards denser sources of energy such as fossil fuels and their derivatives, and electricity. The somatic biomass fuels which are derived from photosynthesis cannot compete with fossil fuels and centralised electricity generation in the amount of energy they contain, and the area needed to grow and harvest them.

Pachauri and Jiang (2008) also show that energy use in the countryside in India varies little in its makeup between rich and poor households. The rich consume more, but the proportion derived from biomass remains similar across all incomes. For urban Indian households, though, the preference for electricity and LPG is evident as incomes grow. The wealthiest households use these fuels almost exclusively, while the poorer the household the more it relies on biomass fuels. These trends are not surprising, given that in wealthy countries domestic energy is derived exclusively from electricity, gas and oil, with wood fires used largely for picturesque effect. The energy density and clean burning of gas and refined oil makes them almost ideal urban fuels for heating and cooking, while the absence of any residues from electricity at the point of consumption, and its instant availability, makes it the universal energy source of choice. As a corollary, because urban houses use modern fuels, they use them more efficiently. The predominance of biomass in the countryside in nations like India means that much of its heat is lost when cooking or heating, so that overall energy use per capita is higher in the country than in the city, with less benefit derived.

Thus the city, in developing countries, offers greater energy security to households in general than the countryside due to its modern distribution network of fuels which contain enormous amounts of energy for their volume, and can be used with optimal efficiency. The provision of electricity is not a particularly challenging undertaking, given the widespread availability of generators and the means to power them. In most countries it is viewed as a critical service, and in some cases the recouping of the costs of generation are pursued selectively (Costa-Jordao 2012). It has been estimated that the electricity utility in Rio de Janeiro endures some 200 million dollars in lost revenue from the illegal connections made to its supply in Rio's favelas. It has continued the supply to its limited paying customers in these slums, but with the pacification process that has brought the favelas into regular municipal control it appears the number of paying customers has risen dramatically (Kaiser 2013).

Despite clear issues with slums and an inability to adequately house its urban dwellers, Brazil generates a great deal of electricity. Its installed generating capacity in 2011 was 119 million kilowatts, greater than Italy, Spain or the UK (Energy Information Administration n.d.). Similar figures prevail in other developing economies. India has a generating capacity twice that of Brazil, and China boasts some 1100 million kilowatts, more than the US (1052 million) or Western and Southern Europe's combined total of 1024 million kW. On a per capita basis the figure for these developing economies is about a third that of advanced economies, but nonetheless they have advanced and large electricity generating plant. The distribution of the power is a trickier issue, but the high percentage of urban households using electricity attests to the uneven split between city and country, and the further split between more or less wealthy households. Load shedding, or rolling blackouts, is also a feature in many parts of India, so the capacity factor or actual usage of installed generating capacity is lower than in developed economies.

The urban bias towards modern fuels is also a function of market efficiency. LPG for home use is supplied in pressurised cylinders, which need to be refilled centrally from large tanks. This is more easily accomplished at urban densities – in the countryside the cost and effort of delivering refilled cylinders over poor roads makes LPG supply a difficult commercial proposition. In India LPG and kerosene are subsidised to encourage a shift from burning biomass. This is not only for convenience: the health impact of cooking with traditional solid fuels indoors is massive and widespread. Estimates put the number of deaths in India that can be attributed to indoor air pollution annually at about 875,000 from infections and obstructive pulmonary diseases. Of these about 140,000 are children under five (Dalberg Global Development Advisers 2013). Traditional biomass cooking is thus a major health hazard, and a leading cause of infant mortality. Even if these figures are exaggerated, they underline the problems of primitive solid fuel stoves.

Unlike the electricity network, the reticulation of gas through pipes in Indian cities is not widespread, although it is increasing. The use of bottled LPG has allowed its market to expand beyond the confines of a piped net-work, using vehicles to transport filled bottles to customers. Gas cylinders of

14.2 kg are the standard size, with smaller 5 kg bottles also available. For slums the LPG bottle is a nimble and versatile solution to energy supply. A deposit is put down on the first cylinder, and subsequent refills charge only for the gas. This is similar to the Australian "Swap and go" system operated from petrol stations, with the difference that here bottled LPG is mainly a fuel used for leisure.

The takeup of LPG in Brazil shows just how effective it can be as a domestic energy source. Like many countries, urban Brazil has an old piped natural gas network which serves about two million, mainly urban, customers (Iberglobal 2014). This network is currently being expanded, but the high cost of installing gas pipelines has meant that the reach of the network is small, and confined to dense areas where the number of customers per kilometre of pipeline is high. As in India, the pressurised gas bottle or cylinder allowed LPG to be widely distributed independently of the piped network. The Brazilian LPG industry established itself through the 1950s, when the 13 kg refillable cylinder was standardised nationally. In 1955 the national oil company Petrobras began large-scale local production of LPG. The penetration of this energy form has been almost universal, with 98% of Brazilian households using the gas. Its price was subsidised until 2001 to encourage its spread as a relatively clean and powerful fuel for household cooking, as well as for water and space heating. It has also played an important role in industrial processes for textiles, plastics and glass (Lucon, Teixeira Coelho & Goldemberg 2004).

The rise of bottled LPG in India and Brazil has been an interesting corollary of the growth of slums in these two countries. The defining characteristic of slums and other informal dwellings is the lack of security of tenure, as they are not developed within the prevailing land title system. This does not mean that the population is necessarily itinerant, or that title will not be granted at a later stage, but in the initial settlement, infrastructure provision is poor or non-existent, and if rates are not levied then there is little incentive to provide public utilities. The private sector may step in, as may enlightened government, but bottled LPG is an example of a technology that can leapfrog infrastructure provision since all it requires is a deposit on the initial bottle, and a road close enough to enable bottles to be exchanged. The use of LPG as the primary cooking fuel for hundreds of millions of people in India and Brazil is testament to the efficiency of the system, which was then officially recognised and promoted in both countries through government subsidy.

Piped gas is a more convenient form of supply, but the cost of reticulation confines it to dense urban areas, and ties it into neighbourhoods with more established forms of tenure to justify the expense and ensure returns on investment. In new middle-class developments in India, for example, gas piping may be included since it not only eliminates bottle swapping but it also increases the consumption of gas. Within a single city there will be different fuels and distribution networks depending on income and the prevailing form of housing tenure. The energy content of a single 14.2 kg refill of LPG is impressive. It will fuel all cooking in an average household for around six weeks, without the conversion losses that electric cooking is subject to. It is incomparably cleaner than traditional biomass cooking, and the cylinder can be handled by the average adult with relative ease (Figure 6.1).

For many poor urban families in India and Brazil energy needs are provided by electricity for lighting, a fridge and entertainment, while LPG provides heating. The convenience with which overhead power lines can be installed has allowed them to penetrate slums which might still lack to-the-home water supply and sewage. Water is often provided by community standpipes, but sewage management is eclectic and in many places absent. Like all utilities the reticulation and collection networks are far more expensive than the treatment or generation itself. In Australia, for example, generating costs are typically about a quarter of an electricity bill, with distribution costs making up over half (Origin Energy 2015). The remainder are retailer's charges and government levies.

Developing economies, and their cities, are characterised by enormous disparities in wealth. This was true for Manchester in the 1850s, and for Sao Paulo now. The energy budget will differ markedly between a poor and a wealthy household, particularly if only one owns a car. Indian households spend between 7 and 11% of their total expenditure on domestic energy, but car ownership will absorb a significant portion of the remainder for emerging middle-class families. While overall car ownership is low at 13 per 1000 population, the inability of local and state governments to keep infrastructure

Figure 6.1 Power to the people. Gas bottles for home use on sale in Hanoi, Vietnam. This form of gas storage and distribution is widespread in many developing economies.
Credit: Hanoi Photography/Shutterstock.com

provision abreast of demand in urban areas has created voids that are filled by private contractors and privatised solutions. Car ownership reduces dependence on public transport, particularly in those cities where new development takes place away from established routes. The same is true for emerging middle classes the world over. The rate of urbanisation generally exceeds the capacity to provide services or orderly development through a trusted market in land, so piecemeal (and often ingenious) market solutions arise.

In recent years there has been considerable interest in slums precisely for their apparent efficiency and careful use of resources. The Mumbai slum of Dharavi has been the subject of numerous documentaries, its draw summarised in a *National Geographic* article thus: "Indeed, on a planet where half of humanity will soon live in cities, the forces at work in Dharavi serve as a window not only on the future of India's burgeoning cities, but on urban space everywhere" (Jacobson 2007). The change in the perception of slums, from evidence of developmental failure to exemplars of self-help, has been a bellwether of several urban trends. Two books of 2010 mark out the terrain of the debate. Doug Saunders' (2010) *Arrival City* painted slums, and the poorer neighbourhoods of established cities, as integral to the conversion of rural dwellers to urbanites. Saunders is reluctant to differentiate between the illegal slum of the developing city and the French public housing schemes on the outskirts of Paris, since they both served as places of opportunity for new immigrants from rural society. Saunders emphasises that the transformation is not always successful, but this risk is tied into the very existence of arrival cities as places where migrants have taken a calculated gamble with the future.

Saunders' book has the virtue of personalising the experience of urbanisation. He ties the process in with the many indicators that show that urbanisation frees even the poor from the precariousness of rural subsistence, and the lack of opportunities for social mobility. In this the arrival cities mimic the experience of 18th century London or Paris, each with their preponderance of small scale commerce and street-level commercial opportunity.

A reluctance to separate trade from late capitalism marks the other influential book on emerging cities, Mike Davis' *Planet of Slums*. Davis (2006) sees slums as the result of the impoverishment of the nascent technical and middle class in developing countries through the neo-liberal policies of the IMF and World Bank after 1970, which made loans to these countries contingent on the opening up of opportunities to Western investors. Davis sees this as destroying the capacity of the state to protect the gains made by local elites following independence or modernisation.

Davis' bias is towards the state to direct development, rather than the market or large external investors. Slums are symptoms of failure rather than places of opportunity, and their growth entrenches the fallen social status of their residents. He emphasises the displacement of the rural poor when agricultural land is amalgamated for mechanised production, or simply stolen to enlarge existing landholdings. This view, built on a long-held explanation for the wretched situation of the early English urban working class, rests on outrage at the living conditions in slums, which are seen as pulsing indictments of the failures of advanced capitalism.

Late 20th century neo-liberal ideology, which favoured market solutions over planned ones, was in fact wrestling with one of Marx's central concerns – the creation and realisation of value. For Marx (following Adam Smith) the source of value lay in the transformative power of human labour, which is embodied in commodities and realised in exchange. This concept gave conceptual clarity to how value arises, and particular dignity to work itself. The difficulty in service economies is that the clear path of value creation in making and selling is harder to trace and value when dealing with jobs in administration and distribution. The neo-liberal reforms that swept through institutions like the IMF had their roots in the Thatcher and Reagan reforms of the 1970s and 80s, when governments in Britain and in America moved to restore market-based valuations to both products and services. In both countries this took the form of attacks on industries perceived as enjoying historically high wages which were incommensurate with the social value of what they produced. Thus in Britain the coal sector was targeted, because its strong unionised culture had combined with a national interest in maintaining local coal supplies to create an industry that was subsidised beyond its perceived usefulness. In the US the high-profile targets were air traffic controllers, who again had won high wages by leveraging their critical role in air transport.

The same thinking underpinned the conditions of IMF loans to developing countries. Local administrative classes had appeared after independence in many emerging nations, and the value of their work to national development had been clouded by inefficiency and corruption. To counter this, international funding bodies insisted on market mechanisms to determine how aid money could best be spent. Where bureaucracies had become bloated, the reforms cut deeply as spending was tied to demands for greater efficiency. Despite this, the result was still a great divergence in value between locally made and traded products, and aid products and services. The latter remained essentially free, or valued in a lesser way to local products and services. This undermined local production, and provided ample opportunities for graft and profiteering (Easterly 2006).

When the money value economy of the poor is compared to that of the wealthy the results are often startling in the width of the disparities they reveal. Yet this is precisely what globalisation has done. As capital has moved to take advantage of low labour costs in China, it has transformed Chinese cities and local entrepreneurs without patronising them. This harmonisation of the American (or Western) and Chinese economies in terms of labour value has been critical to the economic rise of China. No parallel aid system to China undermined the value of local produce and labour by providing a valueless alternative in local terms.

The very existence of these subsidies of food and equipment is testament to the surpluses produced in developed nations, and is another manifestation of energy abundance in advanced economies. While they may seem insignificant to the donor nations, they can have large distorting effects, as well as beneficial effects, in recipient nations.

Needless to say aid can play an important role in guaranteeing life under certain harsh conditions, but its role in nurturing independent local production has been dismal (Easterly 2006). The same logic prevails in the rich–poor divide in cities of developing countries, where the opportunity for local accumulation of capital has a greater flow-on effect than handouts. Subsidies can aid in improving daily life, but the enormous capital and rent windfall of secure land tenure that can be bought or sold is deeply transformative for its beneficiaries. This is part of the process of urban transformation in rapidly growing cities. The older favelas of Rio, particularly those with views near the picturesque parts of the city, have slowly acquired real estate markets either through legal recognition of title, or through customary acceptance over time (Perlman 2009, loc.904). However, the most spectacular example of the granting of legal title to informal squatter settlements has been in Istanbul, where since 1966 legal mechanisms have existed to grant recognition, if not title, to the informal *gecekondu* neighbourhoods. In 1983 an ensuing law allowed the largely rural settlers of these areas to develop their plots, which saw them transformed from modest informal villas to multi-storey apartments. The improvement of these areas propelled millions of rural migrants into the middle class within a generation, a development that Saunders credits with transforming Turkish politics from the secular elitism of Atatürk to the progressive populism of Erdogan (Saunders 2010, p.172).

Harmonisation of values with the broader economy seems to yield three ways that slum dwellers or urban squatters can earn a living, or even transform their circumstances. They can sell their labour, they can hope for title to be granted to their property, or they can deal in altered consciousness. Most inhabitants try to harness the first by finding jobs in the wider city, and by using education to gain access to higher paid and stable jobs. Within their neighbourhoods there are also opportunities for trading, for carting and hauling goods and for repairs and servicing, to name a few. For long-term residents of older slums like Dharavi in Mumbai and Rocinha in Rio, there is the opportunity to make money from the informal market in dwellings and urban space. Even where this is not legal, the long-term survival of these neighbourhoods has created an expectation of continued use which can be traded. For the generation of the 1970s and 80s settlements in Istanbul, the granting of formal legal title to their informal squats and houses has delivered the best windfall of all.

Sadly the trade in altered consciousness, or rather the drugs that induce it, has proved destructive on an almost unprecedented scale where it has taken root. In India or China the social fabric that is reproduced in informal neighbourhoods and slums seems to be able to contain the drug trade. In

Brazil, though, the very high profits it yields have supported and armed young men who have become dominant within favelas, and have effectively taken them out of the control of civil society. Perlman attests to the enormous transformation this wrought. When she first visited Rio in the 1960s favela life was poor, illegal but vibrant and deeply communal. The inhabitants she interviewed in many cases were proud of their identity, despite being socially and politically marginalised. Subsequent visits in the 1990s left her profoundly aware of the fear that had coloured life in these settlements, as violence became entrenched (Perlman 2009).

These are characteristics of informal settlement around, and in, the largest of cities. If anything the lesson of these cities is that informal settlements, including slums, suffer from many depredations, but absolute energy poverty is not one of them. The extremely high percentage of the population with access to electricity, and the ubiquitous adoption of bottled gas as a heating and cooking fuel where piped gas is not available, have proven remarkably plastic as systems for meeting urban domestic energy demand. Developing cities also produce market solutions for transport when infrastructure provision falls behind settlement growth. In South Africa under Apartheid urban growth took place for most of the 1960s and 70s under planned conditions. The racial homogeneity of neighbourhoods that was the goal of the various Group Areas Acts spawned a period of massive population relocation from the old mixed inner cities to racially segregated townships on the urban periphery. There was also a programme of housing provision for rural to urban migrants as the urban labour market expanded. Acknowledging that the low wages offered could not meet commercial rents, subsidised housing described as "sub-economic" was built by municipal authorities for the lowest income earners. Generally these areas were linked to train lines with a radial structure centred on the city core that precluded journeys across suburbs.

With the growth of informal settlements away from public transport, an opportunity arose in South Africa to fill the gap between public transport and private car ownership, which was beyond most residents. The solution was the taxi minibus, a commuter multi-seat van that travels set routes across the city, and charges standard fares for each route. From being non-existent in 1984, these vehicles have become a critical part of the transport system, and carry some 12 million people daily in South African cities. Their emergence has been marked by violent clashes over routes, but they have become officially accepted as efficient and cost effective. Since they often travel full, they are useful in both energy and economic terms, and fares are low. They can also sustain a finer network of service than large buses, and can be deployed immediately on new routes provided there is a suitable road network.

A 2003 report concluded that the industry was largely informal, that is the drivers did not register to pay tax, nor did they register their employees. However, in less than two decades it had garnered 65% of the public transport market, with 127,000 vans operating nationwide. This compared to market shares of 21% for buses and 14% for trains (Barrett 2003). It has since gained greater official recognition as an industry, but its rapid rise to public transport dominance is instructive. A typical fare for a 10 km journey is R7, equivalent to about 60 US cents (2015 values). These fares are viable for both passengers and drivers, and illustrate a modern transport solution in an economy where enormous income disparities continue to exist.

The market niche between public and private transport has seen forms of minibuses emerge in many other countries (Figures 6.2 and 6.3). The Philippines has had its Jeepneys since the Second World War, and the collapse of the Soviet Union gave rise to the *marshrutka* or share taxi that has enjoyed increasing popularity in Eastern Europe and West Asia since the 1990s. Both represent the same value as the South African minibus – an affordable fare for a set route, operating with greater frequency, and greater dispersion, than conventional public transport. There is no reason to believe that these solutions won't continue to find favour in developing cities where many services lag far behind population growth and geographic spread.

Perhaps the greatest difference between the contemporary developing city, and the older Western cities that were the crucibles of the industrial age, is the speed with which the contemporary city leapfrogs the forms of development that seemed to mark the stages of their older counterparts. The early location of industry close to waterways and coal made for a concentric structure, which was reinforced by tram networks. Later suburban rings, and the move of industry to the city rim, left distinct developmental watermarks on urban form. The contemporary city, though, seems to collapse these stages into decades or years, with squatting and

Figure 6.2 A Jeepney in Manila, part of the private fleet that serves as public transport throughout the Philippines
Credit: saiko3p/Shutterstock.com

Figure 6.3 A motorised trike, which provides a nimble, small-engined transport
option in the Philippines
Credit: saiko3p/Shutterstock.com

illegal structures adding to the city in an apparently organic fashion. At the
same time many of these urban economies are bypassing manufacturing in
favour of trade and service industries. The modern factory can be located
anywhere, as long as it is supplied with transport, power and an available
labour force.

Perhaps the most prominent example of this in recent years has been
Foxconn, the world's largest manufacturer of electronic devices. Founded by
Taiwanese Terry Gou as Hon Hai Precision, the company manufactures
many Apple products, as well as those of Sony, Hewlett Packard and Nokia
(*Forbes Magazine* n.d.). The company employs over one million workers in
China alone, and its output accounts for about 40% of the world market in
electronic consumer goods (Johnson 2011). The company has come to
Western attention in a number of ways in recent years, most notably for a
spate of suicides at its massive Shenzhen plant in 2010. While observer
accounts paint the factory as having among the best facilities in the city, and
statistics indicate that the suicide rate is not unusually high and is lower than
US college figures, the controversy has driven Apple to take steps to audit
its suppliers for compliance with relevant labour laws and practices. However,
the company remains trapped within a dilemma of its business model – the
sophistication of its product requires stringent workplace controls, while the
speed with which it brings new products to production demands high
output generally, and surges in production at product launch time, to capitalise on its status as an innovator (Duhigg & Barboza 2012). Apple also has
enormous power as a buyer, since its rigorous technical standards confer

status on any firm that is selected to supply or manufacture its range of computers, tablets and phones.

The relationship between Apple and Foxconn illustrates the realities of manufacturing in low-labour-cost countries, as well as the transformative power of international investment. While Foxconn may not resemble an American manufacturer in its labour practices, wages or worker power, it has made changes to the facilities and services it provides for its workforce, and it is acutely aware of the ongoing scrutiny it is under from the US media. The Shenzhen plant was built with associated dormitories, kitchens and recreation areas to provide some security of housing and services for its workforce, most of whom migrated from less developed provinces for the prospect of secure employment. Shenzhen itself is a creation of Deng Xiaoping's agenda to encourage investment in Chinese manufacturing, and its location next to Hong Kong, combined with favourable local taxes and an influx of Chinese workers, has seen it grow from a regional village to 12 million inhabitants in three decades. Its status as a Special Economic Zone has fostered these advantages in a location with little historic infrastructure or trade. Foxconn has reaped the benefit of these policies, at the same time as it has brought a highly competitive and profitable enterprise to Guangdong province.

Foxconn's policy for locating its plants appears to capitalise on the magnetic pull of its facilities. In Brazil the company's plants are located away from major cities, but close enough to draw on urban links and expertise. Its major factory is in Jundiai, some 60 km north of Sao Paolo, with a small population but easy access to the regional metropolis. Thus the locational logic of this transnational manufacturer relies on the willingness of workers to move to its plants, and the modern ease with which power and construction materials can be brought to smaller cities and towns (Greene 2012).

The company has come to Western attention because its products are so highly visible in everyday life, and because they are used by the most literate sectors of the economy. For users, the visceral connection electronic products give to their country of origin brings an awareness, or at least a curiosity, as to how they were made, and by whom. For many other products the connection is too attenuated to be of concern. China is the world's largest manufacturer of steel, with production increasing as the economy industrialises and building continues at a rapid pace. This is in line with a general historic trend for steel consumption to increase in the initial years of economic development. However, as with many inputs, this trend reverses as the economy approaches infrastructure saturation, and the volume of steel required per unit of GDP declines. This trend has been marked in the case of both Japan and the US (Holloway, Roberts & Rush 2010). The raw figures illustrate this dramatically – in 2013 China produced 779 million tonnes of steel, over seven times the tonnage produced by the second rank country, Japan (World Steel Association 2014).

The pollution load that Chinese steelmaking creates is massive, and the particulate matter produced is complicit in up to 750,000 premature deaths annually from poor air quality (Alliance for American Manufacturing 2009). Even if the steel industry contributes only 10% of this load, its health effects vastly exceed those of Foxconn and other electronics manufacturers. Chinese steel is found in many of China's exported products, but they fail to attract the same attention as Apple products for those concerned about the human cost embedded in their consumption. The devastation wrought by rare earth mining, a critical ingredient for the permanent magnets needed in low-speed wind turbine generators, has also been observed but has failed to make a significant impact on Western consumers (Kaiman 2014).

As China continues as a major manufacturer of all the commodities, and much of the plant, desired by advanced economies, the precise nature of the dialectical dance of investment, exploitation and transformation remains obscured by national pride and Western selective vision. The vast quantities of coal imported for electricity generation and steelmaking have under-pinned the Australian mining industry for some years, as has the iron ore that feeds its furnaces. Historically these energy-intensive industries should decline in relative importance in the Chinese economy, although the point at which this happens remains unclear. Some estimates predict that China has many years of steelmaking ahead to reach the per capita rates of the US or Japan (Credit Suisse 2012).

Chinese urban form, too, has responded to massive city growth by adopting particular models of development that suit its imperatives, and its building industry. The high-rise gated community has emerged as a popular form of development, not in response to widespread urban crime but rather as a way of privately building and running community facilities ahead of state provision. As in many developing economies, private funding of schools and clinics exists parallel to state funding, and has proved more economically nimble for those who can afford it.

Thus urban development can broadly be categorised into that which takes place within planned and legislated forms, and has sufficient state provision of infrastructure and services to ensure that residents of new areas can move into more or less fully functioning communities, and that which leaps ahead of planning and servicing. The first mode of development happens in cities that have advanced economies and which have undergone their periods of rapid growth. Despite cities like New York or Sydney being faced with increasing populations through international migration, and some internal migration, the problems of their growth are measured against the high expectations of urban amenity that the residents have. For Johannesburg or Manila the questions of amenity are far more basic, and despite the solutions that have arisen for transport and energy supply that rely on diffuse and easily expanded networks such as bottled gas supply or minibus operators, these cities still struggle with sanitation and garbage removal for many inhabitants. These are services that are generally funded through rates, and rely on formal title to land or dwellings so they can be billed to owners. Where occupiers have lived in an area informally for a long time, as in some of

Rio's favelas, cheaper systems of sewage disposal have developed which use shallow excavation and connections that can be done with minimal plumbing skills. Where communities are well organised, these *condominial* systems have proven cheap and effective (Leal 2013).

In most advanced economies the drift to the cities was completed generations ago, and urban growth is a consequence of large immigration programmes. European countries are now faced with illegal immigrants from North Africa, whose numbers have begun to change the population composition in Italy and Spain. In developing economies, however, internal migration from the countryside to towns and cities remains the driver of urban growth. The volume of people leaving the land is the result of many factors, but most significant is the viability of small subsistence farms and their capacity to support those who farm them.

The shift from country to city is clearly a phenomenon that will decline in due course for each country where it has resulted in swelling cities. Eventually the rural population will be reduced to a number that can be employed in the agricultural industry, or can live off smaller viable subsistence farms. The future of small farms has been the subject of considerable debate in recent decades, and the main issues have been elegantly summarised by Peter Hazell and his collaborators. In a clear-eyed analysis they consider the various arguments for and against the preservation of small farms in developing economies. As background, they note the role agriculture plays at various stages of national development. For poor countries agriculture represents a much greater share of economic activity, and involves many more people, than in rich countries. As we have seen, in advanced economies the proportion of the population employed in agriculture can be as low as 1–2%, while in poor countries a majority of the population may be farmers and herders. In general their productivity is low, and small farms are home to half of the world's undernourished people. A rise in agricultural productivity seems to precede economic growth: indeed it appears to be a pre-requisite historically for economic take-off. Once this happens agriculture becomes less important economically. Growing economies diversify quickly, and over time they tend towards services and away from primary production like farming (Hazell, Wiggins & Dorward 2007).

The remarkable success in food production that India and China experienced in the latter decades of the 20th century has not been replicated everywhere, and sub-Saharan Africa in particular has shown little improvement in food security. However, the Asian success has also been accompanied by massive migration to cities, underlining that rural to urban migration is not simply a result of absolute poverty but depends on the degree of opportunity offered by cities and towns. As the prospect for wage employment increases, the draw of the town or city exceeds the inertia of remaining in small-farm employ or subsistence farming.

Equally important are the markets for agricultural products. As Hazell *et al.* point out, the growth of supermarket chains can profoundly influence the farming sector. Supermarkets prefer stable suppliers who can provide volume as well as credence, that is knowledge of how the produce was grown and what chemicals were used. Small farms are not suited to this supply chain, and in countries where the majority of produce is sold in supermarkets it is sourced from larger suppliers, sometimes from distant countries. If this is difficult due to poor transport networks, supermarkets may revert to small suppliers. In either case the farmer is drawn into a more specialised cash economy, producing for money rather than the local consumption of subsistence living.

Like other markers of development such as energy consumption or steel production per unit of GDP, a developing economy exhibits an initial rise in agricultural production as an important driver of growth. As the economy diversifies, and consumers demand a wider variety of foods, the limited staples of the subsistence economy become less important, and the value of the whole sector as a proportion of the economy declines. At this point the power is well and truly with the towns, and the dominance of services in mature economies means that the value of land and houses moves decisively away from the countryside and into the cities. Small farms survive at this stage by producing high-value, niche products like cheese or fine wool, while the staples are provided by conglomerate farms with broadacre farming techniques and massive machines for ploughing and harvesting.

However, Hazell *et al.* conclude that there remains a role for small farms in reducing poverty and fostering some economic growth. Ironically though the greater the role they play in this the more the national economy will grow, and the greater will be the incentive to leave the farm. In addition in the Americas, Australasia and Southern Africa, settler colonies have led to large farms being created from grazing lands, grassland and forests, displacing native cultivators and herders over centuries and creating the bitter legacy of dispossession. Although many of these countries are very efficient agricultural producers, where there are large displaced pre-colonial populations there remains social tension over the loss of traditional rights of possession and use.

Thus despite the enormous social dislocation that moving off the land entails, it can also be a marker of developmental success, as in China. In Brazil the initial movement to cities coincided with a stagnation of political development in the 1960s and 70s, and only in recent years has the economy as a whole shown sign of rapid development, and the associated creation of a growing middle class. This is a common element in the recent histories of the five countries now known as the BRICS: Brazil, Russia, India, China and South Africa. With combined populations of nearly three billion people, this grouping has in common its economic potential and sporadic high economic growth rates. Apart from Russia, each country too is in a process of transition where initial migration from the countryside to towns and cities is occurring at a scale greater than the capacity of the state to absorb it. Thus their cities have extensive squatter and shanty settlements. These countries are also marked by sophisticated elites, reserves of poorly paid workers, and large installed electricity generating capacity that could power increasingly sophisticated manufacturing sectors. Thus they encompass many stages of economic development, from highly educated service sectors to subsistence farming.

The compression of developmental stages these countries are experiencing is also evident in their demographic prospects. The demographic transition is transformative in every sense – it changes the opportunities for children as their numbers are reduced, and it changes the ratio of workers to the elderly as the initial population boom works its way through the demographic profile for each age group. This will have an effect on urban form, since fertility rates tend to be lower in cities than in the countryside. Thus as the rates within cities fall below replacement level, they will either lose population or grow only due to population inflows from the countryside, or from other countries. Russia is already confronted with a shrinking population, as its TFR declined to a low of 1.2 in 1997 after the breakup of the Soviet Union. Its current TFR of 1.6, while showing some recovery, remains well below replacement level (World Bank n.d.).

The TFRs of the remaining BRICS are also at various levels of decline. Brazil currently sits at 1.8, China at 1.7, India at 2.5 and South Africa at 2.4. While these last two are above the replacement level of 2.1, they have declined from 3.1 and 2.9 respectively in 2000. However, these figures mask much greater falls in urban areas. Kolkata's TFR has been below replacement for four decades, and in 2011 stood at 1.2, the lowest in India. Mumbai and Chennai have rates of 1.4 (2011), low enough for their impact to become evident in falling school enrolments if rural to urban migration is too low to add net citizens to these cities (Basu 2014; Census India n.d.). Thus at the same time as India deals with slums and informal settlements that resulted from massive population shifts to cities, it is also confronted by a rapidly ageing urban population and the concomitant problems of a declining workforce relative to the number of those retired.

A similar pattern is evident in Brazilian births. The TFR for the region of Rio de Janeiro is 1.63 (2009 figures), 0.17 below the national average (Knoema n.d.). The drift to lower fertility rates in urban areas appears to be almost universal, and marks wealthy as well as poorer countries. As we shall see in the next chapter, its implications are far-reaching for any speculation on the future of urban systems as they deal with demographic change.

In the case of developing economies the effect is part of the overall simultaneous existence of a number of stages of economic development. While Kolkata muses over its historically low birth rates, elsewhere in India subsistence farmers continue to wrestle with the viability of their small-holdings, and whether to move to the overall protection that urban infra-structures offer over the seasonal uncertainty and conservative social mores of rural life. Each decision has implications for how they draw their energy, and the systems that provide it.

Whether India or China, or any other developing countries, will reach the embodied energy rates of advanced nations before their demand for steel or concrete tapers off is unclear. While some analysts have concluded that China is still well below peak per capita use of steel compared to the US or Japan, and still needs much more infrastructure to reach the service level of these two developed economies, these conclusions depend on the assumption that China will follow their trajectory of development. Given the desire to attain a comparable standard of living to the US, for example, this seems reasonable to assume. However, the limits that energy availability might put on this process are unknown. Should China or India succeed in rolling out safe and efficient nuclear power plants they may displace coal-fired generation, and perhaps guarantee electricity production into the future. However, iron making still requires large quantities of fossil fuels. Advanced processes have done away with the traditional reduction of iron ores using coke, but they still need coal or natural gas to heat the ores. This initial stage of steel production uses more energy than any other, consuming between 10 and 18 GJ per tonne of finished iron depending on the process used. The other processes – steelmaking, casting and rolling – together can use anywhere between 3 and 10 GJ per tonne. While electric arc furnaces have given electricity a greater role in steelmaking, the whole process remains fossil-fuel intensive (Price *et al.* 2001).

These are critical questions for the volume of energy consumed in developing economies. For the next decades India and China, with Brazil, seem destined to consume large amounts of fossil fuels for construction and building industrial capacity. Compared to advanced economies they still have a long way to travel if they are to match them in buildings, bridges, roads, train lines and factories. It is hard to imagine that the expectation of parity will be relinquished, and therefore their appetite for fossil fuels will continue. In building infrastructure, China, India and Brazil, and others, will be creating new middle classes whose living standards will exceed those of their parents by any measure. Whole classes will be raised, presuming the resources are available and administrations remain progressive. However, in advanced economies energy politics have a different hue, as their economic achievements remain subject to a continuing supply of high-grade energy.

Note

1 Refers to location numbers in the Kindle edition.

Bibliography

Alliance for American Manufacturing (2009). *An assessment of environmental regulation of the steel industry in China*. Retrieved August 3, 2015, from https://s.bsd.net/aam web/main/page/file/304b12b05c7fed2498_qdm6biar8.pdf

Barrett, J. (2003). *Organizing in the informal economy: A case study of the minibus taxi industry in South Africa*. Geneva: International Labour Organization.

Basu, M. (2014, December 25). *Falling total fertility rate in Kolkata sets alarm bells ringing*. Retrieved August 3, 2015, from www.livemint.com/Politics/9jV7AFSSMgeCrJ qyPgNwFI/Falling-total-fertility-rate-in-Kolkata-sets-alarm-bells-rin.html

Census India (n.d.). Estimate of fertility indicators. Retrieved August 20, 2015, from www.censusindia.gov.in/vital_statistics/SRS_Report_2012/10_Chap_3_2012.pdf

Costa-Jordao, T. (2012, February 17). *Water and energy for favelas*. Retrieved July 30, 2015, from http://projekty.upce.cz/groff/ms2012/lectures/costa-jordao-17.pdf

Credit Suisse (2012, March 8). *Have we reached "peak steel" demand in China? We think not*. Retrieved August 20, 2015, from https://doc.research-and-analytics.csfb.com/doc View?language=ENG&format=PDF&document_id=804893350&source_id=em& serialid=ljR8/PmJnc6nRhduTod7Cl3gVu2YcKPXFh6f2SZ0pvc=

Dalberg Global Development Advisers (2013, February 21). *India cookstoves and fuel market assessment*. Retrieved July 30, 2015, from http://cleancookstoves.org/resour ces/204.html

Davis, M. (2006). *Planet of slums*. London: Verso.

Duhigg, C., & Barboza, D. (2012, January 25). *In China, human costs are built into an iPad*. Retrieved August 3, 2015, from www.nytimes.com/2012/01/26/business/ieco nomy-apples-ipad-and-the-human-costs-for-workers-in-china.html

Easterly, W. (2006). *The white man's burden: Why the West's efforts to aid the rest have done so much ill and so little good*. New York: Penguin Press.

Energy Information Administration (n.d.). Retrieved August 20, 2015, from www. eia.gov

Forbes Magazine (n.d.). Terry Gou. Retrieved August 3, 2015, from www.forbes. com/profile/terry-gou

Greene, J. (2012, April 12). *Could Foxconn's factory in Brazil be a model for Apple production?* Retrieved August 3, 2015, from www.cnet.com/au/news/could-foxconns-factory-in-brazil-be-a-model-for-apple-production

Hazell, P., Wiggins, S., & Dorward, A. (2007). *The future of small farms for poverty reduction and growth*. Washington, DC: International Food Policy Research Institute.

Holloway, J., Roberts, I., & Rush, A. (2010, December 1). *China's steel industry*. Retrieved August 3, 2015, from www.rba.gov.au/publications/bulletin/2010/dec/ pdf/bu-1210-3.pdf

Hu, R. (2013). Drivers of China's urbanisation and property development. *Australasian Journal of Regional Studies*, 19(2), 156–180.

Iberglobal (2014, January 14). *INI: Natural gas sector overview in Brazil*. Retrieved July 30, 2015, from www.iberglobal.com/files/brasil_gas.pdf

Jacobson, M. (2007, May 1). *Dharavi: Mumbai's shadow city*. Retrieved July 30, 2015, from http://ngm.nationalgeographic.com/2007/05/dharavi-mumbai-slum/jacobson-text

Johnson, J. (2011, February 28). *1 million workers. 90 million iPhones. 17 suicides. Who's to blame?* Retrieved August 3, 2015, from www.wired.com/2011/02/ff_joelinchina/all

Kaiman, J. (2014, March 21). *Rare earth mining in China: The bleak social and environmental costs*. Retrieved August 3, 2015, from www.theguardian.com/sustainable-bu siness/rare-earth-mining-china-social-environmental-costs

Kaiser, A. (2013, January 22). Favelas with UPP see illegal electric drop. *Rio Times Online*. Retrieved July 30, 2015, from http://riotimesonline.com/brazil-news/rio-politics/upp-lowers-illegal-electricity-use/#

Knoema (n.d.). *Rio de Janeiro – Total fertility rate*. Retrieved August 3, 2015, from http://knoema.com/atlas/Brazil/Rio-de-Janeiro/Total-fertility-rate

Leal, S. (2013). *Cooperative sanitation in Brazil's favelas*. Retrieved August 3, 2015, from http://revista.drclas.harvard.edu/book/cooperative-sanitation-brazil's-favelas

Lucon, O., Teixeira Coelho, S., & Goldemberg, J. (2004). LPG in Brazil: Lessons and challenges. *Energy for Sustainable Development*, 8(3), 82–90.

Origin Energy (2015, February 18). *Energy bill charges: Know the facts*. Retrieved July 30, 2015, from www.originenergy.com.au/blog/lifestyle/understanding-the-ins-and-outs-of-your-electricity-bill.html

Pachauri, S. (2012). Demography, urbanisation and energy demand. In F. Toth (Ed.), *Energy for development resources, technologies, environment*. Dordrecht: Springer. Kindle edition.

Pachauri, S., & Jiang, L. (2008). The household energy transition in India and China. *Energy Policy*, 36(11), 4022–4035.

Perlman, J. (2009). *Favela: Four decades of living on the edge in Rio de Janeiro*. New York: Oxford University Press. Kindle edition.

Price, L., Sinton, J., Worrell, E., Phylipsen, D., Xiulian, H., & Ji, L. (2001). *Energy use and carbon dioxide emissions from steel production in China*. Ernest Orlando Lawrence Berkeley National Laboratory.

Saunders, D. (2010). *Arrival city: How the largest migration in history is reshaping our world*. New York: Pantheon Books.

United Nations Population Division (2014). *World urbanization prospects: The 2014 revision, highlights*. New York: United Nations.

Wells, M. (2014, March 24). Gangs reassert themselves in Rio's 'pacified' favelas. *InSightCrime*. Retrieved July 30, 2015, from www.insightcrime.org/news-analysis/gangs-reassert-themselves-in-rios-pacified-favelas

World Bank (n.d.). *Fertility rate, total (births per woman)*. Retrieved August 3, 2015, from http://data.worldbank.org/indicator/SP.DYN.TFRT.IN

World Steel Association (2014). *World steel in figures 2014*. Retrieved August 3, 2015, from www.worldsteel.org/dms/internetDocumentList/bookshop/World-Steel-in-Figures-2014/document/World Steel in Figures 2014 Final.pdf

Yap, K. (2012). The challenges of promoting productive, inclusive and sustainable urbanization. In K. Yap & M. Thuzar (Eds), *Urbanization in Southeast Asia: Issues & impacts*. Singapore: Institute of Southeast Asian Studies.

7   Speculations on urban form, energy and sustainability

The survey to date of the interaction of energy sources and cities has attempted to draw out some historical lessons about the form cities take as they are sustained and powered by a range of technologies and food sources. The issue has particular current relevance, as part of a broader debate about the future use of the fossil fuels that have so comprehensively shaped the modern city. It is not my intention to frame a series of prescriptions of how the modern city should develop. I believe it would be far more useful to set out a series of propositions derived from the preceding historical overview. I refer to them as propositions although they are, in reality, broad rules and historical processes that I believe can be gleaned from the historical record of cities, read in conjunction with economic and technical indicators that describe the modern era. Taken together I imagine that these propositions can be applied to prospective scenarios, and they may serve as a useful set of principles by which to evaluate alternate paths of development and planning. I offer them as my considered opinion only, and they will no doubt change as new data comes to light, and the unexpected triumph of technologies still on the periphery changes the picture in coming years.

1. Technology is always a social phenomenon, subject to the laws of physics

To describe technology as a social phenomenon is not to imply that its basic principles are not enduring, and in the course of everyday life, immutable. Rather it seems that the uptake and implementation of technology is determined by social structures and needs, rather than those needs being driven by technological advances themselves. Thus technological invention is not a driving force of change in and of itself, but rather its application and the way it enables certain social phenomena to be magnified in scope and effect is what we see as progress (Heilbroner 1994).

The city is perhaps the clearest example of this. The pre-industrial city in Europe had distinct social classes, but the physical separation of social classes was limited by the poor transport networks and the need for physical closeness when conducting business and moving traded goods. Port cities, or cities on major rivers, could move goods by water into the heart of the trading or provisioning areas. Private carriages gave some of the wealthy access to suburban estates, but for most of urban history the wealthy lived close to where business was done. In the late 18th century Paris had rich and poor living within the same buildings, and class distinctions were played out in behaviour, dress and command of resources rather than through physical location.

The advent of suburban railways, then trams and later motor cars allowed the city to physically develop along class lines which created areas that were homogenous by class, and separately located. This was shaped by the amenity offered by proximity to the city centre, density of services and transport corridors, and the physical attractiveness of parks or shoreline. Thus the advent of new forms of transport did not simply scatter urban dwellers randomly across a larger area, it allowed issues of class to re-arrange the city physically in a more thorough way. This is encapsulated in the real estate maxim of "location, location, location" as the most important factor determining value.

The same is true of all modern technologies. Computers were invented as a tool to assist in complex calculations, but their proliferation is not because all households need to perform complex calculations. Rather their power has been used to mimic existing functions such as writing, or drawing, or speaking, and to reconfigure these into more malleable forms that can be manipulated and transmitted with unique ease. In architecture, for example, complex buildings such as Antoni Gaudi's *Sagrada Familia Basilica* in Barcelona, commenced in 1882, and Hans Scharoun's *Berlin Philharmonic Hall* of 1963 were built before the advent of computer-aided design. Frank Gehry may have demonstrated what modern computer-aided design can achieve, but in general buildings are no more structurally complex or ambitious in the era of computers than they were before. Gehry's buildings serve to distinguish his clients from similar institutions through their distinctive appearance, a social function architecture has undertaken for millennia.

While technology itself may not determine how its use unfolds, once it is established its absorption into society normalises its presence. The vast and deep energy networks of modern cities have become almost invisible, and they are taken for granted. The magnitude of these networks is poorly appreciated even by those involved in planning cities and their expansion. Public transport, for example, makes significant energy demands. While it may reduce the use of private vehicles, dense train or tram networks require lots of electricity. Simply expanding their range produces its own distinctive energy demands, and when lightly used these may exceed the cars they replace. In addition the almost infinite flexibility of travel that private cars provide is reduced for those who only use public transport, and the options for where people might choose to live and work are restricted. The motor car enables great variety in where workers and jobs might choose to locate, and physically enables maximum freedom of choice. Shifting to public transport brings a social cost in this respect, which makes public transport attractive only to those whose work/living locations are on well serviced and comfortably connected routes. Thus the very patterns of everyday life are reliant on a certain quantum of energy, and re-arranging or changing it forces shifts in those patterns as they adjust to changes that may be barely perceptible on the surface.

2. Energy closes class gaps

This proposition is a corollary of the above, and determines the sometimes vehement class politics that surround energy decisions. The sheer magnitude of energy available to the modern citizen means that the highly skewed disposition of motive power that allowed nobility to lead such different lives to ordinary folk in pre-industrial times has all but disappeared. In a modern economy, apart from those who have fallen through societal networks due to illness, misfortune or a history of colonial subjugation, most people lead similar lives in their access to sufficient calories, travel opportunities, electricity, media or the ability to own a car and the enormous motive power it provides. The societal surplus is enough to feed even the poorest, to the point where widespread starvation is absent from all advanced economies.

This has been perhaps the greatest transforming effect of the energy bounty of fossil fuels. Again, it is so widespread as to be almost invisible, but the perception that it may be withdrawn through CO_2 reduction policies informs the sometimes virulent tenor of contemporary energy debates. An intuitive understanding of energy quanta can explain both why the issue is so polarising, and why it has real effects.

While most proposals in energy policy derive from the prospect of destructive climate change caused by man-made carbon dioxide emissions altering the spectral transparency of the atmosphere, and hence trapping more incoming solar heat, the specific proposals put forward to counter this show a much poorer understanding of what might be achieved. One might say that the basic science may be settled, but the engineering is not. The sheer amount of energy derived from fossil fuels at present puts any sharp transition to non-carbon-dioxide-producing energy sources beyond the capacity of even the most advanced societies. The reason can be framed in terms of power densities, a concept popularised by Vaclav Smil through his extensive writings, and taken up by others such as Robert Bryce, David MacKay and Peter Seligman (Bryce 2010; MacKay 2009; Seligman 2010). The basic question determining power density is: how much power does a particular fuel source produce from a specific area or volume? Thus if a forest yields ten tonnes of firewood annually per hectare, and each kilogram of wood provides 18 MJ of energy when burned, then the energy yield of each hectare is about 180,000 MJ, or 18 MJ per m^2. This equates to a constant rate of about 0.6 W per m^2 of solar energy that the forest is storing in the form of combustible wood. As we have seen, this low rate of energy conversion made early cities dependent on vast tracts of woodland to meet their energy needs.

Since most renewable energy sources are converting solar energy, either through photovoltaics or sun-driven wind movement, their power densities are generally low because their energy source is dispersed. For modern wind farms, when the energy produced is divided by the area they occupy, the results lie between 1 and 2.5 W/m^2. Photovoltaics fare a bit better, but not by orders of magnitude. Desert-based generating farms may average 20 W/m^2, but in European countries this is more likely to be around 5 W/m^2. Wilson contrasts this with a small propane-driven generator, which can produce well over 1000 W/m^2 when its footprint is taken into account (Wilson 2013). Large nuclear power stations have power densities ten times greater again when the electricity they produce is divided by the area they occupy.

The issue has been written about extensively in recent years, as it defines very clearly the size of renewable energy sources as expressed in the area required for their production. At current rates of consumption, countries like Japan or Korea could not meet all their energy requirements even if their entire land surfaces were covered by wind turbines (Wilson 2013). In countries like Australia, with large surface areas in relation to population, it may be theoretically possible to move to renewable or somatic sources, but the expenditure and scale of wind farms or photovoltaic arrays, and the network of powerlines needed to link them, would likely exceed the invest-ment capacity of either government or private capital. While it may seem physically feasible to supply the 232 GJ each Australian citizen uses annually with solar panels in a country over 7.5 million square kilometres in size, the capital cost at current rates is staggering. At an optimistic 20% capacity taken over the whole day, each resident would need a 37 kW solar system to generate their total energy needs, including domestic power, transport and manufacturing. At commercial rates this might cost AU$1.50 per watt to install, for an initial cost of AU$55,000 per person or a total cost of AU$1320 trillion – nearly the entire Australian GDP for one year. This is an optimistic figure, given the cost of design and infrastructure, but it underlines the basic magnitude of the problem. Against this it is reasonable to assume a significant reduction in energy requirements – perhaps 30% – because a large proportion of energy in coal-generated electricity is lost as heat, a conversion cost that would be much lower with photovoltaic or wind generation. There would also be some efficiency gained in moving to electric vehicles.

Even assuming the cost of this smaller project could be met by the country spending a third of all government revenue for ten years on the project, the roughly 750 gigawatt arrays required for a population of 26 million would be about twice the 2013 worldwide photovoltaic manufacturing capacity for those ten years (Roney 2013). And this is only to meet the requirements of a single country of moderate population size. An array of this size would also need regular cleaning and maintenance, a massive task with large ongoing costs.

The point is that energy sources that derive their power from the sun or wind are, by definition, dispersed and have low yields per unit area. At between 1 and 2.5 W/m^2 on average, a wind farm is more productive than woodland, but not by orders of magnitude. Although they have the advantage of being able to be used for agriculture as well as for energy, since the turbines themselves have relatively small concrete bases and are spread apart, the size of such farms would need to be gigantic. A typical 1.5 MW turbine produces about 3285 MWh of electricity per year in a good location. Each resident of Australia needs about 64 MWh per year in total, so each turbine serves perhaps 52 people. A modern wind farm has about four turbines per square kilometre, so with 461,000 turbines needed for the country, an area of 100,000 km^2 would be given over to wind farming. This is slightly larger than Portugal, and given the size of the Australian landmass it seems highly feasible. But annual global production of turbines totalled about 51,500 MW in 2014, so again Australia would soak up more than all the turbines produced worldwide at current rates for ten years in order to achieve a shift to wind power, since current installed wind capacity contributes only about 5.5% of national electricity (Global Wind Energy Council 2015; Pitt&Sherry 2015).

These figures are, of course, simply to establish the scale of shifts to somatic power sources. Their sheer size is why most serious energy commentators cannot envisage a quick shift away from fossil fuels back to somatic, or sun-driven, sources despite the inevitable expansion of the wind and solar sectors. The volumes of required energy to sustain contemporary life are too great to be sourced from non-fossil fuel sources using proven technologies in the next decades, nuclear excepted (Figures 7.1 and 7.2). For China and India this argument underpins their energy policy, in which research into

Figure 7.1 The Grohnde nuclear power complex on the River Weser in Germany. It is amongst the most efficient units in the world, producing 1,360 MW of electricity, or as much as 300 square kilometres of solar panels. The plant occupies about 9.7 hectares, giving it a power density of 14,000 watts per square metre. It is due to be shut down in 2021 as a consequence of the 2011 decision by the German Government to phase out nuclear power
Credit: Frank Oppermann/Shutterstock.com

Figure 7.2 The power generating section of the Itaupu Dam on the border of Brazil and Paraguay. The 20 generator units have a total capacity of 14,000 MW, with power split between the two countries. The dam supplies one fifth of Brazil's electricity through a network of long-distance transmission lines. It is the second largest hydroelectric dam in the world by generating capacity, exceeded only by the 22,400 MW of China's Three Gorges Dam. If the power produced is divided by the area of the lake behind the dam, it has a power density of about 10 watts per square metre.
Credit: Iuliia Timofeeva/Shutterstock.com

fourth-generation nuclear power plants, including thorium-fuelled reactors, is a major plank. For countries that are winding down their nuclear generating capacity, or those with none, a shift away from fossil fuels can only mean a reduction in the volume of available energy in the medium term. If, as proponents of compact cities argue, this can be offset by the elimination of cars and a move to apartment living, then the impact must invariably be shaped along class lines. If relative energy scarcity becomes a reality, then the rich will have greater access to it and will shape their lifestyles accordingly. But the mobility brought to the masses in Australia, Canada, the US and increasingly Brazil and European countries through car ownership will be curtailed unless a public transport system such as that enjoyed by Japan can be constructed. However, this is difficult and expensive in countries with low population densities and little track record in building dense and complex infrastructure.

This innate understanding that energy scarcity will play out according to market forces has driven much of the unexpected opposition to energy policies that appear progressive. In Australia a carbon tax to encourage a move away from fossil fuels as energy feedstocks for industry is credited with removing the Labor government from office in 2013 (Thals 2015). The vehemence with which the issue fractured the Labor alliance of working-class Australians and progressive urban intellectuals has left the party with the challenge of healing this rift before it can formulate a cohesive new energy policy. It remains to be seen whether this can be achieved, or whether the effects of urban consolidation and fossil-fuel replacement remain inimical to traditional working-class aspirations.

These, of course, are not static or unchanging. They do, however, have considerable historical momentum. The assumption that cities must become denser, and people be encouraged to forsake their cars, carries with it clear demographic consequences. In modern cities areas of greater density have lower fertility rates than suburbs, and in almost all cases they are demographically unsustainable. The general demographic pattern in these cities is that their core populations are replenished by migration inwards from suburbs, or by international or rural to urban migration. Thus the life that is being lived in the core of modern cities is one where the cultural advantages of these locations are enjoyed and a diverse range of good job opportunities present themselves, but they are regarded as poor places to have children in any great numbers. As developing countries undergo profound demographic transitions, it is possible that the city core may be the most fulfilling place to live, but it will settle into a symbiosis with suburban or rural areas which will replenish its population from their higher fertility rates. However, absolute energy scarcity may make the prospect of having children even in these outlying areas too unattractive, as physical mobility is curtailed and city centres become ever more attractive for the resources they command in close proximity. This would leave few options for those who want to have more than two children without incurring the high costs of large apartments in good urban locations, further accelerating demographic decline as the seed-bed of middle-sized working-class families disappears.

3. Developing cities can undergo faster rates of transition than developed ones

This proposition subverts traditional ideas of urban development that are predicated on the history of the large capital cities of the early 20th century. It is a function of the relationship between urban development and national development. The key to this phenomenon seems to be the many stages of technological sophistication that exist in developing cities, which allow them to develop simultaneously in many ways. Whereas the development of Paris or Berlin relied on technologies that required enormous resources devoted to infrastructure, a developing city in Asia or South America can swell through informal settlements that quickly adopt supple forms of energy and communication such as bottled gas, diversion of electric power supply and mobile phones. If granted formal title, informal settlements quickly become sources of development capital for their owners in a windfall process. This can unleash a dynamism that can be hard to direct, and its transformative power can be seen in the changing skylines of cities such as Istanbul. The population, too, is profoundly changed, particularly in regard to fertility and aspirations.

The advent of media like television is also highly transformative. The stories and images of other lives that are watched everyday in all parts of the city create collective experiences that inevitably are aspirational. Thus the dwellers of Mumbai or Manila develop an expectation of consumption, often on meagre resources. The care that urban workers take in their appearance often belies the amount of money they have available to spend.

On the other hand the enormous resources that cities in China are willing to spend on their urban infrastructure matches any similar programmes of the past, such as the construction of the underground rail lines in Paris, London and New York in the early 20th century. These current projects have the advantage of utilising modern tunnelling and shoring techniques, as well as linking to high speed rail built following French and Japanese precedents.

This is, of course, not universal. Cities like Manila may have vibrant cores for the wealthy, but struggle with low rates of sewered dwellings. This is a reflection of Philippine national wealth, with its productive capacity still unable to generate the amount of public money needed to put in basic services despite relatively low labour costs. But the converse is not necessarily better: developed economies such as the US and Australia struggle to upgrade their infrastructure despite their wealth, high tax rates and sophisticated governance. High costs of labour, of land acquisition and political resistance to new projects, as well as a reluctance to take on public debt, have made the construction of new mass transit lines in major cities a slow and expensive process.

4. Capitalism is inherently technologically progressive

While it may not be inherently socially progressive over all its cycles, capitalism displays a propensity to innovate and to encourage resource efficiency that belies its exploitative nature. This point should be understood in relation to the first proposition, that technology is a social phenomenon. The obvious extension of this point is that, for manufacturing, energy is a cost of production. In a competitive environment lowering production costs conveys an advantage, and the capital cost of upgrading equipment is returned in the form of lowered production costs. This is evident in the falling amount of energy required to produce each dollar of GDP in advanced economies.

However, it appears this is also a function of a maturing economy: in its early years a state may use enormous amounts of dirty and inefficient energy to produce steel and electricity as it scales up production, with a corresponding decrease in air quality. The cleanup can be hastened by legislation, forcing industry to adopt cleaner fuels and processes, but this is only possible as these technologies become available. Legislation is often credited with making this change, but any shift over the long term towards a service-based economy, and the adoption of the most energy efficient processes in manufacturing and power generation, will produce a similar effect.

However, the relationship between the legal framework and industrial development is not a fixed one. There is a balance between the harm a process or industry might do, the cost of compliance to reduce that harm, and the continued profitability of that process or industry. Risk elimination can be undertaken with little cost up to a point, but to reduce risk to zero requires exponential increases of time and money. Industrial risk is low in advanced service economies not only because they have the legal frameworks to prosecute shoddy practices, but also because the risk inherent in manufacturing, whether it comes from coal extraction, overcrowded workplaces or chemical exposure, has been shifted to poorer countries.

How does this affect modern cities? In advanced economies cities enjoy clean air and water because they rely on modern plant and generators that create little pollution, and they contain modern cars that run relatively cleanly, with few particulate emissions. The great demand for steel that characterises early urban infrastructure has passed, and the proportion of the population in service jobs may approach 80%. In the developing world, with its low labour costs, the arrival of manufacturing jobs is profoundly transformative. Capital investment and the desire for a measure of certainty force changes to local practice, and spur infrastructure development. This may initially be cheap and dirty, but over time if state resources increase then parts of the infrastructure may become very sophisticated. Developing states are characterised by unevenness of resource allocation and spread of wealth, but with sufficient economic expansion the portion of the city that is middle class will expand to include all the elements of a consumer society, often on average incomes that would be a hallmark of urban poverty in developed societies. Brazil is a current case in point.

The result is that cities, as they get wealthier, initially become dirtier and then become cleaner. The air quality in Tokyo is currently better than it was in 1990 on almost every indicator (Tokyo Metropolitan Government 2010). The same is true for all major advanced cities. A 2009 study of six major air pollutants in the five largest cities of New York State found significant downward trends for all pollutants between 1980 and 2007 (Buckley & Mitchell 2010). In all cases this has been aided by legislation that set limits on permissible pollutant levels, but the fact that this legislation supported a trend inherent in transport and manufacturing has meant a swift transition to better urban air quality.

5. Cities will develop to the lowest density that their infrastructure and governance can sustain

The work of Angel and his collaborators has charted this trend in the modern era, and it is as widespread as it is consistent (Angel 2012). In some cities we are witnessing a reversal of this tendency, as the provision of services becomes more costly and the political will to expand urban boundaries declines. Sydney is a case in point. Post-war suburbanisation proceeded in Sydney through government utilities providing sewerage, water, power and roads for new developments. This effectively socialised the costs of these new suburbs, with existing ratepayers and utilities customers subsidising new homeowners. Slowly, however, the infrastructure costs of new development were shifted to the individual buyer, with levies on new house blocks driving up land costs to the highest levels in Australia. This reduced the attractiveness of fringe urban development, since new development in old suburbs could tap into existing infrastructure without these additional charges. As the political will to transform rural properties on the urban fringe into suburbs declined, apartments built on amalgamated lots or re-zoned industrial land became the dominant form of new housing. With a public transport system operating at capacity during peak times due to high usage rates, and with no government appetite for borrowing, housing located close to the city centre continues to climb in desirability. As a result the urban density of Sydney has increased due to a combination of infrastructure costs imposed on urban fringe housing, limited expansion of public transport and a policy shift towards urban consolidation as manufacturing disappears from the urban core, and is replaced by sophisticated consumption in the guise of "lifestyle".

Other Australian cities such as Perth have yet to experience this increase in density, as they have yet to reach the thresholds of cost that turned around Sydney's density decline. It should be noted that it is not an absolute failure in public transport or infrastructure provision that has contributed to Sydney's transformation. It has the highest usage of public transport in Australia by far, and it has the largest population. Rather it is that its dynamism has outrun its natural advantages, and the city has been strangled by its own success. The scale of new investment needed to ease its traffic, for example, is beyond the capacity of state coffers in the current era, and hence the premium people are prepared to pay to be close to work and leisure continues to rise.

6. Urban living negates natural variability through collective infrastructure

For most city dwellers the most visible aspect of natural variability is the occasional imposition of water restrictions. However, this is more of an inconvenience than a threat to life, since so much urban water of drinking quality is used to water gardens and in industrial processes. Bottled water is also widely available, and it seems inconceivable to a city dweller that a year of poor rainfall could mean death through thirst or crop failure as for a subsistence farmer. The collective might of the city has insulated even the poorest against these consequences, largely through the application of energy to filter and pump water and to import large quantities of food and shift them to where they are needed.

While urban poverty remains widespread and evident in developing countries, even in the cities where it is prevalent the overall advantages of modern infrastructure and transport mitigate the effects of climatic variability. This correlates with increasing urbanisation: in Asia between 1991 and 2015 the prevalence of undernourishment declined from 23.6% to 12.1%, with corresponding declines from 27.6% to 20% in Africa, and 15.1% to 5.3% in South America (FAO n.d.). Thus the transfer of poor people from countryside to city demonstrates that the urban poor are better off in terms of food security than the rural poor. UN Water also concludes that more urban dwellers (96%) have access to improved water sources than rural inhabitants (81%). These figures explain, in part, some of the most basic motivations for moving from country to city (UN Water n.d.).

7. Lower energy densities mean lower mobility

Any assessment of the relationship between energy and urban life in modern cities needs to take into account the many ways energy is used in contemporary life, and the various amounts involved. The use of solar power to achieve domestic self-sufficiency is feasible if it is used for lighting, especially with low-consumption LED lights now widely available. Computers, televisions and mobile devices could all run off a small solar storage system. With modern cooktops it is even possible to cook from a set of solar-charged batteries, a significant advance since heat conversion is one of the largest draws on domestic power. Long-duration heat exchange, like reverse-cycle air conditioning, is generally beyond the capacity of domestic solar systems, hence the emphasis on passive heating and cooling in the design of contemporary buildings. Hot water can be supplemented by direct heating through roof-top absorption, which brings significant reductions in power usage.

Thus it is possible, as demonstrated by Mobbs, to achieve great gains in energy efficiency in an urban household if it has sufficient roof and ground area for a localised photovoltaic system, supplemented by battery storage (Mobbs 2010). But this is only a fraction of the total energy consumption of a household. The bulk of its energy usage lies in the supply chains that provide food, clothing and consumption goods, and the cars and infrastructure that allow the household to exploit the opportunities of the city. Even if only used for part of the day, the great power densities of modern cars, even small hybrid vehicles, represent the most concentrated form of on-demand power available to consumers. Only in limited cases can these be forgone with no corresponding loss of amenity.

It is useful to think of a city as subject to centrifugal forces that tend to drive it towards lower densities, and cohesive forces that encourage compaction. These are rarely in equilibrium. Cities grow and shrink, and house more or fewer inhabitants. Private vehicles may be thought of as a centrifugal force, in that they enable people to cover large distances quickly and with little physical effort. Yet they only work this way insofar as they enable the opposite: ready access to the many different opportunities in work, consumption and self-fulfilment that provide the centralising forces in urban life. The idea of the walkable city as advocated by new urbanists like Leon Krier proposed that the radius of an easy walk would encompass all those urban functions needed and desired on a daily basis. This seems to me to severely underestimate the breadth of appeal of the modern city.

Reducing energy consumption through increasing urban densities, and hence encouraging a shift to public transport, might seem effective in that inner-city dwellers historically use cars less. But this assumption, pursued by Newman and Kenworthy (1999), was tested using historical data by Michael Breheny. He concluded that "energy savings from urban containment are likely to be disappointingly low" (Breheny 1995, p.99). This is crudely reflected in per capita energy consumption figures. Singapore, with its predominantly apartment living and extensive public transport, uses about the same energy per capita as the Netherlands, and more than New Zealand. Hong Kong is more frugal, with usage similar to Portugal's. Highly urbanised Japan is similar to France and Germany (World Bank n.d.).

Apart from road maintenance, which is not a trivial cost to taxpayers, most costs of private car ownership are borne by the individual motorist. Capital costs, depreciation, maintenance and fuel are all privatised. The transfer of these motorists to public transport would involve the socialisation of these costs, with partial cost recovery through fares and taxes on private transport. However, few public transport lines run profitably, and shifting people from their cars to public transport also involves shifting much of the cost of transporting them from their own wallets to the public purse. In real terms it is hard to replicate the convenience and personal comfort of the private car convincingly even if the motorist could be persuaded to pass the considerable annual outlay on their car to the state for investment in public transport.

All of these factors militate against a complete shift of urban dwellers from private vehicles to public transport. Apart from issues of cost, the prospect of using solar or wind energy to power electric vehicles seems remote due to the low energy densities these technologies generate, and the complexities of distributing and storing that energy. While it is practically possible using current technology, in real terms this is unlikely to displace the much greater energy density of fossil-fuel engines (Smil 2010). Thus, using the contemporary city as a baseline, restrictions on the use of fossil fuels will result in an overall reduction in personal mobility.

There is, of course, plenty of scope for increasing the efficiency of the current fleet of private vehicles. For a single occupant, a one litre modern fuel-injected engine provides adequate power to travel safely around city streets and on freeways. Services such as Uber and minibus routes have the potential to add further niches to efficient point-to-point transport. Without moving away from fossil fuels there are many avenues for significant reductions in the amount of fuel consumed in urban life. However, compared to the current mobility enjoyed by the population as a whole, in advanced countries constraining the availability of fossil fuels will result in less personal travel, and a smaller travel radius, for most people.

8. Energy extraction costs will effect their own transition

As we have seen, in market economies, the tendency to greater efficiency means a reduction in energy usage per unit of production over time. For mature economies with little population growth, this may manifest in an absolute reduction in the amount of energy used annually across the whole economy. Growing economies may become more efficient per unit produced, but because of expanding production they will consume more total energy each year. As extraction costs become higher for resources such as oil, the market will encourage alternate fuels that become economic at certain price thresholds. It is hard to predict exactly what these may be, since there are so many variables in the production and distribution of energy. Natural gas is a current example. Large finds are being commercially exploited and shipped internationally from Australia, whose political structure and geographic location make it an attractive energy supplier. Shale gas extracted by drilling and fracking across America has also transformed its energy market.

Jesse Ausubel has argued that energy transitions have been marked by a decarbonisation of fuels over time, from the high prevalence of carbon over hydrogen in wood burned for fuel, to the ratio of one carbon atom to four of hydrogen in methane. Thus in his view methane will be a transitional fuel towards a hydrogen economy, driven by the increasing energy density of fuels that are mainly composed of hydrogen, and culminating in hydrogen itself as the dominant fuel in several decades (Ausubel 2003). While current methods of making hydrogen use more energy than that yielded by the hydrogen as a portable fuel, it is conceivable that future nuclear reactors could supply the heat needed for hydrogen production through steam reforming of methane.

While this view has proven historically accurate, there is no guarantee that the shift to hydrogen will be the dominant market response to higher oil extraction prices. Each possible alternative has practical limitations that determine how widely they are taken up. While current technology has a host of energy sources that could be used where cost is no constraint, in reality the sheer scale of energy extraction and distribution in the contemporary world has been achieved through accumulated investment over decades. Whatever happens will piggyback off existing infrastructure and know-how, but declines in oil supply will be met by the market in ways that are difficult to predict.

There is no evidence that the predictions of catastrophic collapse made by Peak Oil theorists, who envisage a dramatic decline in productive capacity and social organisation as oil runs out, will come to pass. These millenarian sentiments have been effectively critiqued, and provide a poor framework for energy thinking (Smil 2010). Whether aided by legislation or not, fuel substitution and the urban changes that will accompany it will emerge most effectively through market dynamics rather than through ideological commitments to one form of energy over another.

Where, in the broadest sense, the public good requires action, national strategies have been devised to prevent these issues escalating. A case in point is the poor air quality in large Chinese cities, where surrounding heavy industry and growing vehicle numbers have diminished the quality of life for all. A concerted national effort involving decentralising industry and jobs, as well as expanding nuclear generating capacity, has been launched to rectify this. While the tendency over time is for urban air quality to improve, legislating for air quality can force the level of investment needed to improve things to occur more quickly. Given the capacity of China's government at all levels to direct economic activity, it remains to be seen whether the pressing political issue of air quality is sufficient to force the massive shift to modern factories on the urban periphery, and new generators relying on fuels other than coal, that is needed to address the problem quickly (Johnson 2015).

9. The business of cities is business

Western views of urban planning in the latter half of the 20th century were dominated initially by analyses of cities as places that built on traditional models of urban space and urban life, or later as places distinguished by class divisions emblematic of wider problems within capitalism (Sandercock 1976; Lynch 1960; Castells 1978). Consequently the first impulse of reforming planners was to correct the deficiencies of the capitalist city through redistribution of resources and housing using the state as a vehicle, building on earlier critiques that argued that capitalism is incapable of housing its citizens because it relies on market mechanisms, with winners and losers. However critical this approach may have been, it tacitly accepted the rates and tax base that funded the state and provided funds for public housing.

The resulting ambivalence towards the city as a place of capitalist production was bridged by constraining business and industry through legislation to promote the public good, and by expanding the tax base on both business and personal income to fund state projects that mitigated some of the harsher tendencies of capitalism. The most visible aspects of this in developed economies was the expansion of universities and technical colleges to allow young people from all levels of society to access the financial advantages of higher education. In addition public housing was built so that the state could subsidise those priced out of desirable areas, or who were unable to get into rental housing at all. Both of these were the target of massive spending, often with very progressive results. When done well, large public housing schemes certainly aided the poor to live in some comfort and security close to work. When poorly done, the resulting housing projects isolated their inhabitants from the normalcy of traditional street life, and produced pockets of fear and crime.

The market, of course, continued to provide the bulk of housing in forms that proved attractive to the burgeoning middle class. But the state had emerged as a major player in land use planning and housing development, and ideological goals rather than market forces determined how state funds were spent. This vast fund spurred lively debate about spending for the public good, supported by rising productivity and developing markets through the 1960s and 70s.

This alternative debate that rested on public funding was, inevitably, not overly concerned with the continued viability of the city as a place of capitalist production. As manufacturing moved to lower wage countries, the growth of service jobs made the physical planning of cities less taxing because highly polluting crude industry was disappearing. Zoning laws that separated industry from housing, and commerce from education, lost their effectiveness for the public good. The city became attractive again as a place of consumption as much as one of production.

It is no accident that the urban design that emerged under the rubric of the New Urbanism uses the pre-industrial city as its model. The benign nature of the artisanal way of life it rests on is a far cry from the manufacturing city that Mumford so decried. Craft, entertainment and eating are now the centrepieces of urban renewal, since they are the public activities of the service economy. But the true economic function of the city remains one of free exchange and association, its allure composed of the myriad combinations of work, housing and self-actualisation that the modern city contains. These are accessed through a variety of modes – walking, driving, public transport in various permutations. To imagine the city as composed of self-sufficient quarters is to miss its historical role as a place of exchange of ideas, goods and identities. Any development that restricts mobility around the city also undermines its historical agency.

10. Greater density means less sunshine and land

Urban consolidation, with more people living in apartments and greater densities of inhabitants per unit area, is incompatible with increased household energy autonomy. This is one of the key points in Patrick Troy's trenchant critique titled *The Perils of Urban Consolidation* (Troy 1996). Solar power may be useful in supplementing the electricity a household draws from the grid, and a large enough array with sufficient battery storage may make the household independent of the grid. But it would need to be a large system indeed to achieve this over the course of the year, particularly in winter. In apartment blocks the area exposed to the sun per apartment is very small, and decreases with greater density. Solar power may not be able to power a modern city in all its needs, but increasing density reduces its possible contribution. Generating banks of wind turbines or solar panels would need to be located remotely, and apartments lock people into highly serviced environments. These require continuous power for lifts and services, and per capita use of water is surprisingly high (Talent, Troy & Dovers 2013).

The same is true for all decentralised systems of harvesting water and dealing with waste. A suburban house has far more potential for the installation of local systems than an apartment block, purely by virtue of its land area. Thus as cities increase in density they lock in centralised systems and preclude those that operate at household scale. This is not necessarily bad as centralised systems have greater efficiency and are better operated and maintained, but their critical role in maintaining urban densities must be acknowledged. All proposals that promote decentralised electricity generation and storage at household level decrease in viability as urban densities increase.

11. The modern city relies on the pacification of the modern state through energy

As noted by Saskia Sassen, modern cities play critical administrative and symbolic functions within modern states (Sassen 2008). Tokyo is emblematic of modern Japan, London of modern Britain and so on. Regardless of their standing as international cities that provide services and havens for international capital, they are first and foremost the creation of local history, and the bulk of their services are for local consumption. Their international standing rests on their national standing, and they are sustained by their respective economies and institutions in food, power, education and law and order.

This is not exclusively true, as the case of Hong Kong can attest. But each of these cities is marked by an orderly functioning of daily life that allows their higher international calling to be met. The integration of the city into its locality, which supplies water and power as well as some local food, cannot be exposed to social unrest or criminality if it is to remain viable in the modern sense. Ancient cities expended large resources to protect themselves from attack, and the vulnerability even of Rome to piracy underlines the difference that a pacified modern state can make to the flourishing of its cities.

This raises the large questions that pertain to the formation of the modern state and its role in urban formation. While these are beyond the scope of this book, it seems important to note that without the historically unprecedented pacification that modern equipment and policing can bring, the contemporary city would not be viable.

Pacification is one of the undervalued aspects of the modern democratic state. It allows efficient distribution of goods and labour, without the distorting effects of extortion or corruption. In a modern state, where the public realm is ideally constituted by the rule of law, equitable taxation and equally fair distribution of state resources, loyalty to the state must be coaxed as much as demanded. Corruption is corrosive to markets, because it is capricious and discourages transparent interactions as well as adding non-productive costs.

All modern states rely heavily on energy for policing. This has been used in both the oppressive and the constructive sense. Saul Dubow has shown that the consolidation of the Apartheid state in South Africa in the 1950s and 60s went hand in hand with a policy of modernisation and infrastructure building (Dubow 2014). It may have been rooted in racism, but in its execution it was a thoroughly modern phenomenon. But even the most enlightened state is impossible to imagine without a supporting apparatus of patrol cars, helicopters, guns, intelligence units and electronically controlled prisons. While it may be desirable to imagine the fading away of these instruments of legal enforcement, it is undeniable that they have contributed to the general reduction in violence that marks modern times (Pinker 2012).

In addition there is the vast energy directed to military use. The national military, in democratic states, exists as the ultimate guarantor of property rights. The stability and endurance of the law and private property is protected by the military from drastic alteration through invasion. This imperative is held high in most countries, as reflected in their relative military spending. The military is also custodian of the vast potential energy held in explosives and nuclear weapons where they exist. The capacity to quickly and accurately deploy energy is critical to military success, and it seems unlikely that the energy resources and stocks held as insurance by militaries worldwide are going to be relinquished quickly.

There are some promising signs. The huge stockpile of nuclear warheads held by Russia and the US is being partly dismantled and used as nuclear fuel for generating electricity. But tactical advantage remains a driver of military energy thinking, and destructive capacity is rarely sacrificed to save money or energy. The innovations of the military have also been testing beds for applications taken up elsewhere. Nuclear submarines proved the viability of large, complex electric or steam-driven vessels running on small nuclear reactors measuring some 10 m by 10 m. This in turn established the basic design of the pressurised water reactors that provide most nuclear-generated electricity.

Energy transitions and urban form

It seems perhaps evasive that a book on energy and urban form does not end with some kind of predictions about contemporary cities. But each city has a history and a context, and these are powerful determinants for how its development unfolds. I have lived in cities all my life, and believe that they offer the greatest opportunity for self-fulfilment for the greatest number of people. Based on the principles above, a number of tendencies in both policy and practice can be identified.

For the purposes of any discussion it is worth retaining the simple division of cities according to whether they are part of advanced economies, fast-developing economies or economies yet to achieve rapid development. In the first batch we can include cities in the US, Europe, Canada, Australasia and Japan, in the second countries like China and Brazil, and in the last regions of sub-Saharan Africa and parts of the Middle East. While it may be a truism of development studies that there is no pre-ordained course of national development that will inevitably unfold for each country, it seems equally true that aspects of modernity and modern life have penetrated into almost every region on earth. Generators of various sizes are found everywhere, as are motor vehicles and outboard motors. Technologies with small energy requirements, like telecommunications, can arise quickly as they have in Africa. But those with larger energy needs, like industry or mass transit, cannot bypass basic energy rules. Intermittent generation, called load shedding in India and Pakistan, can still power a mobile phone network with its dispersed consumers and batteries, aided by backup generation for transmission. However, without power a factory or a suburban train quickly grinds to a halt.

Many cities within developing economies have intermittent power supply, which casts doubt on official figures for people who have access to electricity (Tongia 2014). Cities in advanced economies generally have a secure power supply, with interruptions limited to a few hours per year. They also have larger power usage per capita. The true picture of electricity availability in a country is not given by installed generating capacity *per se*, but rather by how much is available for how long. Thus developing economies have a great incentive to increase both installed capacity, and to shift to systems that are more reliable. For developing cities the combination of services that emerges through modernisation may include a sophisticated mobile phone network with high penetration, but poor public transport and interminable traffic jams, as in Lagos, Nigeria.

The biggest challenge facing developing economies is the consolidation of an effective state. Without one, the lack of political and legal certainty needed for capital investment, including infrastructure, severely hampers the creation of productive and wealthy cities. In countries without an effective and legitimate state, the penetration of technologies will always remain at a local level. This suits phones and minibuses, but not high-speed rail. An interesting case in point is Brazil, where in recent years the quasi-military police units of BOPE in Rio de Janeiro state have been used to bring favelas in Rio city back under state control. Drug traffickers and citizen groups obligated to them have held effective control in these areas in recent years. This is perhaps the most dramatic example of urban state pacification in recent years, as both Rio and Brazil consolidate gains made in productivity and middle-class advancement. The survival of pockets of a modern city still outside of official control is an embarrassment to a modern state, a loss to utility revenues and local rates, and an impediment to the growth of the urban real estate market. Taking these areas by force creates conditions for the elimination of all three.

Countries like Nigeria, with its great mineral wealth, face an ongoing battle to consolidate an effective state. Fractured by sectarian violence and hampered by corruption, the enormous potential of a nation just a five hour flight from Southern Europe remains only partially fulfilled, even as its people sign up for mobile phone packages. But developments over the decade to 2015 have brought significant changes, as the service sector expands in Nigeria. Better governance is also a general trend in the region, and some observers claim that sub-Saharan African economies will diversify more rapidly than they might grow (*The Economist* 2015).

The imperative for better governance is strong: there is yet to be an example of an advanced economy emerging without state guidance and infrastructure building. This in turn affects the provision of services to major cities. Whereas telecommunications may be able to be provided through a privately built network alone, distributing water and collecting sewage are best handled through a network built by the state. It is possible to have privately distributed energy as in the case of bottled gas, but this too needs an efficient road network to make it viable. It is hard to imagine a safe and efficient city built by private interests, without state subsidy and assistance to allow its poorer citizens to access daily necessities.

Developing economies also do not have the benefit of an inter-generational accumulation of infrastructure. In Europe and America, for example, generations of spending on roads, electricity generation and rail has left a legacy of networks that may require maintenance, but are larger than could be built within a short span of time regardless of how many resources are thrown into the effort. Thus infrastructure provision might absorb a growing proportion of national budgets in some African countries, but it cannot in one generation match the accumulation over several generations that developed economies enjoy.

The result is that developing cities have an unevenness in the infrastructure they enjoy, which diminishes in the energy-intensive services that require central government assistance. Manila enjoys great media and telecommunications coverage, but only a fraction of its houses are sewered. Yet the city holds together because its limited supply of power and food, together with its fleet of private vehicles, is enough to transcend the limitations of the pre-modern city. Even relatively poor countries like the Philippines are massive beneficiaries of modernity.

Operations in poor cities can also be rendered extremely efficient through poverty. Because of this, and poor government provision of infrastructure, it is possible to imagine slum areas of cities developing economies consisting largely of post-industrial technologies that can be provided with little government involvement. While services as a proportion of GDP might grow to expand banking or aid mineral exports, day to day life will be marked by small-scale transactions and entrepreneurs who can nimbly operate through what have been termed disruptive technologies in countries where there is a substantial sector to disrupt. This might be supplemented by some targeted manufacturing to take advantage of low labour rates, but growth in this sector would depend on infrastructure projects such as roads, airports and harbours as well as power generation. If the state can reach this threshold, as in China, then manufacturing becomes viable and can be an armature for further economic development. However, in Nigeria state revenues in 2014 amounted to US$15.45 billion, out of a total GDP of US$569 billion, or just over 2.7%. It is hard to imagine expansive infrastructure being built with such a small proportion of national economic activity (Trading Economics n.d.). In developed economies government revenues can account for up to a quarter of GDP.

The point here is that energy and urban form cannot be divorced from greater historical questions. A vision for Portland, Oregon, may be pointless in Kigali, Rwanda, because the infrastructure base onto which it needs to be grafted is totally different, and much poorer. What will succeed in Kigali will acknowledge its particular history, constraints and potential. There is no lack today of publications outlining the generic problem of growing cities, most framed in terms reminiscent of Alvin Toffler's *Future Shock*. The acceptance of modernity as a term that describes the relentless change of modern life has given way to a fetishising of change *per se* as the only framework of analysis or indeed description of modern cities. This has not only produced the breathless books and studies that conflate similar issues across all modern cities, but has also divorced the field from a critical sense of history (Burdett & Sudjic 2007).

Perhaps the most important shift in urban studies in recent years is the decline of the paradigm that growth is inevitable and has its own momentum. We now have a complex situation where population growth in all developed economies has ceased, save for those with large immigration programmes. This is also true for developing countries like China and Brazil, with overall fertility rates of 1.55 and 1.79 respectively (Central Intelligence Agency n.d.). Thus urbanisation is not driven by national population growth but by more complex factors like mechanised agriculture and the pursuit of opportunities in cities and towns. Understanding this provides a critical human dimension to a problem often presented as a blind fleeing towards cities driven by lack of choice. While this is true in some cases, it ignores the aspirational move to the city that propels so many millions, and the hopes that go with it. New urban dwellers are not simply numbers that need to be accommodated through rationalist blocks of apartments: they are people who have come to participate in the complex exchange of ideas, goods, services and class position that the city offers. They have industry, nous and often surprising self-discipline.

In a world where all regions except Africa will be in population decline by 2050, living in the city will be the norm for two-thirds of humanity. Most of these will be smaller and mid-size cities on current trends (United Nations

2014). It is difficult to see the disparity between developing and developed economies disappearing in three and a half decades, despite the high rates of growth that may occur over certain periods. Thus disparities in city wealth and energy use will persist. However, certain countries with modern infrastructure but declining populations may be forced to adopt immigration policies to prevent their dependency ratios – the number of children and old people per productive worker – becoming unmanageable. The economic consequences of these developments are uncharted. While the tax base may have to expand from income taxes to consumption taxes as the number of workers declines, the scarcity of labour could cause a massive wealth transfer from the elderly as they depend on the young for services. This may parallel the situation after events such as plagues in Medieval Europe, where survivors could look forward to high wages and good working conditions due to a scarcity of labour.

An ageing population also means less energy consumption in certain sectors (Institute for Future Energy Consumer Needs and Behavior 2014). Older people drive less, and spend more time at home. Their greatest demand is in health services, food and international travel. In Japan oil consumption generally declined from the late 1990s as the population aged, but slow economic growth has confounded this picture. Studies in the US have shown that as people age they do indeed drive less, but use more energy at home. However, research in Switzerland concluded that young and old households consume about the same amount of energy per capita (Institute for Future Energy Consumer Needs and Behavior 2014). Since the detached house is most suitable for solar power, this may be the age group who can most easily convert their houses to solar. However, their ageing will have little influence on the energy inputs to their food supply, travel or medical procedures (Brooks 2010).

For the working population, the idea that cities need to grow more compact in order to reduce private vehicle usage and increase walking or transit use has been influential for over three decades. In its extended form this argument proposes polycentric cities, where employment is concentrated in a number of nodes and away from the city centre. Development is also encouraged along transit routes, as these are well served by public transport. This model of urban development arose in the 1970s in response to the inflation of oil prices in 1973, and was intended to reduce fossil fuel use in anticipation of a decline in recoverable oil supplies which would, it was thought, become evident by the year 2000 (Rygole 1978). In recent years the argument for reducing fossil fuel use has, of course, been driven by concerns over carbon dioxide as a greenhouse gas, and the effect of increasing CO_2 levels on global temperatures. Regardless of the motivation, the arguments as to how cities might function with less reliance on fossil fuels remain the same.

When cities in advanced economies are made more compact, a number of things happen. The first is that the fertility rate declines even further than that for the city as a whole. Why this is so reflects many factors, but in simple terms societies with expectations of high living standards will not have large families in small apartments. This exacerbates the underlying population-wide trend to lower birth rates, so that the dense areas of cities will experience net population decline over time. This may result in small household sizes within each apartment, leading to an increase in energy consumption per capita because the energy costs of servicing high-rise apartments remain fairly constant regardless of how many people actually live in each apartment.

A similar pattern has been observed in the dense historical cores of European cities. Cities like Milan and Venice lost a large proportion of their working-class families from the 1960s onwards, with corresponding decreases in population density. While the number of dwellings in their centres may not have changed substantially, the number of people living there dropped dramatically. These areas became desirable and expensive, and the deserted lanes of contemporary night-time Venice are a salutary lesson in urban transformation.

Thus dwelling density is a poor indicator of how effective a city is in housing people, and in reducing their energy consumption. The equation is also skewed by class factors. Exotic tastes incur large energy costs for food, clothing, whitegoods and travel. For the wealthy the convenient but restricted life in an apartment is offset by a country or coastal property, and by the means to commute between the two.

In Sydney the highest urban birth rates are to be found in a ring of suburbs developed after the Second World War, and now home to lower-middle-class and working families, many started by immigrants (Figures 7.3 and 7.4).

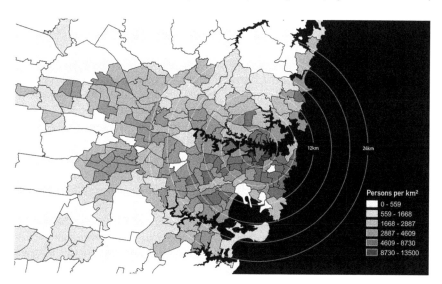

Figure 7.3 Population density for Sydney region, 2011, persons/km2
Based on Australian Bureau of Statistics data: ABS (2013, Table 1)

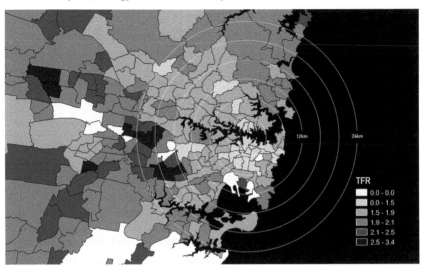

Figure 7.4 Total Fertility Rate for the Sydney region, 2011
Based on Australian Bureau of Statistics data: ABS (2014, Table 3.1)

These are also the households that have been identified as most at risk from higher oil prices, due to their high dependence on cars for transport (Dodson & Sipe 2008). Yet they remain a vital animating force in the city, a talent pool and vigorous crucible of small business responsible for much of the city's population replenishment. That they do so despite their vulnerability to oil price shocks and mortgage rates speaks to the role of simple aspiration in driving generational renewal.

The arguments for urban consolidation that originated in the 1970s also acknowledged that highly serviced apartments do not provide the most energy efficient form of housing. The compact pied-à-terre, or terrace house, has often emerged as the most versatile form, with lower per-capita energy requirements than detached houses or apartments, and the potential to capture some solar energy and rainwater, and in more sophisticated cases to dispose of waste onsite (Mobbs 2010). This housing type, common all over the world in the late 19th century, can produce places of great charm and utility.

The second consequence of making cities denser through restricting sub-urban development, it has been argued, is that property prices rise much faster than incomes. This has been suggested as being particularly acute in English-speaking countries, where housing affordability has declined since 1990. If true, this again may have the reverse effect of forcing working-class families to live beyond the urban boundary where property is more affordable, but also forcing them to commute considerable distances by car to the urban labour market.

However, the question of how to reduce energy use in cities must be framed around the relative magnitude of proposed reductions. Conversion efficiencies – how much thermal energy is actually converted into electricity or motive power – have probably plateaued in most technologies. The enormous gains of the 20th century will not be repeated, and advances will be incremental. Credible assessments conclude that any transition to different energy sources will be slow, given the magnitude of the investment and engineering required to shift all power generation away from the current mix, with its heavy reliance worldwide on coal (Smil 2010; International Energy Agency 2014). Some countries are geographically and historically positioned to do this. Canada is a case in point. In 2014 its most populous province, Ontario, retired its last coal generators. But Canada is endowed with enormous hydropower potential, much of it already harnessed. Dams provide over half of Canada's electricity production, and a long programme of pressurised water reactor development has given the nation a large nuclear-generating capacity through its refined CANDU reactors. These supply 55% of Ontario's power, with hydro adding 22% and gas another 16.5%. The remainder, around 6.5%, comes from wind, with a small contribution from biofuels (Canadian Nuclear Society n.d.).

Few nations have access to this sort of energy diversity. The US has altered its energy mix through the exploitation of shale gas, but this has required the drilling of upwards of 32,000 sophisticated wells across the country, with their associated high-pressure fracking plant (FracTracker 2014). Wealthy countries always have an advantage in this sector, with advanced engineering capabilities and enforceable legal rights combining to give some certainty to investors and developers. While the shale gas industry has generated enormous controversy, and widespread resistance, its contribution to current US energy stocks is dramatic.

Substitution of one energy source by another also carries the risk of overly optimistic accounting in the planning phase. Because of their low energy yields by area, renewable energy sources produce low returns on the energy invested in their production. The production of ethanol from corn in the US has been a case in point. There have been a number of attempts to calculate whether this fuel contains more available energy when it is burned than has been consumed in its production. The energy accounting is complex because the energy used in its production includes all the inputs to the growing of the corn, including diesel fuel for the farm equipment and energy used in fertiliser production. An assessment of the various calculations proposed over time concluded that "production of corn ethanol within the United States is unsustainable and requires energy subsidies from the larger oil economy" (Murphy, Hall & Powers 2010). Even photovoltaics can be marginal. A study of the energy accounting of the solar panel industry concluded that when the energy generated by panels worldwide is balanced against the energy consumed in their production, it is possible that until 2010 it resulted in a net loss of energy. Even as the industry slowly moves into energy positive territory, this study underlines the dangers of assuming that renewables represent free energy (Dale & Benson 2013).

If energy availability were to be scaled back dramatically in advanced economies, beyond the natural declines in consumption that occur when a population ages, market allocation of resources would have to follow an atavistic regression, that is a withdrawal of energy from activities seen as less critical to more critical ones as determined by the historical transition to modernity. In the case of cities there appears to be some elasticity in the system, since even poor cities in the modern era can grow to many times the historical limit of the pre-industrial city.

Under such a scenario the modern agricultural sector would need to survive more or less intact, along with the industrial processes that make fertiliser and convert primary products into an array of foods, and the distribution networks that bring them to market. This is the single largest guarantor of the survival of cities, and the means to supply the requisite calories to their inhabitants. The energy sector itself would also be protected, as the primary supplier of the motive force of modern life. Within cities class differences would re-assert themselves, but the particular form this might take is moot. Many cities contain wide differences in social class without excessive friction or violence. It seems unlikely that cities could disaggregate into smallholdings capable of sustaining themselves, like the villa-estates that surrounded ancient Rome. The sheer size of such agglomerations, and the inefficiencies of small-scale agriculture, would likely keep this development to hobby scale. The end result might come to resemble modern Japan, with its densely settled flatland interspersed with rice fields and free-standing houses in a landscape rarely without inhabitation, except in the mountainous regions. Space standards are small, but housing varies from villas through small suburban houses to apartment blocks of every scale, bound by superb infrastructure that has almost eliminated rush-hour traffic from Tokyo's streets. But Japan has a vast appetite for electricity, seen in the endless power cables that enmesh the country, and the exploitation of every suitable alpine river for hydropower. It also has a distinctive social cohesion that bridges gaps of class and opportunity.

However, given the technical and financial impediments to a rapid transition from one energy mix to another, a regime that was deeply punitive of fossil fuels would in the short term induce energy austerity. For advanced countries this might take the form of a severe tax on CO_2 emissions, which would favour a shift towards natural gas as a fuel, with nuclear expanding more slowly due to its long construction time. Gas turbines could provide supplementary power generation relatively quickly, and urban transport might revert to a greater share of motorcycles, which are more fuel efficient. This is the dominant form of private transport in dynamic emerging cities such as Hanoi. Urban transit might resort to gas-powered buses, which can be deployed along existing street networks without the disruption and cost of laying tram lines. Taxi regulation might also be loosened to allow minibus fleets to expand in developed cities.

Energy austerity would likely depress the fertility rate even further in all affected cities. It would favour the young and the childless, since they can walk or cycle more easily than the old and can live in small quarters near work. The scope of suburban life would shrink faster than that of urban life, as mobility became more constrained by the increasing costs of travel. This might be offset by the slow market penetration of cheap electric cars, whose range of less than 150 km and long charging time will decrease the distance travelled overall by cars every year. The retirement of coal generators will make home charging an imperative unless additional dense generating capacity can be quickly brought online. Solar powered home chargers will only suit dwellings with large roof areas, since the amount of power generated per unit area is low. The considerable additional cost of the solar system would also add to the capital cost of private vehicles. With its intermittent generation, additional battery packs may be required to make it workable. A small enclosed motor tricycle running on petrol or LPG would be a more viable vehicle in many respects.

The level of personal discomfort would also rise. Air conditioners have become among the most sought after items in Asian households, with 64 million units sold in China in 2013 (Davis 2015). They have also been instrumental in the shift in the US population southwards, and constraining energy use would make the running of these most energy-hungry of appliances more costly.

While these may be some of the practical consequences of restricted energy use, at a broader level the critical question that remains to be answered is one at the core of materialist thinking. In this tradition the maxim of *being precedes consciousness* is often cited to underline how the material circumstances of everyday life are the main determinants of ideas and ideals. Thus for Marx the rules of everyday life, with its power structures and skewed ownership of productive industries, needed to be changed before a liberated human could emerge. The converse view sees ideas and institutions as more critical for social and personal development (Fukuyama 2011). Using these two viewpoints, what might the relationship between energy and social cohesion be? Has the huge energy bonanza of the past century, distributed to citizens through the modern state, produced a world of increasing civility? And conversely, would that civility be reversed if energy became less abundant? The answers to these questions would obviously vary from place to place, dependent on how legitimate the state is considered, and how far people identify with a greater cause or identity. Japan and China have long histories of strong collective identities, for example, and can harness these towards state-directed objectives even when these involve hardship. But these identities are not constants, and the individualism fostered by consumer society erodes the collective. Conversely countries like Australia and the US have been very successful in maintaining state legitimacy among diverse immigrant groups, based on the perception that their societies are socially permeable according to individual merit and effort.

My own view is that the establishment of enduring social institutions that are competent, fair and transparent, and are viewed as such, is of paramount importance. For advanced economies where these exist, they convey an inestimable advantage in dealing with energy transitions as well as the possible consequences of climate change. A rich country with good governance, a broad tax base and an advanced engineering sector can respond to disasters and exigencies far better than a poor one without these advantages. Societies with strong informal identities, and a developed sense of national purpose, would also seem to be at an advantage. This may mean the loss of much of the individualism within Western nations. Living big as an expression of one's personality might have to yield to a more self-disciplined society in order to cope with the fine-tuning of energy consumption and the restraint and bargaining this would entail.

In the meantime the process of redistribution of populations from areas of poor infrastructure towards better endowed areas proceeds regardless. Within countries this takes the form of the rural to urban trek. Between countries this takes place through the immigration programmes of traditional destinations like the US, Canada and Australia, and the often tragic but relentless journeys of Africans to Europe. As the towns of Italy or Spain decline through falling household formation and low birth rates, immigrants desperate for a better life will slowly invigorate them. Despite the social tensions that the process brings, they will repopulate these towns and revive the schools, and provide the labour and industry to maintain the economy. As populations begin to decline in all advanced countries, the social and political capital invested in their cities will become too precious to simply fall away. The infrastructure will be avidly taken over by immigrants, and if the social institutions are well founded they will be vigorously upheld by these immigrants. In this we find the obverse of the inevitable slowness of energy transitions. The legacies of culture and infrastructure from the past century, with all its drama, have a momentum that will continue through upcoming demographic changes. There is every likelihood that we will pass peak energy needs, peak infrastructure building and peak population in the next 80 years, and enter a paradigm for which we have almost no predictive tools. Only history, in its long sweeps, can offer any clues.

Bibliography

ABS (Australian Bureau of Statistics) (2013). *Population estimates by statistical area level 2, 2011 to 2012*. Retrieved September 7, 2015, from www.abs.gov.au/AUSSTATS/abs@.nsf/DetailsPage/3218.02011?OpenDocument
ABS (Australian Bureau of Statistics) (2014). *Births, summary, statistical area level 2 – 2001 to 2013*. Retrieved September 7, 2015, from www.abs.gov.au/AUSSTATS/abs@.nsf/DetailsPage/3301.02013?OpenDocument
Angel, S. (2012). *Planet of cities*. Cambridge, MA: Lincoln Institute of Land Policy.
Ausubel, J. (2003). *Decarbonization: The next 100 years*. Retrieved August 13, 2015, from http://phe.rockefeller.edu/PDF_FILES/oakridge.pdf

Breheny, M. (1995). The compact city and transport energy consumption. *Transactions of the Institute of British Geographers*, 20(1), 81–101. doi:10.2307/622726

Brooks, G. (2010, October 28). *Musings: Population demographics, energy consumption*. Retrieved August 3, 2015, from www.rigzone.com/news/article.asp?a_id=100738

Bryce, R. (2010). *Power hungry: The myths of "green" energy and the real fuels of the future*. New York: PublicAffairs.

Buckley, S., & Mitchell, M. (2010). Improvements in urban air quality: Case studies from New York State, USA. *Water, Air, & Soil Pollution*, 214(1–4), 93–106. doi:10.1007/s11270-11010-0407-z

Burdett, R., & Sudjic, D. (Eds) (2007). *The Endless City*. London: Phaidon.

Canadian Nuclear Society (n.d.). *Electricity generated in Ontario*. Retrieved August 4, 2015, from http://media.cns-snc.ca/ontarioelectricity/ontarioelectricity.html

Castells, M. (1978). *City, class, and power*. New York: St Martin's Press.

Central Intelligence Agency (n.d.). *Country comparison: total fertility rate*. Retrieved August 3, 2015, from www.cia.gov/library/publications/the-world-factbook/rankorder/2127rank.html

Dale, M., & Benson, S. (2013). Energy balance of the global photovoltaic (PV) industry – Is the PV industry a net electricity producer? *Environmental Science and Technology*, 47(7), 3482–3489. doi:10.1021/es3038824

Davis, L. (2015, April 27). *Air conditioning and global energy demand*. Retrieved August 4, 2015, from https://energyathaas.wordpress.com/2015/04/27/air-conditioning-and-global-energy-demand/

Dodson, J., & Sipe, N. (2008). *Unsettling suburbia: the new landscape of oil and mortgage vulnerability in Australian cities*. Retrieved August 4, 2015, from www.griffith.edu.au/__data/assets/pdf_file/0003/88851/urp-rp17-dodson-sipe-2008.pdf

Dubow, S. (2014). *Apartheid, 1948–1994*. Oxford: Oxford University Press.

FAO (n.d.). *Food security: World*. Retrieved August 3, 2015, from http://faostat3.fao.org/browse/D/*/E

FracTracker (2014, March 4). *Over 1.1 million active oil & gas wells in the US*. Retrieved August 4, 2015, from www.fractracker.org/2014/03/active-gas-and-oil-wells-in-us

Fukuyama, F. (2011). *The origins of political order: From prehuman times to the French Revolution*. New York: Farrar, Straus and Giroux.

Global Wind Energy Council (2015, March 1). *Global wind report 2014*. Retrieved August 3, 2015, from www.gwec.net/wp-content/uploads/2015/03/GWEC_Global_Wind_2014_Report_LR.pdf

Heilbroner, R. (1994). Do machines make history? In M. Smith & L. Marx (Eds), *Does technology drive history?: The dilemma of technological determinism*. Cambridge, MA: MIT Press.

Institute for Future Energy Consumer Needs and Behavior (2014). *Energy consumption patterns of an aging population*. Retrieved August 3, 2015, from www.fcn.eonerc.rwth-aachen.de/cms/E-ON-ERC-FCN/Forschung/Projekte/~evmj/Energy-Consumption-Patterns-of-an-Aging/lidx/1/

International Energy Agency (2014). *World energy outlook factsheet: How will global energy markets evolve to 2040?* Retrieved August 24, 2015, from www.worldenergyoutlook.org/media/weowebsite/2014/141112_WEO_FactSheets.pdf

Johnson, I. (2015, July 11). *Chinese officials to restructure Beijing to ease strains on city center*. Retrieved August 12, 2015, from www.nytimes.com/2015/07/12/world/asia/china-beijing-city-planning-population.html

Lynch, K. (1960). *The image of the city*. Cambridge, MA: MIT Press.

MacKay, D. (2009). *Sustainable energy – Without the hot air*. Cambridge, UK: UIT.

Mobbs, M. (2010). *Sustainable house* (2nd ed.). Sydney: Choice Books.

Murphy, D., Hall, C., & Powers, B. (2010). New perspectives on the energy return on (energy) investment (EROI) of corn ethanol. *Environment, Development and Sustainability*, 13(1), 179–202. doi:10.1007/s10668-10010-9255-9257

Newman, P., & Kenworthy, J. (1999). *Sustainability and cities: Overcoming automobile dependence*. Washington, DC: Island Press.

Pinker, S. (2012). *The better angels of our nature: A history of violence and humanity*. London: Penguin.

Pitt&Sherry (2015). Retrieved August 13, 2015, from www.pittsh.com.au/assets/files/ Cedex/CEDEX Electricity Update August 2015.pdf

Roney, J. (2013, July 31). *World solar power topped 100,000 megawatts in 2012*. Retrieved August 3, 2015, from www.earth-policy.org/indicators/C47/solar_power_ 2013

Rygole, D. (1978). Energy and urban form: The need for energy conscious urban planning (unpublished report). Baltimore: Center for Metropolitan Planning and Research, The Johns Hopkins University.

Sandercock, L. (1976). *Cities for sale: Property, politics and urban planning in Australia*. London: Heinemann.

Sassen, S. (2008). Cities in today's global age. In C. Johnson, R. Hu, & S. Abedin (Eds), *Connecting cities: Networks*. Sydney: Metropolis Congress 2008.

Seligman, P. (2010, July 2). *Australian sustainable energy – By the numbers*. Retrieved August 3, 2015, from www.energy.unimelb.edu.au/documents/sustainable-energy-numbers

Smil, V. (2010). *Energy myths and realities: Bringing science to the energy policy debate*. Washington, DC: AEI Press.

Talent, M., Troy, P., & Dovers, S. (2013). *Canberra residential energy and water consumption baseline report*. Canberra: Australian National University.

Thals, K. (2015, July 15). *Labor denies carbon tax plan*. Retrieved August 12, 2015, from http://thenewdaily.com.au/news/2015/07/15/labor-denies-new-carbon-tax-plan

The Economist (2015, January 10). *The twilight of the resource curse?* Retrieved August 3, 2015, from www.economist.com/news/middle-east-and-africa/21638141-africas-growth-being-powered-things-other-commodities-twilight

Toffler, A. (1970). *Future shock*. New York: Random House.

Tokyo Metropolitan Government (2010). *Changes in annual average of concentration*. Retrieved August 3, 2015, from www.kankyo.metro.tokyo.jp/en/attachement/Air Quality of Tokyo.pdf

Tongia, R. (2014, October 7). *Electrified but without electricity*. Retrieved August 3, 2015, from www.brookings.in/electrified-but-without-electricity

Trading Economics (n.d.). *Nigeria: economic indicators*. Retrieved August 3, 2015, from www.tradingeconomics.com/nigeria/indicators

Troy, P. (1996). *The perils of urban consolidation: A discussion of Australian housing and urban development policies*. Sydney: Federation Press.

UN Water (n.d.). *Water and urbanization*. Retrieved August 3, 2015, from www.unwa ter.org/topics/water-and-urbanization/en

United Nations (2014). *World urbanization prospects: The 2014 revision (highlights)*. Retrieved August 3, 2015, from http://esa.un.org/unpd/wup/Highlights/WUP 2014-Highlights.pdf

Wilson, R. (2013, August 8). *The future of energy: Why power density matters*. Retrieved August 3, 2015, from www.theenergycollective.com/robertwilson190/257481/why-power-density-matters

World Bank (n.d.). *Energy use (kg of oil equivalent per capita)*. Retrieved August 24, 2015, from http://data.worldbank.org/indicator/EG.USE.PCAP.KG.OE

Index

For Product Safety Concerns and Information please contact our EU
representative GPSR@taylorandfrancis.com
Taylor & Francis Verlag GmbH, Kaufingerstraße 24, 80331 München, Germany